BEST *of the* BEST *from*

COOKBOOK

❄ ❄ ❄ ❄ ❄

Selected Recipes from
ALASKA'S FAVORITE
COOKBOOKS

Mount McKinley, the highest mountain in North America, provides a stunning background for a large bull moose in Denali National Park. Denali, the "High One," is the name the native Athabascan people gave the massive, snow-covered peak.

BEST *of the* BEST *from*

ALASKA

COOKBOOK

❄ ❄ ❄ ❄ ❄

Selected Recipes from
ALASKA'S FAVORITE COOKBOOKS

Edited by
GWEN McKEE
and
BARBARA MOSELEY

Illustrated by Tupper England

QUAIL RIDGE PRESS
Preserving America's Food Heritage

Library of Congress Cataloging-in-Publication Data

Best of the best fr om Alaska cookbook : selected recipes from Alaska's favorite cookbooks / edited by Gwen McKee and Barbara Moseley ; illustrated by T upper England.
   p. cm.
   ISBN 1-893062-42-2
   1. Cookery, American 2. Cookery—Alaska. I. McKee, Gwen. II. Moseley, Barbara.

TX715.B48563614 2003
641.5978—dc21   2002036904

QUAIL RIDGE PRESS
P. O. Box 123 • Brandon, MS 39043 • 1-800-343-1583
email: info@quailridge.com • www.quailridge.com

CONTENTS

Alaska is populated by more than 98% of the U.S. population of brown bears. Lucky for Editor Gwen McKee, this bear is stuffed!

PREFACE

Searching for cookbooks in Alaska was a fascinating experience. Tasting the local fare, meeting so many friendly people, and seeing the extraordinary scenery along the way was truly a memorable adventure.

The first time we saw salmon jumping, it was almost like a personal welcome! That certainly was the case in Ketchikan. Creek Street, even in the rain, had the wooden-plank feel and rushing-creek sound that put you into another era, and being wet and a little uncomfortable made it all the more authentic. We found the most charming bookstore where narrow wooden stairs led us to one cozy cubbyhole of lovely books after another. The cookbook section was my sit-down spot, of course, and I soon found out what they do with all those salmon!

Juneau, the state capitol, had so much to offer, and within a few miles you can be walking through a rain forest, gazing at a glacier, or ordering an Alaskan brew at the Red Dog Saloon! The Red Dog still has sawdust covering the floor . . . and stuffed bears, mounted fish and moose heads all around. The sign says: "If our food, drinks and service aren't up to your standards, please lower your standards." But the fare was indeed very much up to our standards.

In Sitka we met with Gayle Hammons, a local schoolteacher and cookbook collector. She provided us with valuable information on Alaskan cookbooks, and gave us a copy of a rare out-of-print one from Sitka that is her personal favorite. Likewise, when we met Cheryl Berger at the Purple Moose in Skagway, we were instant friends. She stocks cookbooks from all over Alaska—talk about hitting the Mother Lode! I am so pleased to be able to pass along these treasures for so many to enjoy. Thank you, Gayle and Cheryl.

In Seward we were directed to the Showcase Lounge (the owner showcases his amazing collection of Jim Beam bottles) to watch a football game at 10 a.m. on a Sunday. "Who do you pull for?" we asked, since Alaska does not have a team. "Whoever you like," the colorful owner replied. The luncheon special was a superb halibut dish. Halibut was our favorite fish and we ate it often . . . so fresh and delicious.

From there we headed up the Seward Highway toward the Kenai Peninsula. Oh, my! What spectacular, gorgeous, beautiful scenery!

Turnagain Arm takes you around a lovely loop that turns again and again onto yet another incredible view. One of our stops was at Portage Glacier, where we enjoyed the icebergs and glacier views. The little eatery there had the creamiest, most delicious clam chowder . . . and peach ice cream . . . and a gift shop with cookbooks! All my favorite things! The staff there was friendly and anxious to talk. Loved it.

Anchorage, Alaska's largest city, offered a variety of treats. We enjoyed reindeer sausage from a sidewalk vendor, and a marvelous dinner at Simon & Seaforts. Chef Matt Little Dog allowed us to include his incredible bread pudding recipe in the book (see page 248). Yum!

One of the most enjoyable times of our Alaskan research trip was to spend a day at the Alaska State Fair in Palmer. The numerous booths at the fair featured delicious examples of local cuisine. In the exhibit area, we viewed the prize-winning produce and were amazed at the 90-pound head of cabbage!

Beyond the delicious fare within these pages, you'll also find beautiful photographs from around the state and a collection of quips scattered throughout the book that provide interesting facts about Alaska. (Did you know Alaska oil production can generate more revenue in a single day than the entire cost of acquiring this vast territory in 1867?)

A special Catalog of Contributing Cookbooks Section in the back of this book provides a description and ordering information on each contributing cookbook.

We wish to thank everyone who contributed to the development of this book: the food editors and the bookstore and gift shop managers who guided us to the state's most popular cookbooks; the personnel at Alaska's tourism departments, Chamber of Commerce offices, and museums who provided valuable historic and informative data; Tupper England, who added the charming illustrations; Lauren Jones for her poignant photographs; and especially all the great cooks in Alaska who shared their recipes. Thank you all.

We invite you to put yourself in Alaska through the pages of this book, and enjoy this tasteful journey to the Last Frontier.

Gwen McKee and Barbara Moseley

CONTRIBUTING COOKBOOKS

Alaska Backyard Wines
Alaska Connections Cookbook III
Alaska Cooking: Featuring Skagway
Alaska Gold Rush Cook Book
Alaska Magazine's Cabin Cookbook
Alaska Shrimp & Crab Recipes
Alaska Women in Timber Cookbook
Alaska's Cooking Volume II
Alaska's Gourmet Breakfasts
The Alaskan Bootlegger's Bible
Alaskan Halibut Recipes
All-Alaska Women in Timber Cookbook
Be Our Guest
The Best of the Blueberry Bash, 1994–2002
Best Recipes of Alaska's Fishing Lodges
Blueberry Pride: Blueberry Bash Recipes 1989–1993
A Cook's Tour of Alaska
Drop the Hook, Let's Eat
Eskimo Cookbook
Eskimo Cookbook by Alexandra
Favorite Recipes from Alaska's Bed and Breakfasts
Grannie Annie's Cookin' at the Homestead
Grannie Annie's Cookin' Fish from Cold Alaskan Waters
Grannie Annie's Cookin' on the Wood Stove
Huna Heritage Foundation Cookbook
Just for the Halibut
Kay's Kitchen
Ladies of Harley Cookbook
Let's Taste Alaska

CONTRIBUTING COOKBOOKS

License to Cook Alaska Style
Literary Tastes
Methodist Pie
Moose & Caribou Recipes of Alaska
Moose in the Pot Cookbook
Moose Racks, Bear Tracks, and Other Alaska Kidsnacks
Nome Centennial Cookbook 1898-1998
The Original Great Alaska Cookbook
Our Cherished Recipes
Our Cherished Recipes Volume II
Panhandle Pat's Fifty Years
Pelican, Alaska: Alaskan Recipe Cookbook
Pioneers of Alaska Auxiliary #8
Recipes from the Paris of the Pacific
Recipes to the Rescue
Salmon Recipes from Alaska
Sharing Our Best
Simply the Best Recipes
A Taste of Kodiak
A Taste of Sitka, Alaska
Tasty Treats from Tenakee Springs, Alaska
33 Days Hath September
Upper Kenai River Inn Breakfast Cookbook
We're Cookin' Now
Welcome Home
What's Cookin' in the Kenai Peninsula
Wild Alaska Seafood—Twice a Week

BEVERAGES *and* APPETIZERS

Each year thousands of tourists from around the world visit Alaska aboard magnificent ships that cruise Alaska Marine Highway's Inside Passage from April through September. Skagway, the northernmost stop, can hold up to seven cruise ships a day.

Rhubarb Punch

We used to call this "Missionary Lemonade" in Sitka. It was as close as we came to the real thing.

6 cups cut-up rhubarb
4 cups water
$1^1/_2$ cups sugar
$^1/_3$ cup orange juice

$^1/_4$ cup lemon juice
Dash salt
Water or ginger ale

Cook rhubarb in water until soft. Strain through sieve. Should have 5 cups of juice. Add sugar and bring to a boil. Add orange juice, lemon juice, and a dash of salt. Chill the mixture or freeze. Dilute punch with equal parts water or ginger ale to serve.

All-Alaska Women in Timber Cookbook

Bishop's Punch

2 (12-ounce) cans frozen pink
  lemonade concentrate
1 (12-ounce) can frozen orange
  juice concentrate
1 (64-ounce) can grapefruit juice

8 ounces cranberry juice
3 quarts cold water
3 quarts ginger ale
Ice

In gallon jug, mix all juices; add enough water to make 1 gallon of concentrate. When ready, pour concentrate into punch bowl. Add 3 quarts cold water, 3 quarts ginger ale, and ice. Depending on their thirst, recipe will serve 20–30 people.

Pioneers of Alaska Auxiliary #8

Instant Russian Tea Mix

This is an old standard that helps get you through long winter nights.

2 cups instant tea with lemon
2 cups sugar
2 cups Tang

1 teaspoon cinnamon
$^1/_2$ teaspoon ground cloves
$^1/_2$ teaspoon nutmeg

Mix ingredients together and store in dry container. Mix 3–4 tablespoons with 8 ounces of boiling water per serving.

Recipes From the Paris of the Pacific—Sitka, Alaska

Rose Hip Wine

The prickly rose grows everywhere in Alaska. Beautiful to look at, a wild rose is a real treasure house for wine makers. The petals, gathered on sunny summer days make an exquisitely scented, clear, pale pink wine. The fruit, plucked in the cool crisp of autumn, makes a tawny wine. The "hip" is the fruit of the plant, the part of the flower that's left on the bush after the petals drop. When ripe, it tastes a little like an apple.

5 pounds rose hips
1 pound raisins
2 lemons
1 gallon boiling water, divided

$3^{1}/_{2}$ pounds sugar
1 gallon boiled water, cooled
Yeast

Pick rose hips in the fall, when they are red and fairly firm. Wash them and grind them up with raisins and lemons. Put the mixture into a crock or other container and cover with boiling water (cool remaining water to use later). Cover and let stand for 4 days. Strain liquid into a clean container and discard the solids.

Add sugar to the liquid and stir until it is dissolved. Sprinkle yeast over the surface of the must,* cover the container, and let stand for 4 days. Siphon into fermentation bottle and top up with cool boiled water, if necessary. Insert air lock, and ferment to a finish in a warm place. Rack and place in a cool, dark storage area for 3 months. Rack again and store for another 3 months. Repeat once more. Rack and bottle.

*Must is the freshly pressed juice of grapes or other fruit before fermentation occurs.

Note: Grapes do not grow in Alaska, of course, nor do many of the fruits, vegetables and flowers listed in other books about wine making. But many plants suitable to wine making do grow in the far north, and from these, the Alaskan wine maker can produce home wines that rival any produced anywhere in the world.

Alaska Backyard Wines

Editor's Extra: "Rack" means to siphon wine into another container leaving sediments behind.

Strawberry Wine

Strawberries do grow wild in Alaska, but my experience has been that they are few and far between. Fortunately, domestic varieties excel in Alaskan gardens. They make a fine, clear, rose wine.

4 pounds strawberries
2¹/₂ pounds sugar
1 Campden tablet, crushed
1 tablespoon citric acid
¹/₂ teaspoon yeast energizer

¹/₂ teaspoon grape tannin
1 teaspoon pectin enzyme
Wine yeast
1 gallon boiled water, cooled

Wash and hull strawberries and layer with sugar and crushed Campden tablet in a clean container. Cover and let stand for 48 hours. Strain juice into fermentation vessel. Add boiled water (about a cup) to pulp and stir; strain and add liquid to juice in fermentation bottle. (Pulp can be used in cooking later.) Add citric acid, yeast energizer, grape tannin, pectin enzyme, yeast, and cool, boiled water to top up. Insert air lock and place in a warm spot to ferment to a finish. Rack and store in a cool, dark place until clear. Rack again and bottle.

Alaska Backyard Wines

Editor's Extra: Campden tablets are a form of sulphur dioxide, used to prevent bacteria and oxygen from spoiling your wine with funny flavors and to preserve color.

Raspberry Wine

Red raspberries grow profusely throughout coastal Alaska and up into the Matanuska Valley, the Alaska Range, and the Yukon River district.

1¹/₂–3 pounds raspberries	¹/₂ teaspoon yeast nutrient
4 pints boiling water	Pectin enzyme
2–2¹/₂ pounds sugar	Wine yeast
2 pints cold water	Water, boiled and cooled
2 Campden tablets	

Cover raspberries with boiling water. Add sugar and cold water and stir until sugar is dissolved. Add Campden tablets and yeast nutrient and stir. Cool mixture to body heat; add pectin enzyme and activated yeast. Cover and ferment on pulp for 1 week, stirring daily. Strain into fermentation bottle, then top up with boiled water, if necessary, insert air lock, and set in a warm place to ferment to a finish. Rack and store in a cool, dark place until clear. Rack again and bottle.

Alaska Backyard Wines

Raspberry Liqueur

4 cups raspberries, mashed	3 cups vodka
¹/₂ lemon peel, scraped	³/₄ cup Simple Syrup

Mix raspberries, lemon zest, and vodka. Steep 3 weeks; strain and filter. Add Simple Syrup, and age 1 month.

SIMPLE SYRUP FOR LIQUEURS:

It is one of the basic ingredients of many liqueur recipes. It is made by simmering equal volumes of water and sweetener for about 5 minutes. Sweeteners can be cane sugar, brown sugar, or honey. Powdered sugar is not suitable because it has a starch filler and will make a cloudy syrup.

The Alaskan Bootlegger's Bible

Coffee Liqueur

Boil 1 pound of drip-grind coffee in $1^1/4$ quarts of water, and simmer 40 minutes. Strain liquid (for grounds) through cheesecloth. Dissolve 3 pounds sugar in 1 quart of water and boil 5 minutes. Add coffee concentrate and cool. Add $1^1/4$ quarts of 180 proof alcohol and 2 ounces vanilla extract. Yields about $2^1/2$ quarts.

The Alaskan Bootlegger's Bible

Chocolate Moose Latté

$^1/2$ ounce chocolate syrup
2 shots of coffee
1 cup steamed milk

1 large scoop of whipped cream
6 raisins

Add chocolate syrup, coffee, and steamed milk together in coffee cup. Top with bull-sized (large) scoop of whipped cream and raisins.

Moose in the Pot Cookbook

Bailey's Irish Cream

1 can sweetened condensed milk
$1^3/4$ cups Irish whiskey
4 egg whites
1 cup heavy cream

1 tablespoon chocolate syrup
1 tablespoon instant coffee
1 teaspoon vanilla extract
$^1/4$ teaspoon almond extract

Combine ingredients in a blender and blend until smooth. Bottle and steep in the refrigerator for 1 week. Will last up to 1 month refrigerated.

The Alaskan Bootlegger's Bible

Egg Nog

You can vary the strength of this is a basic recipe. Makes about 1 gallon.

12 eggs, separated
1 pound (2¹/₂ cups) sugar
  (cane or powdered)
2 quarts whipping cream

¹/₂–4 cups brandy, cognac, rum,
  bourbon or rye whiskey*
1 teaspoon nutmeg (or ¹/₂ nutmeg
  and ¹/₂ cinnamon)

Beat egg yolks and gradually blend in sugar, cream, and liquor. Beat egg whites until stiff, then blend into other ingredients. Refrigerate for 3–4 hours, then serve sprinkled with nutmeg/cinnamon or blend in before refrigerating.

*You may use a blend of the liquors or even use fruit-flavored brandies, but take note of the strength of what you use. Some rye whiskey runs to 110 proof and 4 cups in a gallon may give you "Nuclear Nog."

The Alaskan Bootlegger's Bible

Peg's Frozen Smoothie

This is a great way to use bananas that are getting too ripe. Bananas keep frozen for about a month.

2 peeled and frozen bananas,
  cut in quarters
2 tablespoons sugar

1 teaspoon almond extract
2 cups milk

Put all ingredients in blender and blend until smooth. Any frozen fruit works well.

Upper Kenai River Inn Breakfast Cookbook

Inuits have more than 1,000 different words for ice but not one word for hello! Inupiaq is spoken throughout much of northern Alaska and is closely related to the Canadian Inuit dialects and the Greenlandic dialects, which may collectively be called "Inuit" or Eastern Eskimo, distinct from Yupik or Western Eskimo.

Grandma's Crab Goodies

1 (6-ounce) can crabmeat
1½ jars Old English cheese
1 stick margarine, softened

¼ teaspoon garlic powder
1 package English muffins, cut in
   half, then quartered

Combine all ingredients, except muffins. Spread mixture over muffin quarters. Freeze at least 20 minutes before cooking. Bake at 400° for 15 minutes.

We're Cookin' Now

Crab Stuffed Mushrooms

12 medium mushrooms
3 tablespoons butter
1 cup crabmeat, flaked
¼ cup cracker meal
2 tablespoons mayonnaise
¼ teaspoon white pepper

1 tablespoon dry white vermouth
1 tablespoon grated Parmesan
   cheese
Salt to taste
1 cup milk
Fresh parsley for garnish

Remove stems from mushroom caps and discard. Wipe caps with a damp sponge and set aside.

Melt butter and mix with crab, cracker meal, mayonnaise, pepper, vermouth, grated cheese, and salt. Stuff each cap with mixture. Place caps in baking dish. Pour in milk to just below the stuffing. Bake at 300° approximately 45 minutes. Remove to serving dish. Garnish with parsley. Serves 6.

Alaska Shrimp & Crab Recipes

Joyce's Crab Dip

3 (8-ounce) packages cream
  cheese, softened
1 medium onion, chopped
$^1/_4$ bottle Worcestershire sauce

7 ounces crabmeat, flaked
1 bottle chili sauce
Horseradish to taste

Mix cheese, onion, and Worcestershire sauce. Spread into 9x9-inch dish. Sprinkle crab over cheese mixture. Combine chili sauce and horseradish. Spread over top of crab. Serves 4.

Alaska Shrimp & Crab Recipes

King Crab and Artichoke Dip

During one fishing season in Kodiak, we canned king crab legs, thinking that we would have the summer's abundance for winter feasting. Our family's over indulgence of fresh crab had spoiled our enthusiasm for canned crab. Our very happy yellow Labrador dogs gobbled up the crab without complaint. Their beautiful, sleek coats at the end of the summer were testaments of the nutrients and value of the crabmeat. Two cans of crab legs ended up in our winter fish supply, and on Superbowl Sunday, I made this recipe. Everyone wished we had every can of crabmeat back!

1 (8-ounce) package low-fat
  cream cheese, softened
1 cup low-fat mayonnaise
1 cup crabmeat

$^1/_3$ cup chopped green onion
1 (13$^3/_4$-ounce) can artichoke
  hearts, drained and chopped
$^1/_2$ cup shredded Parmesan cheese

Preheat oven to 375°. Blend cream cheese and mayonnaise in a bowl. Stir in all remaining ingredients. Spread evenly into an ovenproof baking dish. Bake uncovered for 15 minutes, until heated through and golden brown on top. Serve with sliced baguettes and cut vegetables such as carrots, celery, red bell peppers, and cucumbers.

Wild Alaska Seafood—Twice a Week

Crab Deviled Eggs

6 eggs, hard-boiled and peeled
1 (6¹/₂-ounce) can crabmeat,
  drained
¹/₂ cup chopped Spanish green
  olives
¹/₃ cup chopped celery

¹/₄ cup mayonnaise
¹/₄ teaspoon dry mustard
Paprika for garnish
Flaked crabmeat or sliced green
  olives for garnish

Slice hard-boiled eggs in halves. Remove yolks and mix with remaining ingredients, except garnish. Place the mixture into the egg white halves. Sprinkle with paprika and crabmeat or green olives.

All-Alaska Women in Timber Cookbook

Halibut Puffs

¹/₂ pound mashed, cooked
  halibut
1 (8-ounce) package cream
  cheese, softened
¹/₂ teaspoon salt

2 teaspoons minced onion
¹/₄ teaspoon garlic powder
40 wonton skins
1 egg, slightly beaten
Vegetable oil

Mix mashed halibut, cream cheese, salt, onion, and garlic powder. Brush a wonton skin with egg. Place heaping teaspoonfuls of halibut mixture in center of wonton skin. Top with another wonton skin, press edges to seal. Brush a dab of egg on center of each side of puff. Make a pleat on each edge, pressing to seal. Repeat with remaining wonton skins. Fry puffs in vegetable oil until golden brown (about 2 minutes), turning 2 or 3 times. Drain and serve with desired sauce.

Just for the Halibut

Deep Fried Fiddleheads in Beer Batter

You just can't stop eating fried fiddlehead fern. For something uniquely Alaskan, serve these as hors d'oeuvres.

1 quart fresh fiddleheads	**2 teaspoons salt**
(3-inch necks)	**1 teaspoon pepper**
1 cup flour	

If fern is not completely dry, blot dry with paper towels. Put dry mixture (flour, salt, pepper) into paper bag and shake a little of the fern at a time, as you would chicken.

BEER BATTER:

4 egg whites	**1 cup flour**
1 bottle beer	

Beat egg whites until stiff. Add beer and flour. Whip until stiff. Dip fiddleheads by holding tips of stems. Deep fry until golden brown.

PANCAKE BATTER:

Prepare fern and cook according to recipe above, using pancake batter rather than Beer Batter. Krustease Pancake Batter works beautifully (if available). It also gives a slightly sweet taste, enjoyed by children and grown-ups alike.

Let's Taste Alaska

The Alaska state flower is the Forget-me-not, which grows well throughout the state. Growing 18-inches tall, this small, delicate plant has clusters of small bright blue or white flowers. The tall, stately Sitka spruce, the official tree of Alaska, is found in both national forests of the state. The wood is light, soft and relatively strong and flexible and is used for general construction, ship building and plywood. The wood also has excellent acoustic properties and is used to make sounding boards in pianos and other musical instruments such as violins and guitars.

Salmon Balls

Canned salmon is fine for these delectable salmon balls, though freshly caught and cooked salmon tastes even better.

1 (1-pound) can salmon	1 teaspoon prepared horseradish
1 (8-ounce) package cream cheese, softened	1/4 teaspoon liquid smoke
	1/4 teaspoon salt
2 teaspoons lemon juice	Chopped pecans or walnuts
3 teaspoons grated onion	Chopped olives (optional)

Drain and clean, as needed, a can of salmon. Combine cream cheese, salmon, lemon juice, grated onion, horseradish, liquid smoke and salt. Mix carefully to a smooth consistency and form into balls. Roll balls in finely chopped nuts, or roll in chopped olives. Refrigerate for several hours before serving. These balls can be successfully frozen.

Alaska Magazine's Cabin Cookbook

Alaska Day Festival is held in October of each year in Sitka to celebrate the actual transfer in 1867 of Alaska from Russia to the United States. Celebrations include ceremonies, a period costume ball, dances, dinners, contests and a parade. Sitka's Keystone Kops (local women dressed as police officers) will threaten to put ANYONE in jail during the festival, but if you purchase an Alaska Day Pin, it serves as your "get-out-of-jail-free card." People in period costumes are usually left alone by the Kops. But if you donate enough money to have someone arrested, the Kops will toss just about anyone in the clink! To get out of jail, a bail is set and the jailed person must plea to passersby to pay their bail. The money collected supports the Festival.

Smoked Salmon Paté

2 cups crumbled smoked salmon
1/2 teaspoon lemon juice
2 tablespoons chopped onion
1 (8-ounce) package cream
   cheese, softened

1/4 cup mayonnaise
1/2 tablespoon horseradish
Finely chopped walnuts
Crackers or breadsticks

Sprinkle crumbled salmon with lemon juice. Add onion and cream cheese. Mix together with fork and combine with mayonnaise and horseradish. Form to make a round ball. Roll in finely chopped walnuts. Serve with crackers or breadsticks.

Alaska Women in Timber Cookbook

Super Salmon Spread

2 envelopes unflavored gelatin
3/4 cup white cooking wine
1 cup boiling water
1 (16-ounce) carton sour cream

1/2 cup chili sauce
1 (15 1/2-ounce) can salmon,
   drained and flaked

In a large bowl, sprinkle unflavored gelatin over wine; let stand 1 minute. Add boiling water and stir until gelatin is completely dissolved. With wire whisk or rotary beater, blend in sour cream and chili sauce. Stir in salmon. Turn into 6-cup mold or bowl; chill until firm. Makes about 5 1/4 cups spread.

Salmon Recipes

Smoked Salmon Dip

4 ounces boned, smoked salmon
1/4 medium onion
1/2 teaspoon lemon juice
1/4 teaspoon pepper
1 (8-ounce) package cream
 cheese, softened

1/2 cup milk
1 tablespoon red salmon caviar,
 divided
1 teaspoon scallion greens, thinly
 sliced for garnish

Purée salmon, onion, lemon juice, and pepper until smooth. Cut up cream cheese and add to salmon; pour in milk and process until well blended. Stir in 2 teaspoons of the caviar and scrape Dip into an attractive bowl. Cover and refrigerate 2 hours, or up to 2 days. Garnish top with remaining caviar and scallion greens. Makes 2 cups.

Salmon Recipes

Spicy Hot Salmon Dip

1 pint canned salmon, drained
 and dark pieces taken out
1/4 cup finely chopped onion
1/4 cup finely chopped green or
 red pepper
1/2–1 teaspoon hot horseradish
4–6 shakes Tabasco

1 teaspoon lemon juice
1/2 fresh jalapeño, chopped or
 1–2 tablespoons canned
1/2 teaspoon garlic salt
2 tablespoons mayonnaise or sour
 cream or cream cheese

Stir until blended; place in a pretty bowl. Sprinkle with black pepper. Serve with crackers.

Grannie Annie's Cookin' Fish from Cold Alaskan Waters

Valdez Marinated Shrimp

1¼ cups vegetable oil
⅓ cup vinegar
½ cup ketchup
2 teaspoons sugar
3 teaspoons Worcestershire sauce
2 cloves garlic
2 teaspoons dry mustard

¼ teaspoon pepper
⅛ teaspoon hot pepper sauce
3 pounds cooked shrimp, peeled
1 large onion, sliced thin and
 separated into rings
4 bay leaves

Combine all ingredients, except shrimp, onion, and bay leaves, in a food processor and blend until smooth. Add shrimp, onion, and bay leaves. Marinate in the refrigerator for 2 days. Serve cold. Serves 12.

Alaska Shrimp & Crab Recipes

Hot and Spicy Shrimp

10 peppercorns
4 cloves garlic
1 teaspoon whole cloves
3 lemons, sliced
¼ teaspoon cayenne pepper
1 large green pepper, chopped

4 bay leaves
1 tablespoon salt
1 teaspoon celery seed
1 cup vinegar
1½ gallons water
3 pounds raw shrimp with shells

Combine all ingredients, except shrimp, in a large pot and bring to a boil. Boil for 15 minutes. Add shrimp and cover. Simmer for 8 minutes. Drain and serve immediately. Serves 5.

Alaska Shrimp & Crab Recipes

The second largest earthquake ever recorded in world history occurred on Good Friday, March 27, 1964, in Prince William Sound. The energy released in this earthquake was equivalent to approximately four trillion pounds of explosives. The motions on the fault lasted four minutes, rupturing an area about 497 miles long and 155 miles wide.

Coconut Shrimp
with Sweet Dipping Sauce

2 pounds unpeeled large fresh
   shrimp (48 shrimp)
2 cups all-purpose flour, divided
1 (12-ounce) can beer (1^1/$_2$ cups)
^{1}/$_2$ teaspoon baking powder
^{1}/$_2$ teaspoon paprika
^{1}/$_2$ teaspoon curry powder

^{1}/$_4$ teaspoon salt
^{1}/$_4$ teaspoon ground red pepper
1 (14-ounce) package flaked
   coconut
Vegetable oil
Sweet Dipping Sauce

Peel and devein shrimp and devein, leaving tails intact. Combine
1^1/$_2$ cups flour, beer, and next 5 ingredients. Dredge shrimp in
remaining ^{1}/$_2$ cup flour, dip in batter and roll in coconut. Fry
shrimp in batches in deep hot oil (350°) until golden. Serve with
Sweet Dipping Sauce. Yields 12 appetizer servings.

SWEET DIPPING SAUCE:
1 (10-ounce) jar orange
   marmalade

3 tablespoons Creole mustard
3 tablespoons prepared horseradish

Combine all ingredients, stirring until smooth.

A Taste of Kodiak

Tarragon Shrimp

1^1/$_3$ cups olive oil
^{2}/$_3$ cup tarragon vinegar
^{1}/$_2$ teaspoon salt
^{1}/$_2$ teaspoon pepper
^{1}/$_4$ teaspoon paprika
1 clove garlic, mashed
1 large onion, chopped

1 tablespoon German-style mustard
3 tablespoons Dijon mustard
2 tablespoons horseradish
1 tablespoon powdered thyme
1^1/$_2$–2 pounds large shrimp,
   cooked and peeled

Mix everything except the shrimp in a blender. Pour this mixture
over the shrimp and marinate overnight in the refrigerator. Serve
shrimp on a large platter with toothpicks.

Be Our Guest

Pickled Shrimp & Avocado

1¹/₂ cups distilled white vinegar
2 onions, sliced
10 cloves
³/₄ teaspoon peppercorns, cracked
1 tablespoon sugar
4 teaspoons salt

1¹/₄ teaspoons red pepper flakes
1¹/₂ pounds shrimp, shelled and deveined
2 avocados
3 tablespoons minced fresh coriander leaves
Sprigs of coriander for garnish

In a stainless steel or enameled saucepan, combine the vinegar, onions, cloves, peppercorns, sugar, salt, and red pepper flakes. Bring vinegar mixture to a boil and simmer for 10 minutes. Add shrimp; bring back to a boil and simmer for 2 minutes. Let the mixture cool; pour it into a ceramic or glass bowl and chill, covered, overnight.

Halve avocados lengthwise. With a melon ball cutter, scoop out balls of avocado and fold gently into shrimp mixture along with the minced coriander. Transfer shrimp and avocado with a slotted spoon to chilled glass bowls, discarding the pickling liquid, seasonings, and onion slices. Garnish each serving with a sprig of coriander. Serves 8–10 as a first course.

We're Cookin' Now

Annie's Salsa on the Wood Stove

6–8 large tomatoes, diced and drained
1 large onion, chopped
2 stalks celery, finely chopped
1 carrot, grated
2 jalapeños, chopped
2 (16-ounce) cans tomato sauce
1 can tomato paste
1 can water
1 teaspoon garlic salt (or more)

1 tablespoon apple cider vinegar or1 tablespoon lemon juice
1 teaspoon black pepper
$\frac{1}{2}$ teaspoon cayenne pepper
2 teaspoons basil
2 teaspoons parsley
1 teaspoon oregano
1 teaspoon Italian seasoning
2 teaspoons minced garlic
1 teaspoon sugar

Place all ingredients in a large glass cooking pot or stainless Dutch oven. Put on wood stove to simmer all day (and into the nigh, if the tomatoes are still firm). Cook down until thick, and taste for salt; usually if it tastes "flat," it's because there is not enough salt; add a small amount at a time.

If you are canning, bring to boil on regular stove and can as directed in your canning book. If you do like I do, cool, put in containers and give out to your friends. This will last at least 2 weeks in the fridge.

Tasty in omelettes, chili, or spaghetti sauce; try it with a green salad with Ranch dressing; and try a big spoonful on top of tacos, burritos and enchiladas; try it on a grilled hamburger topped with Co-Jack cheese, salsa, onion, lettuce, and mayonnaise.

Grannie Annie's Cookin' on the Wood Stove

BREAD and BREAKFAST

During gold rush days, every cabin had a cache much like this one to keep perishable goods and foodstuffs safe from predators.

Sourdough Bread

Sourdough is as much a part of Alaska as gold, salmon, and dog mushing— and sourdough cookery is easy, once you get the hang of it. To start, you need a "Starter." I value my Starter so highly that I always store at least 2 extra cups in the freezer.

STARTER:

2 cups flour

2 cups warm water

1 cake yeast (or package of dry yeast)

Combine flour, warm water, and yeast; stir and allow to sit all night in a warm place. First of all, treat your Starter with tender loving care, and it will do wonders for you and for your friends who will undoubtedly ask for a share of your pot of sourdough. Be kind and generous as well and you will be rewarded by some scrumptious fare from your own kitchen.

My "working stock" of Starter stays in a clean 2-quart crock, free from unfriendly bacteria. Friendly bacteria comes in cans of evaporated milk, so I always use this rather than fresh or powdered milk. Basically, Starter is wild yeast. To "set," you add $1/2$ cup milk and enough flour and water to make a thick batter. This means 2 or 3 cups flour for pancakes; 4 or 5 cups flour for Sourdough Bread. Let batter rise overnight in a warm place, covered.

In the morning, take at least 1 cup of the Starter for "seed" and store in clean crock, using the rest of the Starter for the recipe. I prefer to keep at least 2 cups of Starter in the crock, keeping it scrupulously clean and sweet. If green or orange mold forms on the sides of the jar, scrape it off and pour off excess liquid. The inside part is still good.

Whether you use it or not, renew the Starter by "setting" it at least every 2 weeks.

SOURDOUGH BREAD RECIPE:

Starter

9–11 cups flour, divided

1 cup milk, divided

$1^1/2$ tablespoons sugar

$2^1/2$ teaspoons salt

1 package dry yeast

$1/4$ cup warm water

At night: Add Starter to 4 or 5 cups flour, $1/2$ cup milk, and enough water to make a thick batter. Let rise in covered pot in a warm place

(continued)

Sourdough Bread (continued)

overnight. In the morning: Leave 1 cup in the Starter as before. Combine 5–6 cups flour, sugar, and salt. Place in large bowl and make a well in the center.

Soak 1 package dry yeast in ¼ cup warm water, add to mixture with 4 cups Starter in bowl. Combine remaining ½ cup milk and the yeast mixture, and pour into well in flour mixture. Mix thoroughly. The batter should be thick, but not dry. Add a little water, if necessary. Set in covered bowl in warm spot until double, about an hour or so.

Pour onto floured board and shape into 3 loaves. Put into greased loaf pans, cover and let sit until double, about 1–2 hours, if needed. Bake at 425° for 15 minutes, then bake at 400° for 30 minutes. Bread is done when tapping side of loaf sounds hollow. Brush tops with margarine while hot.

Tasty Treats from Tenakee Springs, Alaska

Sourdough Starter

2½ cups warm water
1 package active dry yeast (not
  quick rising)

2½ cups unbleached white flour

Put warm water into large bowl and sprinkle yeast over; let stand 5 minutes. Add flour ½–¾ cup at a time, beating well with each addition. When batter is beaten smooth, cover bowl with cheesecloth or loose fitting foil and let stand in warm place 24–48 hours, stirring occasionally (always with a clean wooden spoon). Starter will be very bubbly.

When fermentation is complete, pour Starter into glass jar or earthenware crock. Cover. Refrigerate.

A Cook's Tour of Alaska

Russian Black Bread

Russian Black Bread commemorates the "breaking of bread" fellowship that has resumed between the United States and Russia. This dark bread is delicious with soup and cheese.

2 cups lukewarm water
1 tablespoon sugar
1/4 cup molasses
2 packages active dry yeast
1 tablespoon instant coffee
  granules
3 cups rye flour, divided
3 cups unbleached white flour,
  divided
1 cup bran

1/4 cup baking cocoa
1 tablespoon dried onions
2 teaspoons crushed caraway seeds
1 teaspoon crushed fennel seeds
1/4 cup vinegar
1/4 cup vegetable oil
2 teaspoons salt
1 teaspoon cornstarch
1/2 cup cold water

Mix lukewarm water, sugar, and molasses. Add dry yeast. When yeast mixture is foamy, add coffee, 2 cups rye flour, 1 cup white flour, bran, cocoa, dried onions, caraway, fennel seeds, vinegar, vegetable oil, and salt. Stir vigorously, about 200 strokes.

Gradually stir in 1 cup rye flour, and 2 cups white flour until a kneadable dough develops.

Knead, adding white flour until dough is smooth but still slightly sticky. Place in an oiled bowl, cover, and let rise in a warm place until doubled in bulk. Punch down and divide dough in half.

Shape each half into a round, tucking seams underneath. Grease 2 (9-inch) cake pans or pie tins. Place each round in a pan. Cover and let rise in a warm place until almost doubled. Bake at 350° for 40–45 minutes.

To glaze tops, mix cornstarch and cold water in a small saucepan. Cook over medium heat, stirring constantly until mixture boils, thickens, and clarifies. As soon as bread is baked, brush mixture over tops of loaves and return to the oven for 2–3 minutes. Makes 2 large round loaves.

Best Recipes of Alaska's Fishing Lodges

Indian Fried Bread

4 cups all-purpose flour
1 cup nonfat powdered milk
8 teaspoons baking powder
2 teaspoons salt
2 cups warm water

Sift all dried ingredients together. Add warm water gradually. Mix and knead dough lightly until dough is soft, but not sticky. Shape into balls about 2 inches in diameter. Flatten by pressing between thumb and forefinger. If too sticky, work in a little more flour. Fry in deep fryer about 375° until nicely browned.

Methodist Pie

Green Chile-Cheese Cornbread

$^1/_2$ cup canola oil, divided
1 cup yellow cornmeal
1 cup unbleached white flour
1 teaspoon baking soda
1 teaspoon baking powder
$^1/_4$ teaspoon salt
1 cup buttermilk
1 egg
1 (4-ounce) can green chiles, chopped
1 cup whole-kernel corn, cut off the cob or frozen
1 cup grated Cheddar cheese

Preheat the oven to 400°. Pour $^1/_4$ cup of oil into a 10-inch cast-iron skillet and place in the oven to heat. Combine dry ingredients in a bowl and stir. Add milk, remaining $^1/_4$ cup oil, egg, chiles, corn, and cheese; mix well. Pour batter into heated skillet and reduce oven heat to 375°. Bake for 30 minutes until golden brown and done in the center. Yields 6–8 servings.

Drop the Hook, Let's Eat

At their closest, America and Russia are a mere 2.5 miles apart—the distance between Little Diomede Island, Alaska, and Big Diomede Island, Russia. The two islands sit astride the U.S./Russian maritime border in the middle of the Bering Strait. When the Bering Strait freezes, you can walk between the two islands—from America to Russia—and thus, because you would cross the international date line, from today to tomorrow. Or walk from Russia to America and travel from today to yesterday. But don't try it. The frozen Bering Strait can have huge ice ridges as well as open holes of water.

60-Minute Rolls

We had a very large Sunday dinner after church each week. It was a rare time we didn't have these rolls. They are wonderful the next day, too!

¹/₄ cup warm water
2 packages yeast
3 tablespoons sugar, divided
1¹/₄ cups milk

4 tablespoons butter
1 teaspoon salt
4–5 cups bread flour

Place warm water in a large mixing bowl; sprinkle yeast and 1 table-spoon sugar on top and let yeast proof. Place milk, butter, 2 table-spoons sugar, and salt in microwave cup or bowl. Heat until butter, sugar, and salt are melted and dissolved. Add to proofed yeast (make sure milk is not too hot).

Add enough flour to make soft dough. Knead in mixer, or by hand, about 10 minutes. Put bowl in warm place and let rise about 15 minutes. Punch down; shape into rolls and place on greased baking sheet. Let rise 15 minutes and bake at 400° for 8–10 minutes.

Welcome Home

1-2-3 Biscuits

As soon as my children were old enough to count, they started making these quick and simple biscuits.

1 teaspoon salt
2 cups flour
3 teaspoons baking powder

¹/₃ cup oil
²/₃ cup milk

Mix salt, flour, and baking powder together in a bowl. Mix oil and milk, then add to dry mixture. Mix briefly. Place on ungreased baking sheet, about 3-tablespoons size (the size of a small child's fist). Bake at 375° for 10–12 minutes until golden brown. Serve warm. Makes about 12–15 biscuits.

Nome Centennial Cookbook 1898-1998

Fireweed Herb Garden Focaccia Bread

This bread starts off in the bread machine.

³/₄ cup lukewarm water
2 cups white bread flour
³/₄ teaspoon salt
2 tablespoons sugar
³/₄ teaspoon fast-rise yeast
Olive oil
Fresh herbs, chopped (oregano, rosemary, basil, thyme, parsley)

Cracked pepper
Kosher salt, sea salt or garlic salt
¹/₂ teaspoon minced garlic
Parmesan cheese
1 medium tomato, diced (optional)
Sliced olives
3–4 tablespoons chopped onion

Combine water, flour, salt, sugar, and yeast, and put in bread machine. Set on dough setting. Oil a medium-sized pizza pan with olive oil. Set oven at 400°. Take dough out of machine at the end of the cycle and press into the oiled pizza pan. Dimple the top of the dough by pushing tips of fingers into dough. Let dough rise for 20–30 minutes. Gently re-dimple. Drizzle 3 tablespoons olive oil over top and bake at 400° for 15 minutes. Remove from oven and top with remaining ingredients. Put bread back in oven just 10 minutes to warm up the herbs and bring out the flavor. Serve warm and enjoy!

Grannie Annie's Cookin' at the Homestead

Fireweed is a vibrant flower that blooms in late summer and autumn, painting the roadsides in rich hues of pink and magenta. As legend has it, when fireweed reaches its full splendor, the six-week countdown to winter begins.

Buttermilk Cinnamon-Nut Bread

4 cups unbleached flour
2 teaspoons baking soda
1 teaspoon salt
1/2 cup vegetable oil
2 1/2 cups sugar, divided

2 cups buttermilk
2 eggs
2 tablespoons chopped walnuts
1 tablespoon cinnamon

Mix flour, soda, and salt. Combine oil and 1 1/2 cups sugar. Add buttermilk and eggs. Mix well. Stir into dry ingredients; add nuts. Pour batter into 2 loaf pans. Mix cinnamon and leftover sugar. Sprinkle over batter. Swirl batter with a knife. Bake at 350° for 40–45 minutes.

Upper Kenai River Inn Breakfast Cookbook

LAUREN JONES

Along the Denali Highway between Mount McKinley and the Talkeetna Mountain range stands Igloo City Resort, where you can gaze at the amazing view, buy gifts and T-shirts, buy a drink, get fuel for your car, and refuel your helicopter.

Sour Cream Cranberry Nut Bread

1 cup margarine, softened
2 cups sugar
1 teaspoon salt
4 eggs, beaten
2 cups mashed ripe bananas

1 cup sour cream
4 cups all-purpose flour
2 teaspoons baking soda
1 cup chopped walnuts
2 cups cranberries

Preheat oven to 350°. Cream margarine and sugar in large bowl. Add salt, eggs, bananas, and sour cream. Beat until smooth. In separate bowl, combine flour and soda. Gradually add to creamed mixture. Mix in walnuts, then gently add cranberries. Prepare 2 (9x5x3-inch) loaf pans by coating with nonstick cooking spray. Divide batter evenly between pans. Bake for 50–60 minutes, or until top springs back when touched lightly. Yields 2 loaves.

Alaska's Gourmet Breakfasts

Cranberry Apple Nut Bread

3 eggs
1 teaspoon vanilla
3/4 cup vegetable oil
1/2 cup milk
3 cups flour
1 3/4 cups sugar
1 teaspoon baking soda

1 teaspoon salt
1/2 teaspoon cinnamon
3 cups diced Granny Smith apples
1 cup chopped walnuts
1 1/2 cups cranberries (Alaskan
   low-bush)

Mix liquids together in one bowl and dry in another. Gradually add dry to liquid until mixed, and beat on low speed for 3 minutes. Stir in apples and nuts. Last, fold in cranberries. Spoon into sprayed loaf pans (any size) to about 1/2 full. Bake at 350° for about 1 hour, or until browned, and bread pops back when touched. Spoon Glaze over top, if desired. Yields 16 servings.

GLAZE:

1 cup powdered sugar

2 tablespoons lemon juice

Recipe from Alaskan's Lazy Daze B & B, North Pole
Favorite Recipes from Alaska's Bed and Breakfasts

Cranberry Orange Bread

2 cups sifted flour
³/₄ cup sugar
3 teaspoons baking powder
³/₄ teaspoon salt
¹/₂ teaspoon nutmeg
Grated rind of 1 orange

³/₄ cup orange juice
1 egg, slightly beaten
2 tablespoons salad oil
1 cup chopped cranberries (if
   wild, leave whole)

Sift dry ingredients into bowl. Add orange rind; mix. Combine orange juice, egg, and salad oil. Add to dry ingredients, stirring just until flour is moistened. Fold in cranberries. Spread in greased 9x5x3-inch loaf pan. Bake at 350° for 60–70 minutes. Serve with Orange Honey Butter.

ORANGE HONEY BUTTER:
¹/₂ cup margarine, softened
2 tablespoons honey

1 teaspoon grated orange rind
¹/₂ teaspoon coriander and ginger

Combine all and mix well.

Note: May be baked in 12-ounce juice cans or small muffin tins.

Alaska's Cooking Volume II

Of the 20 highest peaks in the United States, 17 are in Alaska. Denali (dunäl´E), the "High One," is the name Athabascan (athubas´kun) native people gave Mount McKinley, the massive peak that crowns the 600-mile-long Alaska Range. Mount McKinley's altitude is 20,320 feet, making it the highest mountain in North America. Temperatures at the summit are severe even in summer. Winter lows at just 14,500 feet can plummet below -95 degrees Fahrenheit! Permanent snowfields cover more than 75% of the mountain and feed the many glaciers that surround its base. The mountain's granite and slate core is, in fact, overlain by ice that is hundreds of feet thick in places. Mount McKinley National Park was renamed Denali National Park and Preserve in 1980 when the boundary was enlarged by four million acres. At six million acres, the park is larger than Massachusetts. It remains largely wild and unspoiled, as the Athabascans knew it.

Banana Nut Whiskey Bread

1 1/2 cups sugar
1/2 cup butter or margarine
3 eggs
3 cups flour
1 1/2 teaspoons baking soda
3/4 teaspoon salt
1 1/2 teaspoons baking powder

1/2 cup water
1 teaspoon vanilla
1 cup R&R Canadian whiskey
   (blended bourbon), optional
3 bananas, mashed
1/2 pound chopped walnuts
   (optional)

Preheat oven to 350°. Cream together sugar, butter, and eggs. Mix in the remaining ingredients, adding mashed bananas last, and beat together. Add nuts, if desired. Bake in greased loaf pans for 45 minutes.

Note: Batter should be creamy and pourable. If sticky, add more whiskey or water to make batter creamy. If you don't use the whiskey, use more vanilla for flavor.

Ladies of Harley Cookbook

Sour Cream Banana and Berry Bread

1 cup margarine, softened
2 cups sugar
4 eggs
1 teaspoon salt
1 teaspoon vanilla
2 cups mashed bananas (very
   ripe is best)

4 cups sifted flour
2 teaspoons baking soda
1 cup sour cream
1 cup chopped nuts
2 cups cranberries (frozen
   work best)

Beat margarine until soft; add sugar, eggs, salt, vanilla, and bananas and blend together. Add dry ingredients alternately with sour cream, blending well after each addition. Fold in nuts and cranberries. Bake at 350° in greased and floured loaf pans until toothpick inserted in the middle comes out clean. Do not overbake. Bread in small pans will bake about 40–50 minutes.

What's Cookin' in the Kenai Peninsula

Sweet Berry Bread

2 cups flour
$^1/_2$ teaspoon salt
1 teaspoon baking powder
1 teaspoon baking soda
$^1/_2$ cup butter or margarine,
   softened

1 cup sugar
$^1/_2$ teaspoon almond extract
2 eggs
1 cup crushed, hulled, fresh
   strawberries*

Stir together flour, salt, baking powder, and baking soda. Set aside. In medium bowl, cream together butter, sugar, and almond extract. Add eggs, one at a time, beating thoroughly after each. Add flour mixture and berries, mixing only until blended. Grease an 8x4x2-inch loaf pan, then line with greased waxed paper. Turn batter into pan; smooth top evenly with spoon. Bake at 325° for 50–60 minutes or until pick inserted in center of loaf comes out clean. Let bread stand in pan on rack for 10 minutes. Turn out on rack, peel off paper, and turn bread, right-side up, to cool completely. When cold, wrap airtight. Let bread stand for 1 day before slicing. Makes 1 loaf.

*If fresh berries are unavailable, thawed, frozen, unsweetened berries can be substituted. If too much juice, drain some off.

Huna Heritage Foundation Cookbook

The state of Alaska superimposed on a map of the lower 48 states illustrates the awesome size of the 49th state.

Lingonberry Loaf
Alaska Low-Bush Cranberries

This makes a good loaf in appearance and taste.

2¼ **cups all-purpose flour**
2¼ **teaspoons baking powder**
¼ **teaspoon baking soda**
¾ **teaspoon salt**
3 **teaspoons shortening**
¾ **cup sugar**

1 **egg, beaten**
¾ **cup orange juice**
½ **cup chopped walnuts**
1 **cup lingonberries**
½ **cup minced pineapple**

Grease and flour 9x5x3-inch loaf pan. Sift flour; measure and resift 3 times with next 3 ingredients. Cream shortening and sugar well; add egg and beat until smooth and fluffy. Add orange juice and sifted dry ingredients alternately in 3 portions, beating smooth after each. Fold in nuts, lingonberries, and pineapple. Turn into prepared pan and let set for 15 minutes. Cover with another pan and bake for 20 minutes in 350° oven. Remove top pan and bake for 50 minutes longer.

TOPPING:

½ **cup orange juice**
¾ **cup sugar**
2 **tablespoons grated orange rind**

½ **teaspoon vanilla**
½ **teaspoon rum extract or**
1 **tablespoon rum**

Mix Topping and spoon over hot loaf while still in pan. Remove warm loaf; cool on rack. Wrap in plastic wrap or aluminum foil.

Pioneers of Alaska Auxiliary #8

Alaska contains 586,412 square miles and is one-fifth the size of the Lower 48 states, 488 times larger than Rhode Island, two and a half times larger than Texas, and larger than the next three largest states in the U.S. combined. East to west (including the Aleutian Islands), Alaska measures 2,400 miles—roughly the distance between Savannah, Georgia and Santa Barbara, California.

24-Karat Sourdough Sunshine Muffins

1 cup flour
1/4 cup oat bran
1/4 cup brown sugar
1 teaspoon baking powder
1/2 teaspoon baking soda
1/4 teaspoon salt
1 teaspoon cinnamon
2 large eggs, or 4 egg whites

1/4 cup vegetable oil
1/2 cup Sourdough Starter* (see starter recipe on page 31)
1 1/2 cups grated carrots (about 2 medium)
1/2 cup crushed pineapple
1 teaspoon grated orange peel
1/2 cup walnuts

Preheat oven to 375°. Measure all the dry ingredients into a large bowl, or the work bowl of a food processor. Mix to blend well.

In a second bowl, stir together the eggs, vegetable oil, sourdough starter, carrots, pineapple, orange peel, and walnuts. Dump the whole bowl of wet ingredients on top of the dry ingredients and mix with a mixer or by pulsing the food processor just to blend well.

Spray 18 muffin cups with nonstick coating, and scoop the batter evenly into the muffin tins. Bake 25–30 minutes at 375°. Makes 18 muffins.

*Bring starter to room temperature before using, and replenish with equal parts of warm water and flour.

Alaska Cooking: Featuring Skagway

Banana Sunshine Muffins

1/2 cup uncooked oatmeal
1/2 cup milk
1 cup unbleached flour
1/4 cup sugar
1 1/2 teaspoons baking powder
1/2 teaspoon baking soda
1/2 teaspoon salt

1/2 teaspoon cinnamon
1/4 teaspoon nutmeg
1/4 cup butter, melted
1 egg
1 cup mashed bananas
1/2 cup shelled sunflower seeds

Mix oatmeal and milk and set aside. Mix dry ingredients. Add butter, egg, bananas, and sunflower seeds. Stir in oatmeal mixture. Add to dry ingredients. Bake in greased (12-cup) muffin tin at 350° for 25–30 minutes.

Upper Kenai River Inn Breakfast Cookbook

Russian River Cranberry Muffins & Honey Orange Butter

2 cups unbleached flour
1 cup sugar
1¹/₂ teaspoons baking powder
¹/₂ teaspoon baking soda
1¹/₂ teaspoons nutmeg
1 teaspoon cinnamon
¹/₂ teaspoon ginger

¹/₂ cup shortening
³/₄ cup orange juice
1 tablespoon vanilla
2 teaspoons grated orange zest
2 eggs
1¹/₂ cups chopped cranberries
1¹/₂ cups chopped walnuts

Mix dry ingredients and cut in shortening. Mix orange juice, vanilla, orange zest, and eggs. Stir into flour mixture. Fold in cranberries and nuts. Spoon batter into buttered muffin cups and bake at 350° for 25 minutes. Serve with Honey-Orange Butter.

HONEY-ORANGE BUTTER:
1 cup butter, softened
¹/₂ cup honey

2 tablespoons grated orange zest

Beat butter till fluffy. Add honey and zest. Beat well. Makes about 1¹/₄ cups.

Upper Kenai River Inn Breakfast Cookbook

Sourdough English Muffins

1 package dry yeast
1 teaspoon sugar
¹/₄ cup warm water
¹/₂ cup scalded milk
1 cup water
¹/₂ cup Sourdough Starter
   (see page 31 for recipe)

¹/₄ teaspoon baking soda
1 rounded teaspoon salt
4 cups sifted flour (or can use
   2 cups white and 2 cups wheat),
   divided
3 tablespoons melted shortening

Sprinkle yeast and sugar over warm water. Heat milk to lukewarm, add water, Sourdough Starter, baking soda, salt, and yeast which has been allowed to get bubbly. Add half the flour and beat well with either an electric beater or a wooden spoon. Let rise to double in bulk. Add melted shortening and remaining flour. Beat and knead thoroughly. Let rise until double in bulk. Place on board dusted slightly with corn meal and flour. Flatten with rolling pin to ³/₄-inch thickness. Let stand until light. Cut with a 2¹/₂-inch diameter cutter. Cook 15 minutes on a hot, buttered griddle (about 340° on an electric skillet) turning several times during cooking. When ready to serve, split in half, toast and butter.

A Cook's Tour of Alaska

Speak the Alaskan lingo: "Breakup" is the end of an Alaskan winter when the ice that has frozen the major rivers thaws. "Ice fog" is a thick, winter fog made of suspended ice particles that leave the trees coated with ice crystals. "Mukluks" are Eskimo moccasins. "Outside" means anywhere but Alaska. Natives call newcomers to Alaska "cheechakos" (chE-chää´kOs), and an Alaskan old timer is called a "sourdough."

Blueberry Scones

²/₃ cup buttermilk or plain yogurt
1 large egg
3 cups all-purpose flour
4 teaspoons baking powder
¹/₂ teaspoon baking soda
¹/₂ teaspoon salt

8 tablespoons (1 stick) cold,
  unsalted butter, cut up
1 cup fresh or frozen blueberries
¹/₂ cup sugar
1–3 teaspoons freshly grated
  orange peel

Heat oven to 375°. Measure buttermilk or yogurt into a small bowl and beat in egg with a fork. Set aside.

Measure flour, baking powder, baking soda, and salt into a large bowl and stir well. Cut in the butter with a pastry blender or rub in with your fingers until the mixture looks like fine meal. Add blueberries, sugar, and orange peel; mix lightly until evenly distributed. Add buttermilk or yogurt and stir until a soft dough forms.

On a lightly floured surface, knead dough 5 or 6 times. For small scones, split the dough into 2 pieces and form each piece into a ball. Flatten each ball with your hands to form a circle; cut each circle into 6 wedges. Place circles on an ungreased baking sheet. For large scones, do not split dough into 2 circles. Make 1 circle and cut into 8 wedges. (For crisp sides, separate wedges; for softer sides, leave wedges touching.) Bake for 20–25 minutes, or until light to medium brown. Remove and cool on a wire rack. Allow to cool at least 1 hour before serving. Serve with Orange Butter. Makes 12 small or 8 large scones.

ORANGE BUTTER:

1¹/₂ teaspoons freshly grated
  orange peel

1 stick butter, room temperature
1 teaspoon sugar

Mix ingredients together with a food processor or electric mixer until well blended. Best if allowed to sit before use so flavors can blend.

Blueberry Pride: Blueberry Bash Recipes 1989–1993

Butterhorns

2 sticks butter, softened   **2 cups flour**
12 ounces cottage cheese   **Dash of salt**

Cream butter and cottage cheese, then mix in flour and salt. Place in refrigerator overnight. In morning, divide dough into 3 equal parts, then roll each into a circle on floured surface. Cut each circle into 12 wedges and roll up, starting at wide end. Place on greased sheet. Bake at 350° for 30–40 minutes or until golden. Remove from oven and drizzle with Frosting mixture.

FROSTING:
1 cup powdered sugar   **2 tablespoons milk**
2 tablespoons softened butter   **$^1/_2$ teaspoon vanilla**

Simply the Best Recipes

Snails

1 (2-crust size) box "unfold and   **$^1/_4$ cup sugar**
bake" refrigerated pie crusts   **$^1/_2$ teaspoon cinnamon**
$^1/_4$ cup butter, melted

Preheat oven to 350°. Unfold crusts, brush with some of the butter, and cut like a pie into 8 wedges each. In a small bowl, mix sugar and cinnamon. Sprinkle each pie crust with some of sugar mixture. To make snails, roll each slice from the outer edge toward the tip. Place on ungreased baking sheets, brush with butter, and sprinkle with remaining sugar mixture. Bake for 12–15 minutes. Makes 16.

Moose Racks, Bear Tracks, and Other Alaska Kidsnacks

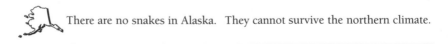

There are no snakes in Alaska. They cannot survive the northern climate.

Blue Ribbon Cinnamon Rolls

This makes 2 pans of extra-large, cinnamon-swirled rolls.

2 packages active dry yeast	10 cups sifted flour, divided
3 cups lukewarm water	1 cup maple-flavored syrup
1 cup butter or margarine, divided	1 cup firmly packed brown sugar
$^1/_4$ cup shortening	$^1/_2$ cup margarine, softened, divided
$^3/_4$ cup sugar	1 cup sugar, mixed with
2 teaspoons salt	2 teaspoons cinnamon
2 eggs	

Sprinkle yeast on lukewarm water; stir to dissolve. Add $^1/_2$ cup butter, shortening, sugar, salt, eggs, and 2 cups flour. Beat with electric mixer at medium speed until smooth. Gradually add enough remaining flour to make a soft dough that leaves the side of the bowl. Place dough in lightly greased bowl; turn over to grease top. Cover and let rise until doubled, about $1^1/_2$ hours.

Combine syrup, remaining $^1/_2$ cup butter, and brown sugar in saucepan. Heat until sugar dissolves, stirring occasionally. Cool to lukewarm and pour evenly into 2 (9x13-inch) baking pans. Divide dough in half. Roll $^1/_2$ into a 12x14-inch rectangle on floured surface. Spread with $^1/_2$ the softened margarine and sugar/cinnamon mixture, reserving half for rest of dough. Roll up like jellyroll from narrow side. Cut into 12 slices.

Place in prepared pan. Repeat with remaining dough. Let rise until doubled, about 45 minutes to 1 hour. Bake at 375° for 30 minutes or until golden brown. Remove from pans by inverting on racks over waxed paper. Makes 24 rolls.

Note: You may use chopped nuts in the syrup mixture or add raisins by sprinkling over dough when adding sugar and cinnamon mixture. The basic dough recipe can be adapted to other sweet rolls.

What's Cookin' in the Kenai Peninsula

Admiralty View Bed and Breakfast Sticky Buns

1 package yeast
$^1/_4$ cup warm water (110°)
1 cup milk, scalded
$^1/_4$ cup sugar
$^1/_4$ cup shortening
1 teaspoon salt
3$^1/_2$ cups flour (sifted all-purpose), divided
1 egg

6 tablespoons butter, melted
2–3 generous tablespoons sour cream
1 cup + extra brown sugar
Chopped walnuts or pecans (optional)
Butter
Cinnamon
Raisins (optional)

The night before: Soften yeast in warm water. Combine milk, sugar, shortening, and salt; cool to lukewarm. Add 1$^1/_2$ cups flour; beat well. Add yeast and egg. Gradually add remaining flour to form a soft dough, kneading well. Place in greased bowl; turn once to grease surface. Cover and let rise until doubled (1–2 hours). Punch dough down and divide in half. Let the dough rest while the Caramel is prepared.

Mix together the melted butter, sour cream, 1 cup brown sugar, and nuts, if using. Divide this mixture in half and spread evenly in the bottom of 2 (9-inch) cake pans. Roll half the dough out into a rectangle shape; butter dough and cover with extra brown sugar and cinnamon (raisins may be added). Roll up and cut into 8 pieces and put the pieces, cut-side down, in the prepared pan. Repeat with second $^1/_2$ of the dough. Cover with plastic wrap and let the buns rise overnight in the refrigerator.

The next morning take the buns out of the refrigerator and put them in a cold oven. Turn the oven on (the buns will continue to rise as the oven heats up) to 350° and bake for 25–30 minutes, or until the buns are golden brown and sound hollow when tapped.

Recipe from Admiralty View B&B, Juneau
Favorite Recipes from Alaska's Bed and Breakfasts

Buttermilk Coffee Cake

1¼ cups flour
½ teaspoon salt
1½ teaspoons cinnamon, divided
1 cup packed brown sugar
¾ cup sugar
¾ cup oil

½ cup chopped walnuts
1 teaspoon baking soda
1 teaspoon baking powder
1 egg, slightly beaten
1 cup buttermilk

Sift flour with salt and ½ teaspoon cinnamon into a large bowl; add sugars and oil. Mix until well blended and feathery. Take out ¾ cup of this mixture and save as topping. Add nuts and 1 teaspoon cinnamon to topping and set aside.

To remaining mixture, add baking soda, baking powder, egg, and buttermilk. Mix until smooth. Pour into a 9x13-inch pan. Sprinkle with topping and press lightly. Bake at 350° for 25–30 minutes.

Our Cherished Recipes Volume II

BARNEY MCKEE

One of the most popular visitor attractions in Alaska is Portage Glacier in Portage Valley. In 1893 the glacier deposited the rocks of what is now the terminal moraine (the farthest advance) at the foot of Portage Lake. Since then the ice has receded three miles up and around a bend in the valley. Boat tours of the berg-dotted lake and glacier are available two miles beyond the center on the lake's south shore.

Overnight Blueberry Coffee Cake

1 egg
¹/₂ cup + 2 tablespoons sugar,
  divided
1¹/₄ cups flour
2 teaspoons baking powder

³/₄ teaspoon salt
¹/₃ cup milk
3 tablespoons butter or margarine,
  melted
1 cup fresh blueberries

In a mixing bowl beat egg and ¹/₂ cup sugar. Combine flour, baking powder, and salt. Add alternately with milk to sugar mixture, beating well after each addition. Stir in butter. Fold in berries. Pour into a greased, 8-inch-square baking pan. Sprinkle with remaining sugar. Cover and chill overnight. Remove from refrigerator 30 minutes before baking. Bake at 350° for 30–35 minutes. Serves 9.

Literary Tastes

Yummy Coffeecake

1 tablespoon vinegar or lemon
  juice
1 cup milk
³/₄ cup pecans
¹/₃ cup brown sugar
1¹/₃ cups sugar, divided
1 teaspoon cinnamon

1 cup butter, softened
2 eggs
2 cups flour
1 teaspoon baking soda
1 teaspoon baking powder
¹/₂ teaspoon salt
1 teaspoon vanilla

Add vinegar to milk and let stand 5 minutes. In a food processor, process pecans, brown sugar, ¹/₃ cup sugar, and cinnamon. Set aside. Cream butter, 1 cup sugar, and eggs; then add milk mixture, dry ingredients, and vanilla.

Pour ¹/₂ the batter in greased 9-inch tube pan. Sprinkle with ¹/₂ the pecan mixture. Pour remaining batter and top with rest of pecan mixture. Bake at 325° for 40 minutes. Cool 10 minutes before removing from pan.

Recipe from Midge's Birch Lane B&B, Fairbanks
Favorite Recipes from Alaska's Bed and Breakfasts

Baked Orange French Toast

3 tablespoons freshly grated
  orange zest
2 cups orange juice
$^{1}/_{4}$ cup sugar
$^{1}/_{4}$ teaspoon vanilla
2 tablespoons Triple Sec
6 large eggs

$^{1}/_{2}$ cup half-and-half
Pinch of salt
8 (1-inch-thick) diagonal slices of
  challah or good-quality Italian
  bread
3 tablespoons unsalted butter,
  melted

In a large bowl, whisk together zest, juice, sugar, vanilla, Triple Sec, eggs, half-and-half, and a pinch of salt. Arrange bread slices in 1 layer in a 9x13x2-inch glass baking dish. Pour mixture over bread, turning slices to coat, and chill, covered, 4 hours or overnight.

Preheat oven to 400° and brush a large baking sheet with butter. Using slotted spatula, arrange bread in 1 layer on baking sheet, leaving at least 2 inches between each slice, and bake in middle of oven 5 minutes. Rotate pan and bake 5 minutes more. Turn bread over and bake 5 minutes more. Rotate pan and bake until bread is puffed and golden, 5 minutes more. Make Sauce while bread is baking.

SAUCE:

2 tablespoons sweet orange
  marmalade

3 tablespoons unsalted butter
1 tablespoon Triple Sec

In a small saucepan, cook marmalade, butter, and Triple Sec over low heat, stirring until butter is melted. Drizzle French Toast with Sauce and serve with maple syrup. Serves 4.

Recipe from Lilac House, Anchorage
Favorite Recipes from Alaska's Bed and Breakfasts

Overnight Blueberry French Toast with Blueberry Sauce

12 slices day-old white bread, crusts removed, divided
2 (8-ounce) packages cream cheese
1 cup fresh or frozen blueberries
12 eggs
2 cups milk
⅓ cup maple syrup

Cut bread into 1-inch cubes; place ½ in a greased 9x13x2-inch baking dish. Cut cream cheese into 1-inch cubes; place over bread. Top with blueberries and remaining bread. In a large bowl, beat eggs. Add milk and syrup; mix well. Pour over bread mixture. Cover and chill 8 hours or overnight.

Remove from refrigerator 30 minutes before baking. Cover and bake at 350° for 30 minutes. Uncover; bake 25–35 minutes more, or until golden brown and the center is set. Yields 6–8 servings.

SAUCE:

1 cup sugar
2 tablespoons cornstarch
1 cup water
1 cup fresh or frozen blueberries
1 tablespoon butter or margarine

In a saucepan, combine sugar and cornstarch; add water. Bring to a boil over medium heat; boil for 3 minutes, stirring constantly. Stir in blueberries; reduce heat. Simmer for 8–10 minutes or until berries have burst. Stir in butter until melted. Serve over French toast. Yields 1¾ cups sauce.

The Best of the Blueberry Bash, 1994-2002

Tlingit [tling git, or kling kit] Chief Kowee led two prospectors to a creek which emptied into the Gastineau Channel, and after a few hours of panning, Joe Juneau and Richard Harris found gold and laid claim on October 4, 1880, to an area they called Gold Creek—thus changing the history of Alaska forever. In 1897, gold was discovered on the Klondike River in Canada's Yukon Territory. Many of the 10,000 fortune seekers hiked from Skagway across the treacherous Chilkoot Trail. In 1898, gold was found on the beaches near Nome. A city of tents sprang up overnight, and by 1900, 232 ships had arrived in Nome carrying nearly 18,000 prospectors.

Peg's Kid-Pleasin' French Toast

$^1/_2$ cup creamy peanut butter	4 eggs
$^1/_4$ cup honey	1 cup milk
8 slices bread	Butter

Mix peanut butter and honey. Spread on 4 slices of bread and top with remaining bread. Trim crusts. Beat eggs and milk. Cut sandwiches into 3 slices. Dip each piece in milk mixture. Cook on hot buttered griddle until browned on each side. Can sprinkle with powdered sugar. It is also good served with honey for dipping.

Upper Kenai River Inn Breakfast Cookbook

Butterscotch Toast

A quick "sweet bread" for breakfast.

$^1/_4$ cup chopped walnuts	$^1/_3$ cup soft margarine
$^3/_4$ cup brown sugar	$^1/_4$ teaspoon nutmeg
1 teaspoon water	Bread slices

Mix first five ingredients well and store in fridge and use as needed. Spread on bread slices and toast or broil in oven till brown and crunchy.

All-Alaska Women in Timber Cookbook

Oatmeal Pancakes

2 cups quick or rough-cut oats
$^1/_2$ teaspoon baking soda
$2^1/_2$ cups buttermilk
1 cup flour

2 teaspoons baking powder
$^1/_2$ teaspoon salt
$^1/_3$ cup oil
2 eggs, beaten

Mix oats, baking soda, and buttermilk; let stand 5 minutes (if using rough cut, soak longer). Stir in flour, baking powder, salt, oil, and eggs; mix well. Drop $^1/_3$ cup batter on medium-hot griddle. (Batter is thick, so pancakes need to "bake," versus fry like regular pancakes.) Cook until bubbles burst, then cook on other side.

Recipes From the Paris of the Pacific—Sitka, Alaska

Sourdough Pancakes

1 cup Sourdough Starter (see
    starter recipe on page 31)
2 cups warm milk
$2^1/_2$ cups sifted flour
2 eggs

3 tablespoons sugar
1 teaspoon salt
1 teaspoon baking soda
5 tablespoons melted butter

Combine Starter, milk, and flour. Leave at room temperature overnight. The next morning add eggs, sugar, salt, baking soda, and butter. Mix well. Drop onto a greased griddle and cook each side until golden brown.

License to Cook Alaska Style

In 1867, U.S. Secretary of State William H. Seward negotiated the purchase of Alaska from Russia for $7.2 million, which breaks down to approximately 2 cents per acre. The treaty was signed on March 30th and ratified by the Senate on June 20th. Formal handover of the territory took place on October 18th. In America, reaction to the purchase was mixed. The *New York Tribune* referred to the new territory as "Walrussia" to define what they deemed as a worthless, frozen territory. Some called it "Seward's Folly" after Secretary of State Seward. Other newspapers praised the acquisition for its possible commercial and strategic benefits.

Speckled Baked Eggs

2 tablespoons canola oil
$^1/_2$ cup chopped onion
1 cup chopped mushrooms
$^1/_2$ cup chopped green pepper
$^1/_4$ cup chopped roasted red
   pepper
12 eggs
6 tablespoons milk

1 teaspoon dried thyme
1 teaspoon white pepper
$^1/_2$ teaspoon ground coriander
Salt
$^1/_2$ cup shredded Cheddar cheese,
   plus 2 tablespoons, divided
$^1/_4$ cup diced fresh tomatoes
   (optional)

Preheat oven to 400°. In a large skillet sauté onions in oil over medium heat until soft. Add mushrooms, green and red peppers, and sauté until vegetables are tender. Meanwhile, whisk eggs in a large bowl, adding milk and seasonings. Pour into a lightly oiled, 2-quart baking dish. Stir in vegetable mixture and $^1/_2$ cup cheese. Cover and bake for 30 minutes. Reduce oven temperature to 350° and bake another 15 minutes until eggs are firm in the center. Sprinkle remaining cheese on top and allow this to melt, covered. If using tomatoes, spread on top of cheese. Serve at once, so that the eggs do not fall. Yields 6 servings.

Drop the Hook, Let's Eat

Bayfield Eggs

1$^1/_2$ pounds sausage
12 eggs
$^3/_4$ pound shredded Cheddar
   cheese, divided
$^1/_2$–1 cup green onions, chopped
$^1/_2$ green pepper, chopped

Small can sliced mushrooms,
   drained
$^1/_2$ teaspoon salt
$^1/_2$ teaspoon pepper
$^1/_2$ pint whole cream

Fry sausage and drain well. Grease 9x13-inch pan. Break eggs into pan. Poke the yolks. Top with all the sausage, $^1/_2$ cheese, all the onions, green pepper, and mushrooms. Sprinkle with salt and pepper. Cover all with cream and remaining cheese. Refrigerate overnight. Bake at 350° for 1 hour. Serves 8.

Sharing Our Best

Chichee Yitsee
Seagull Eggs

Gather from high bluffs in May. Take only 1 or 2 from each nest. Uses are as follows: Boil about 20 minutes; cool, peel, and eat.

Beat 3 eggs well. Add enough flour to make a medium thick batter. Add 1–2 teaspoons baking powder and a bit of salt. Mix well. Drop into a hot pan to which lard has been added. Fry until golden brown on each side. Eat with jelly or jam. Try salmonberry jam with this.

Eskimo Cookbook by Alexandra

Scotch Eggs

8 eggs, hard-boiled, peeled
3 cups herb seasoned stuffing mix
1 pound bulk pork sausage
2 tablespoons finely chopped onion
1 teaspoon ground sage

¹/₄ cup flour
1 egg, beaten with 1 teaspoon water
Vegetable oil
Tomato slices for garnish
Parsley for garnish

Prepare hard-boiled eggs; set aside. In food processor, crush stuffing mix to fine crumbs. In separate bowl, combine sausage, onion, and sage; mix in 1¹/₂ cups stuffing mix crumbs. Divide mixture into 8 portions. Dip each egg in flour. Flatten out each sausage portion and gently press around egg. Dip each coated egg in beaten egg mixture and roll in remaining crumbs. Preheat oil to 375° in large skillet. Fry eggs in oil for 4–5 minutes, turning to cook sausage until browned and thoroughly cooked. Drain. Serve hot, sliced in half, lengthwise, garnished with tomato slice and parsley. Yields 8 servings.

Alaska's Gourmet Breakfasts

Early Morning Quiche

1 unbaked pastry shell
12 strips crisp bacon, crumbled
1/2 cup grated Monterey Jack
  cheese
1/2 cup grated Cheddar cheese
1/3 cup chopped onion

4 eggs, beaten
2 cups whipping cream
3/4 teaspoon salt
1/4 teaspoon sugar
1/8 teaspoon cayenne pepper

Line pastry shell with double thickness of foil. Bake at 450° for 5 minutes. Remove foil and bake another 5 minutes. Remove from oven. Reduce heat to 425°. Sprinkle bacon, cheeses, and onion over crust. Beat eggs, cream, salt, sugar, and cayenne. Pour into crust. Bake for 15 minutes. Reduce heat to 300° and bake 30 minutes longer or until knife inserted into center comes out clean. Serves 6–8.

Upper Kenai River Inn Breakfast Cookbook

Salsa Omelet

1/2 cup mild salsa
1 cup shredded Monterey Jack
  cheese
1 cup shredded Cheddar cheese

8 eggs
1/2 cup small curd cottage cheese
1/2 cup sour cream
Cilantro as garnish

Spray an 8-inch pie pan with nonstick cooking spray. Spread salsa over bottom of pan; sprinkle Monterey Jack and Cheddar cheeses on top. In a medium bowl, whip together eggs, cottage cheese, and sour cream. Pour egg mixture over cheese. Bake in 350° oven for 45 minutes, or until egg is lightly browned and puffy on top. Serve with cilantro garnish. Yields 6 servings.

Alaska's Gourmet Breakfasts

Alaska oil production can generate more revenue in a single day than the cost to purchase this vast territory in 1867.

Moose Racks

1 pound thinly sliced bacon   **1 cup brown sugar**
1 tablespoon sesame seeds

Preheat oven to 375°. Line an 11x15-inch baking pan with foil. Cut bacon strips in half and arrange in prepared pan in a single layer. Bake for 10 minutes, then turn and sprinkle with sesame seeds and brown sugar. Return to oven and bake another 10 minutes. Remove to a slightly greased platter to cool. Makes about 36 slices.

Moose Racks, Bear Tracks, and Other Alaska Kidsnacks

Don's One-Pan Breakfast

This is excellent on a boat trip. I suggest several Bloody Marys while preparing the meal.

1¹⁄₂–2 pounds country sausage   **Eggs**
¹⁄₂ pound mushrooms, sliced

Cook sausage in frying pan until nearly done; pour excess grease off. Add mushrooms and cook until both are done. With large spoon, make some nests (small indentions) in the sausage. Break an egg in each nest; put lid on and cook until firm. Don't overcook eggs.

Alaska Women in Timber Cookbook

 The Mendenhall Glacier walking trail (opposite page) is sometimes closed temporarily after numerous bear sightings. If you encounter a live bear at close distance, remain calm. Attacks are rare. Remember the following:

- Let the bear know you are human. Talk to the bear in a normal voice. Wave your arms. You may try to back away slowly and diagonally, but if the bear follows, stop and hold your ground.
- Don't run. You can't outrun a bear. They have been clocked at speeds up to 35 mph, and they will chase fleeing animals.
- If a bear actually makes contact, surrender! Fall to the ground and play dead. Lie flat on your stomach, or curl up in a ball with your hands behind your neck. Typically, a bear will break off its attack once it feels the threat has been eliminated.

Alaska Department of Fish and Game

Sunshine Pie

2 cups or 1 (15-ounce) carton
  low-fat ricotta cheese
3 eggs
²/₃ cup sugar
2 tablespoons all-purpose flour
2 tablespoons orange juice

2 teaspoons grated fresh orange
  rind
1 teaspoon orange extract
¹/₄ teaspoon lemon extract
1 (9-inch) deep dish pie shell,
  uncooked

Preheat oven to 350°. Beat ricotta cheese in a large bowl with an electric mixer on high speed for 1 minute. Add eggs, sugar, flour, orange juice, orange rind, orange extract, and lemon extract; blend well with electric mixer. Pour into uncooked pie shell and bake for 50 minutes, until a knife inserted comes out clean. Refrigerate overnight; serve chilled the next morning.

A serving suggestion: A small slice (10 servings per pie) on a plate with fresh fruit is a perfect addition to your breakfast menu, or a large slice (6 servings per pie) can be served as your main breakfast dish.

Recipe from Skyline B&B, Homer
Favorite Recipes from Alaska's Bed and Breakfasts

JUDY TYLER

Sometimes signs are posted warning that bears have been recently sighted in the vicinity. Gwen is NOT going beyond this sign.

Fruit Medley with Amaretto Cream

3 cups fresh fruit*

Place fruit (*strawberries, raspberries, blueberries, kiwi, orange segments, melon, grapes, plums, peaches, etc.) into footed dessert or compote glasses. Serve with Amaretto Cream.

AMARETTO CREAM:

1 (8-ounce) package cream cheese, softened

1 cup (8 ounces) amaretto coffee creamer

¹/₂–1 teaspoon amaretto liqueur (optional)

Whip cream cheese and amaretto coffee creamer in a small bowl until thick and creamy. Whip in liqueur, if desired. Store in a pint jar in the refrigerator. Serve with fresh fruit.

Recipe from Southshore B&B, Wasilla
Favorite Recipes from Alaska's Bed and Breakfasts

Rhubarb Jam with Jello

5 cups sugar
8 cups cut-up rhubarb
1 large box Jell-O (strawberry, cherry or raspberry)

¹/₂ box Sure-Jell

Mix sugar and rhubarb and soak overnight. Cook 15 minutes at medium temperature and add box of Jell-O. Mix until Jell-O is dissolved, then add Sure-Jell. Pour into jars and seal.

Our Cherished Recipes Volume II

Fireweed Herb Garden
Alaska Fireweed Jelly

Give this as a Christmas present, tying the jar with a pretty ribbon with the recipe attached.

8 cups fireweed blossoms
  (no stems)
¹/₄ cup lemon juice
4¹/₂ cups water

2 packages Sure-Jell or other
  powdered pectin
5 cups sugar

Pick, wash, and measure fireweed blossoms. Add lemon juice and water. Boil 10 minutes and strain. Reheat to lukewarm, add pectin, and bring to boil. Add sugar and bring to full boil. Boil hard for just 1 minute. Pour into hot clean jars and seal. Makes a pretty pink jelly. Makes about 6 jars.

Grannie Annie's Cookin' at the Homestead

Salmonberry and Rhubarb Jelly

3 cups salmonberry juice
2 cups rhubarb juice
7 cups sugar

¹/₈ cup lemon juice
1 package MCP or ¹/₂ bottle Certo
  Pectin

Place the juices in large kettle; add sugar and lemon juice; mix well. Bring to a boil, stirring constantly. Add pectin and bring to full rolling boil; boil hard for 1 minute, stirring all the time. Remove from heat, skim and pour into hot glasses; seal with paraffin.

Tasty Treats from Tenakee Springs, Alaska

Salmonberries are found in Southeastern Alaska along the Alaskan Gulf Coast. They resemble a boysenberry, except for the color. In late summer or early fall, the berry is translucent and either bright red or yellow.

Clover Honey

2¹/₂ cups water

10 cups sugar

1 teaspoon alum

18 fireweed blossoms

30 white clover blossoms

18 red clover blossoms

In large pot, combine water, sugar, and alum. Boil for 8 minutes. Remove from heat and add blossoms. Soak for 6 hours. Remove blossoms. If thicker honey is desired, boil a few minutes longer. Put in jars and seal. Makes 4 pints.

Simply the Best Recipes

Homesteader's Honey

30 fireweed flowerlets

20 red clover blossoms

20 white clover blossoms

20 rosehip blossoms

10 cups sugar

2¹/₂ cups water

1 teaspoon powdered alum

Gather, rinse and tie all blossoms in cheesecloth or short, clean nylon. Dissolve sugar in boiling water and boil over low heat 25 minutes. Remove from heat, add alum, and emerse blossoms 25–30 minutes for alum to draw out nectar. Pour into sterilized jars. Seal. If it should sugar the second year, set jar in boiling water until liquid.

Let's Taste Alaska

SOUPS, CHILIES *and* STEWS

Called "The Last Great Race," the Iditarod Trail Sled Dog Race is the ultimate test of mushers and dogs. This annual 1,049-mile trek across Alaska starts in downtown Anchorage the first Saturday of March.

Corn Chowder

4 medium potatoes, peeled and
  cubed
4 medium onions, sliced
6 tablespoons butter, divided
4 cups milk
1/2 cup light cream or canned milk

2 cans creamed corn
1/2 teaspoon parsley
1/8 teaspoon thyme
1/8 teaspoon marjoram
Salt and pepper to taste

Boil potatoes in water until soft. Set aside. Fry onions in 2 table-spoons of butter. Warm milk and cream in large kettle. Add drained potatoes (reserving 1 cup of potato water), onions, corn, potato water, 4 tablespoons butter, parsley, thyme, marjoram, salt and pepper. Heat, but do not boil. For best flavor, cool and reheat.

Be Our Guest

Corny-Salmon Chowder

1 can chicken broth
1/2 cup chopped onion
1/2 cup chopped green pepper
1/2 cup chopped celery
3–4 diced new red potatoes with
  skins left on
1 cup chopped carrots
1 teaspoon minced garlic

1 can creamed corn
1 can evaporated milk
2 tablespoons flour (optional)
1/4 cup water (optional)
1 pint salmon
2 tablespoons butter
Pepper to taste

In a glass soup pot with a lid, place broth, onion, green pepper, celery, potatoes, carrots, and garlic. Simmer on wood stove until vegetables are done. Stir in creamed corn and canned milk; thicken with flour and water, if you wish, making sure the milk is very hot—not boiling. Take off stove and stir in salmon (bones and dark parts removed). Stir in butter, if you are not on a diet. Ladle into large bowls and sprinkle with pepper. Pass the saltines and don't forget the homemade dill pickles.

Grannie Annie's Cookin' on the Wood Stove

Leek and Salmon Chowder

Serve it with crusty bread and a nice salad.

12-ounces of salmon filet
3 cups bottled clam juice
1 tablespoon butter, softened
1 tablespoon flour
4 bacon slices, chopped
2 medium leeks, thinly sliced,
   soaked in water for about 10
   minutes

1 large white-skinned potato,
   peeled, cut into $1/2$-inch pieces
$2^1/2$ cups milk
$1/2$ cup whipping cream
2 tablespoons chopped fresh chives
Salt and pepper to taste

Simmer salmon in clam juice in medium skillet, covered, for 10 minutes. Transfer salmon to plate. Reserve clam juice. Flake salmon into small pieces. Mix butter and flour in a small bowl. Cook bacon in large heavy saucepan over medium-low heat until crispy. Transfer bacon to paper towels.

Add leeks to drippings in saucepan and sauté 3 minutes. Add potato and reserved clam juice and bring to a boil. Reduce heat. Cover and simmer until potato is tender, about 10 minutes. Add milk, bring to a boil, and whisk in flour mixture. Reduce heat. Simmer. Soup will thicken in about 3 minutes. Stir in cream, chives, salmon, and bacon. Season with salt and pepper.

Be Our Guest

Everything but the Kitchen Sink Fish Chowder

Accompanied by fresh bread, this makes a hearty meal!

5 slices bacon, cut up
1 large onion, chopped
3 celery sticks, diced
1 garlic clove, minced
1 small can mushrooms, drained
1 cup + 1 tablespoon water, divided
2 tablespoons cornstarch
1 cup white wine
1 (14-ounce) can chicken broth

$^1/_2$ cup half-and-half
$^1/_2$ stick butter
$2^1/_2$ cups milk
Spices: bay leaves, dill weed, cayenne pepper, paprika, celery salt, garlic powder
6 small potatoes, peeled and diced
2 pounds halibut or other fish
Salt and pepper to taste
Parsley

In a large 6-quart pot, cook bacon until crisp. Drain off fat; reserve 1 tablespoon. Crumble bacon and set aside. Sauté onion, celery, garlic, and mushrooms in bacon drippings. Add 1 tablespoon water; thicken with cornstarch. Add wine, chicken broth, half-and-half, butter, and milk. Add any or all of the spices to your taste. Add 1 cup water; stir. Add potatoes and bring to a boil, cooking until potatoes are almost done. Add halibut or other fish or other seafood. You may need to add more water. Season to taste; cook at medium heat until fish is done. Serve in large bowls. Sprinkle chopped fresh parsley and bacon over chowder.

Recipes to the Rescue

The Eskimo Blanket Toss recreates both a traditional hunting tool and modern celebration game used by the Inupiaq and St. Lawrence Island Yupik. The "pullers" represent a group of people that, working together, provides support, trust and safety. The "blanket," usually a large walrus hide, stands for the culture, laws, or beliefs of a community. The "tossee" represents an individual or group of individuals. The blanket toss is an exercise in trust and teamwork.

Halibut Cheese Chowder

2 tablespoons olive oil
1/2 cup chopped onion
1/2 cup chopped celery
1/2 cup chopped carrots
1/2 cup chopped green pepper
1/2 cup chopped red bell pepper
  (optional)
2 pounds fresh halibut, cut in
  bite-size pieces, set aside

3 cups low-fat chicken broth
1/2 teaspoon garlic salt
Sprinkle of cayenne
2 cans evaporated milk
3 tablespoons cornstarch
2 1/2 cups shredded cheese
Croutons

Sauté in olive oil the onion, celery, carrots, green and red pepper. Add halibut and fold into vegetables. Sauté 1 minute. Add chicken broth, garlic salt, and cayenne. Bring to simmer for 4–5 minutes. Add canned milk mixed with cornstarch; bring to simmer until thick. Add shredded cheese. Stir over low heat until melted (watch carefully). Remove from heat. Serve in large bowl; sprinkle with croutons.

This is most delicious with small amount of broccoli in it—just add it to the sauté pan along with other vegetables.

Grannie Annie's Cookin' Fish from Cold Alaskan Waters

Mom's Seafood Chowder

2 slices bacon, diced
1 cup minced onion
$^{1}/_{2}$ cup diced celery
1 leek, white part, washed and
  minced
5 cups clam juice
$2^{1}/_{2}$ cups peeled and diced
  potatoes
$2^{1}/_{2}$ cups whole-kernel corn
$^{1}/_{2}$ whole thyme leaf

1 bay leaf
$^{1}/_{2}$ teaspoon Tabasco sauce
1 teaspoon Worcestershire sauce
4 tablespoons cornstarch
9 ounces evaporated milk, skim or
  low-fat
8 ounces salmon, cubed
1 ounce peeled shrimp
8 ounces halibut, cubed
4 green onions, sliced thin

In a stockpot, render the fat from the bacon over medium heat; add onion, celery, and leek; cook until soft. Add juice, potatoes, corn, thyme, bay leaf, Tabasco, and Worcestershire sauce; simmer until potatoes are done. Mix the cornstarch with the milk; pour slowly into the soup, stirring constantly until it thickens. Add seafood; cook until done. Do not overcook. Check seasoning; adjust to your desire. Serve with green onions on top. Makes 8–10 servings.

Huna Heritage Foundation Cookbook

Alaskan Cioppino

2 tablespoons olive oil
4 cloves garlic, chopped
1 medium onion, chopped
2 medium green bell peppers,
  chopped in coarse chunks
2 cups chopped canned
  or fresh tomatoes
$1/2$ cup tomato paste
2 teaspoons salt
1 teaspoon red pepper flakes
$1/2$ teaspoon paprika
1 teaspoon dry basil

$1/2$ teaspoon dry oregano
2 dozen hard shell clams
Dry white wine (about $1/2$ cup)
Water for steaming shellfish
2 dozen mussels, scrubbed
$1^1/2$ pounds fresh white fish fillets,
  halibut, cod or sea bass
1 pound large shrimp, shelled and
  deveined
2 fresh whole crabs, about 2
  pounds each, cooked, separated
Fresh herb sprigs for garnish

Heat the olive oil in a large skillet and sauté garlic, onion, and bell peppers over medium-high heat until they are slightly softened. Add tomatoes, tomato paste, and seasonings. Simmer over very low heat while you steam the shellfish.

Steam clams with $1/4$ cup of wine and 1 cup lightly salted water for about 5 minutes, covered, until they just pop open. Remove to cool and add the mussels to the boiling wine/water and add a splash of wine and another cup of water. Steam the mussels just until they pop open. Remove to the bowl with the clams.

Strain the steaming wine/water through a double layer of cheese-cloth or dampened paper towels or through a sieve, into the sautéed vegetables and tomato sauce. Stir and pour into a deep, wide serving pot. Bring the sauce to a boil and add the fish, shrimp, crab bodies (not the claws and legs yet). As soon as the pot begins to bubble, reduce the heat to low and simmer about 5 minutes, until the fish is cooked. Jiggle the pot to distribute the cooking evenly, but resist the urge to stir. Add the crab legs, claws, mussels, and clams and a splash more wine. Jiggle the pot, and gently push the shellfish into the broth. Heat partially covered about 1 minute. Garnish with fresh herb sprigs and enjoy at once with lots of sourdough French bread. Serves 6–8.

Alaska Cooking: Featuring Skagway

Barb's Seafood Soup

1–2 tablespoons olive oil
$^1/_2$ cup chopped celery
$^1/_2$ cup chopped onion
$^1/_2$ cup chopped carrots
1 clove garlic, minced
2 (16-ounce) cans chicken or
   vegetable broth
1 can stewed tomatoes or canned,
   diced tomatoes, or 3–4 fresh
   tomatoes, chopped
1 cup water
1 tablespoon parsley
$^1/_2$ teaspoon thyme

$^1/_2$ teaspoon rosemary
$^1/_2$ teaspoon cumin
2 tablespoons Worcestershire sauce
1 tablespoon vinegar
1 tablespoon brown sugar
2 tablespoons ketchup
3 dashes Tabasco sauce
$^1/_2$ cup rice
$1^1/_2$–$2^1/_2$ cups seafood (scallops,
   shrimp, halibut, or salmon)
$^1/_3$–$^1/_2$ cup zucchini, spinach,
   peas, or broccoli (optional)
1 Roma tomato, chopped (optional)

In a large soup pot, heat oil and sauté celery, onion, carrots, and garlic. Add broth, canned tomatoes, and water. Season with parsley, thyme, rosemary, cumin, Worcestershire sauce, vinegar, brown sugar, ketchup, and Tabasco sauce. Simmer over medium-low heat for 1 hour. Add rice after 30 minutes of cooking. Cook seafood (can use microwave) and add to soup. May also add optional green vegetables, if desired. Continue cooking until vegetables are tender. Serve with chopped Roma tomatoes, if desired.

Welcome Home

Alaska was purchased from Russia for $7.2 million in 1867. Russia insisted on the extra $200,000 for "private Russian interests," probably as compensation for the valuable ice trade they had established with the west coast in the years before refrigeration of shipments was possible. The alternative source of ice was from Boston in ships that had to go through the Panama Canal (and warm climates) to deliver the ice (a good portion of which had melted along the way) to the west coast.

Mom's Fish Head Soup

I usually serve this to my guests before I tell them how it's made!

1 large salmon head, cut long
   with front fins left intact
1 or 2 bay leaves
1/2–1 onion, depending on size
   of fish head

Instant potatoes, dry from package
Flour for thickening
Cornstarch for thickening
Salt and pepper to taste

Cook fish head with water (enough to use as the broth later). Add bay leaves, the amount determined by how much you like bay leaves. Cook the head at least 1/2 hour after it boils. Drain broth from head and save the broth for your soup base. Add chopped onion to broth, but be sure to remove bay leaves. Add instant potatoes to broth for thickening. Also add some flour and cornstarch (dissolved in cold water) for additional thickening. Don't use too much of any one of the thickeners, as you might taste them. Cook until it reaches the consistency you like for soup.

Meantime, pick the meat particles from the fish head. Be sure to include meat from fins and the cheek meat. Add this picked meat to fish broth. Salt and pepper to taste.

Panhandle Pat's Fifty Years

Mat-Su Caribou Vegetable Soup

2 pounds caribou roast, cut in
  1-inch cubes
1 teaspoon lemon juice
2 cups water
1/2 teaspoon crushed basil leaves
2 cups beef broth
1/2 cup chopped onion
1 bay leaf

1 (16-ounce) can stewed tomatoes
2 cups sliced celery
1 cup sliced carrots
1 cup cauliflower
1/2 cup sliced fresh mushrooms
4 potatoes, sliced
1 cup chopped spinach
Salt and black pepper to taste

Brown caribou pieces in Dutch oven. Add lemon juice, water, basil, broth, onion, and bay leaf. Bring to a boil. Cover and simmer for 90 minutes. Add tomatoes, celery, carrots, cauliflower, and mushrooms. Cover and simmer for about 40 minutes. Add potatoes and simmer until tender. Add spinach and simmer 5 minutes more. Salt and pepper to taste. Serves 6.

Moose & Caribou Recipes of Alaska

Editor's Extra: If you don't happen to have caribou or moose for any of these recipes, try subbing venison or beef.

Ptarmigan Soup

Remove feathers from ptarmigan. Clean, wash and cut the meat. Put into cooking pot with the water and salt, onion, pepper, and curry powder, also add rice and macaroni. Cook about 25 minutes.

Eskimo Cookbook

Editor's Note: The recipes in this cookbook are somewhat impractical to prepare but are fascinating to read. See the catalog section for a description of this unique cookbook.

Mooseball Soup

MOOSEBALLS:

¹/₂ cup bread crumbs	1 egg
¹/₂ teaspoon salt	¹/₂ teaspoon thyme
1¹/₂ pounds ground moose meat	1 small onion, chopped very fine

Mix bread crumbs, salt, ground meat, egg, thyme, and onion until well blended. Shape into 1-inch balls. Place in a Dutch oven and brown; remove and drain.

SOUP:

1 onion, chopped	2 cans beef broth
³/₄ cup sliced, fresh mushrooms	1 can stewed tomatoes
or 1 small can mushrooms	5 red potatoes with skins left on,
1 tablespoon olive oil	cubed

In the same sauté pan used for meatballs, sauté onion and mush-rooms in olive oil. Add beef broth, stewed tomatoes, and potatoes. Bring to a simmer and add the browned Mooseballs. Simmer until potatoes are done, 30–40 minutes; or if you are doing this on the wood stove, simmer all day until you have the snow shoveled and the wood chopped.

Grannie Annie's Cookin' on the Wood Stove

Broccoli and Hazelnut Soup
Au Gratin

1 tablespoon butter
1 medium onion, chopped
1 large bunch broccoli
3 medium potatoes, peeled and
  diced
6 cups chicken stock
1¼ cups heavy cream
1 cup roasted, finely chopped
  hazelnuts

2 tablespoons cream sherry
¼ cup grated Parmesan cheese
1½ teaspoons salt
⅛ teaspoon freshly ground pepper
1½ cups grated Gruyére cheese,
  divided
1¼ cups coarsely chopped
  hazelnuts, divided

Melt butter in a 4- to 6-quart kettle; sauté onion until softened, about 3 minutes. Cut broccoli into florets and thinly slice tender upper portion of the stems. Add to kettle along with potatoes and chicken stock. Cover and simmer until potatoes and broccoli are tender, about 25 minutes. Purée mixture in several batches in food processor. Return purée to kettle and stir in cream, roasted hazelnuts, sherry, Parmesan cheese, salt, and pepper to taste. Gently heat.

To serve, ladle 8-ounce servings into broiler-safe dishes. Sprinkle each with ½ ounce grated Gruyére cheese and ½ ounce coarsely chopped hazelnuts. Place under broiler until cheese is melted and hazelnuts are browned, about 1 minute. Instead of broiling, you might use a small propane torch to brown the hazelnuts. Yields 10 (1-cup) servings.

Kay's Kitchen

World War II made a supply route to Alaska critical since Alaska was considered vulnerable to Japanese attack. The government built the 1,523-mile Alaska Highway, through Canada to Fairbanks, in just eight months. Road conditions were rough, with 90-degree turns and 25% grades, so the highway was improved in 1943. The United States paid for the Canadian part of the highway and then relinquished it to Canada in April 1946, in exchange for the right-of-way.

Raspberry Fruit Soup

2 tablespoons quick cooking
tapioca
¹/₄ cup sugar
¹/₈ teaspoon salt
¹/₂ cup water
2 (10-ounce) packages frozen
sweetened raspberries, thawed,
undrained, divided

¹/₃ cup reconstituted lemon juice
(if fresh, use scant ¹/₃ cup)
1 tablespoon butter or margarine
¹/₂ cup whipping cream, whipped,
or ¹/₂ cup sour cream
Ground nutmeg
Mint sprigs (optional)

Combine tapioca, sugar, salt, water, and 1 package raspberries in saucepan. Cook, stirring constantly, over medium heat until mixture comes to a boil; reduce heat. Simmer, uncovered, for 5 minutes.

Stir in lemon juice and butter; cool for 20 minutes. Add remaining package of raspberries, stirring to blend well. Chill. Serve in sherbet glasses. Top each serving with a dollop of whipped or sour cream; dust with nutmeg. Garnish with mint sprig. Yields 8 servings.

Our Cherished Recipes Volume II

Salmon Soup Bisque

¹/₂ pound fresh salmon
4 tablespoons butter
¹/₄ cup minced green onion
1 clove garlic, minced
¹/₄ cup flour
2 cups milk
3 cups half-and-half (or substitute
3 cups milk)

¹/₂ cup tomato purée or paste
2 tablespoons dry sherry
(California Chablis)
1 teaspoon salt
1 tablespoon minced fresh dill or
spice dill
¹/₄ teaspoon ground white pepper
Dill or watercress for garnish

Cook salmon, or poach: cool, flake, and set aside. In large saucepan, melt butter; stir in onion and garlic, and sauté till clear. Blend in flour with whisk. Cook 5 minutes on medium heat. Whisk in milk and half-and-half (or milk to total 5 cups); stir until thick (takes a while—don't let it stick). Add remaining ingredients except garnish. Stir well, then add salmon. Simmer 15 minutes, then serve. Garnish with dill or watercress.

Recipes to the Rescue

Mild Moose Chili

1 pound moose steak, cut into
  1-inch cubes
2 tablespoons flour
3 tablespoons oil
$1/2$ cup chili sauce
1 cup chopped onion

$1^1/2$ cups sliced celery
1 cup chopped carrots
$1/2$ cup water
1 can kidney beans
1 green pepper, sliced
Salt and pepper to taste

Coat moose with flour and brown in oil in heavy skillet. Stir in chili sauce, onion, celery, carrots, and water. Bring to a boil; cover and simmer about 50 minutes. Add kidney beans and green pepper. Season to taste. Cover and simmer for another 10 minutes. Serves 4.

Moose & Caribou Recipes of Alaska

Cheesy Chili

1 pound ground beef
1 medium onion, chopped
1 medium green pepper, chopped
1 (6-ounce) can button
  mushrooms, drained
2 cloves garlic
3 cups water
1 (16-ounce) can kidney beans,
  drained
2 (6-ounce) cans tomato paste

1 (16-ounce) can stewed tomatoes
$1/4$ cup diced ripe olives
1 hot pepper, diced
2 tablespoons chili powder
$1^1/2$ tablespoons brown sugar
$1/2$ teaspoon salt
$1/4$ teaspoon garlic salt
$1/4$ teaspoon pepper
$1/4$ teaspoon ground cumin
Shredded cheese

Combine ground beef, onion, green pepper, mushrooms, and garlic in a Dutch oven. Cook until beef is browned, stirring to crumble meat. Drain off pan drippings. Add next 12 ingredients, mixing well. Cover and simmer $1^1/2$ hours. Sprinkle individual servings with cheese. Yields 3 quarts.

Recipes to the Rescue

Lori's Firecracker Chili

1 pound cubed round steak
Oil
2 medium onions, chopped,
  divided
2 cloves garlic, minced, divided
1½ teaspoons cumin, divided
¼ cup chili powder, divided
2 cups water, or as needed
1 pound lean ground beef
1 medium green pepper, seeded
  and chopped
1 stalk celery, chopped

½ teaspoon oregano
2 (16-ounce) cans tomatoes, cut up
1 (15-ounce) can tomato sauce
2–3 jalapeño peppers (¼ cup
  chopped)
1½ teaspoons ground red pepper
1 bay leaf
Salt and pepper to taste
1 (15½-ounce) can red kidney
  beans (optional)
Grated cheese, chopped onions and
  peppers for garnish

In large kettle, brown cubed round steak in oil with ½ the onions, 1 clove minced garlic, ½ teaspoon cumin, and 1 teaspoon chili powder. Add 2 cups water. Bring to boil, reduce heat and cook down until liquid is almost gone. Set aside.

In saucepan, brown ground beef with remaining onion and garlic, plus green pepper and celery. Combine both meat mixtures in kettle. Add oregano, canned tomatoes, tomato sauce, jalapeño peppers, red pepper, bay leaf, and remaining cumin and chili powder. Bring to a boil and reduce heat. Add salt and pepper and simmer at least 1½ hours. Stir occasionally and add water, as needed. If beans are to be used, add them during the last 20 minutes or so. Remove bay leaf before serving. Serve with grated cheese, onions, and peppers. Cornbread is a great complement!

Our Cherished Recipes Volume II

Avalanches are so common in Alaska that avalanche guns are sometimes used to purposely set off small avalanches, rather than waiting until larger ones occur naturally and endanger people. Often small "hand charges" are thrown from safely-accessible ridges onto slopes, or delivered from the open door of a low-flying helicopter.

Mountain Man Chili

1 pound good sausage
$^1/_2$ pound bacon
3 onions, chopped
A big hunk of moose, caribou, or beef (about 3 pounds) cubed
1 (15-ounce) can tomato juice or beef broth
1 large can diced, stewed Mexican tomatoes or 1 (10-ounce) can tomatoes with green chiles

1 (15-ounce) can tomato sauce
1 (4-ounce) can diced green chiles
2 tablespoons minced garlic
$^1/_2$ cup (yes) dark chili powder
1 teaspoon cumin
1 teaspoon coriander
1 teaspoon oregano
1 tablespoon garlic salt
1 teaspoon black pepper
2–6 drops of Tabasco

Cook sausage and bacon, then put the onions and moose in large skillet and brown the meat. Drain off all the fat. Add tomato juice, tomatoes, tomatoe sauce, green chiles, garlic, chili powder, cumin, coriander, oregano, garlic salt, black pepper, and Tabasco. Simmer on wood stove all day or all night—until meat is tender and liquid is thick. You may have to add a small amount of water from time to time. So good with corn bread, hot out of the oven.

Note: For guys who like it spicy and hot, add $^1/_2$ teaspoon habanero chile or $^1/_2$ teaspoon red pepper.

Grannie Annie's Cookin' on the Wood Stove

Grannie Annie's Oyster Stew

This is great in the middle of a dark winter when you are tired, cold and hungry. It does not take very long to prepare.

¹/₂ onion, chopped
¹/₂ cup chopped celery with leaves
2 tablespoons butter, divided
1 can oysters

1 can evaporated milk
Salt and pepper
Oyster crackers

In medium saucepan, sauté onion and celery in 1 tablespoon butter. Add oysters and milk. Heat, but do not boil. Stir in ¹/₂ tablespoon butter. Pour into big soup mugs and dot with remaining butter, salt and pepper and serve with a few oyster crackers. Serves 2 generously.

Grannie Annie's Cookin' Fish from Cold Alaskan Waters

Trail Stew

This is a great camping recipe.

3 tablespoons margarine
1 pound wieners
1 medium onion, chopped
1 tablespoon flour
1 teaspoon salt

1 teaspoon chili powder
2 (15-ounce) cans kidney beans
1 (16-ounce) can tomatoes, undrained
1 (12-ounce) can corn, drained

Melt margarine in kettle. Cut wieners lengthwise into 4 pieces. Sauté onion and wieners in melted margarine. Mix flour, salt, and chili powder and blend into onion-wiener mixture. Add beans, tomatoes (with juice) and corn. Cover and simmer 15 minutes (wieners will curl into rings). Feeds 4–6.

Alaska Women in Timber Cookbook

Baked Venison Stew

2 tablespoons olive oil
2 pounds deer meat, cubed
  (substitute elk or caribou)
2 cups fresh pearl onions, peeled
3 cloves garlic, chopped
1¹/₂ pounds tomatoes, peeled and
  seeded (about 5 medium)
2 teaspoons fresh thyme, minced
  (¹/₂ teaspoon dry)
1 teaspoon fresh oregano, minced
  (¹/₂ teaspoon dry)

1 teaspoon fresh rosemary, minced
  (¹/₄ teaspoon dry)
1 bay leaf
1 teaspoon ground cumin
2 cups canned, unsalted beef broth
1 cup dry red wine
2 tablespoons cornstarch
1 cup diced carrots
1 cup small chunk rutabaga
2 cups diced potatoes

Preheat oven to 200°. In a heavy stockpot, on top of the stove, heat oil until it begins to smoke. Add meat; brown and remove from heat. Add onions to stockpot; cook until nicely browned. Turn heat to low; add garlic, tomatoes, and herbs; stir. Mix broth and wine together, then mix in the cornstarch. Stir the cornstarch liquid into the vegetable/herb mixture; bring to a simmer. Add browned meat, carrots, rutabaga, and potatoes. Stir, cover with lid, place in oven, and cook until done (approximately 3 hours). Makes 6–8 servings.

Huna Heritage Foundation Cookbook

Walrus Stew

Cut the walrus in small pieces and also cut the coke (skin and blubber of walrus). Then put them together in the pot to boil. Add salt and water.

Eskimo Cookbook

Editor's Note: The recipes in this cookbook are somewhat impractical to prepare but are fascinating to read. See the catalog section for a description of this unique cookbook.

Wood Stove Stew

Put all the ingredients in a Dutch oven in the order given; put the lid on, put it on your wood stove and go chop wood or work in your garden—that's more fun!

1 (10-ounce) can beef broth
1 (28-ounce) can whole or stewed tomatoes
1¹/₂ pounds trimmed moose roast, cut in 1-inch chunks (well, beef will do!)
1 onion, chopped
4 carrots, peeled and cut in large chunks
1 medium potato, cut in bite-size pieces

2 ribs celery, cut in bite-size pieces
1 tablespoon Worcestershire sauce
2 tablespoons parsley
1 bay leaf
1 teaspoon garlic salt
¹/₄ teaspoon pepper
2 tablespoons quick-cooking tapioca to thicken (or you can stir 2 tablespoons flour into the beef broth)

Put lid on and set on hottest part of stove and let simmer for 6 hours or until you get the wood chopped or the garden weeded. Serve with homemade bread, real butter, and dill pickles.

Note: If you don't have beef broth, you can use water or even, in a pinch, steal a can of your husband's beer.

Grannie Annie's Cookin' on the Wood Stove

Chulitna Moosemeat Stew

During winter the style of eating changes at the lodge. They no longer have the lush salads of summer, but rely on long-lasting staples. Kirsten cooks big one-pot meals that simmer all day on the woodstove. Moosemeat is plentiful in the winter, but this recipe is equally good made with beef. Kirsten likes to make it thick and serve it with a big bowl of rice. Accompaniments are shredded Cheddar cheese, sour cream and hot corn bread. She serves moose stew to the racers on the Iditaski Race, but state laws require beef to be served to commercial guests.

6 strips bacon, cut into 1-inch pieces
2–3 pounds moosemeat or lean beef, cut in 2-inch cubes
Salt and pepper
10 small white onions, peeled
2 medium potatoes, well scrubbed and cubed
3 tablespoons all-purpose flour
1^{1}/$_{2}$ cups dry red wine
1 cup beef broth

3 tablespoons brandy
2 cloves garlic, pressed
1–2 strips of orange peel
1 teaspoon marjoram
1 teaspoon fresh thyme (^{1}/$_{2}$ teaspoon, if dried)
1 medium-size onion, peeled and studded with 3 cloves
1 pound medium-size mushrooms
4 large carrots, peeled and cut ^{1}/$_{2}$ inch thick

In a large frying pan on medium heat, cook bacon until brown and crumbly. With a slotted spoon, remove bacon from pan and place in a deep casserole dish. Reserve pan and bacon drippings.

Sprinkle meat cubes with salt and pepper. Add to the pan, a few at a time, and cook over medium heat until brown on all sides. Remove meat cubes from pan and add to casserole. To remaining pan juices, add onions. (The easiest way to peel small onions is to drop them whole into boiling water for a few minutes, then remove and peel). Cook onions and potatoes until light brown. Set aside.

Add flour to the remaining pan juices. Cook until bubbly, stirring frequently. Pour in wine, beef broth, and brandy, stirring until sauce is thick. Add garlic, orange peel, marjoram, and thyme. Pour sauce over meat in casserole. Tuck clove-studded onion down in liquid.

Bake in 325° oven for 2^{1}/$_{2}$ hours. During the last ^{1}/$_{2}$ hour of cooking, add mushrooms and carrots, cooking until tender. Remove the studded onion. Serves 6.

Variation: If you prefer rich undertones, add a touch more brandy and mushrooms. If you like more orange undertones, use more orange peel.

Recipe from Riversong Lodge
Best Recipes of Alaska's Fishing Lodges

Vosie's Famous Iditarod Bean Stew

1 good ham bone for broth
6 cups water (more, if needed)
2 cups dried pinto beans
1 pound hamburger meat
1 cup ham pieces
1 or 2 hot sausages, sliced
  (Louisiana-type)
1 green pepper, sliced
2 cloves garlic, chopped

1 cup chopped celery
1 medium onion, chopped
2 cans Italian-style stewed
  tomatoes, crushed
1 teaspoon smoke flavor
2 teaspoons sugar
1 teaspoon salt
1 teaspoon dried oregano
1/3 cup peanut butter

Boil ham bone in 6 cups water and prepare the beans (sort, wash, and soak). Brown hamburger, ham, and sausage in pan and remove from pan when done. Sauté green pepper, garlic, celery, and onion in the same pan and stir for 5 minutes.

In a large pan with a heavy bottom (if it's not heavy, the bottom will burn), combine ham broth and beans and cook for 1 hour. Add meat, vegetables, crushed tomatoes, smoke flavor, sugar, salt, oregano, and additional water, if needed, to cover. Cook for 2 or more hours for thickness. About 15 minutes before done, add peanut butter. Cool slowly and stir often.

Simply the Best Recipes

Interesting facts about the Iditarod:
In 1925, an epidemic of the disease diphtheria loomed over the small town of Nome and the necessary serum was in short supply. Bad weather in the area kept airplanes on the ground, so the serum was instead rushed from Nenana to Nome, about 675 miles, by dog teams. The medicine was relayed the distance in just 127 1/2 hours. The Iditarod Sled Dog Race commemorates the historic serum run.

Spanning 1,100 miles, there are two Anchorage-to-Nome Iditarod trails, the southern route, which is used on odd-numbered years, and the northern route, which is run on even-numbered years.

The approximately 60 competing teams average 16 dogs, which means over 1,000 dogs leave Anchorage for Nome.

From the first 20-day run in 1973, the times have fallen to under 10 days. After the first musher reaches the burl arch in Nome, mushers continue to flow in both day and night for a week and a half. The most mushers to finish a race was 63 in 1992.

Chill Chasing Beans and Ham

1 pound (about 2 cups) dried
  beans, white and red
2 quarts water
2 tablespoons olive oil
3 large cloves garlic
1 medium onion, chopped
1 medium carrot, chopped

1 tablespoon dried Italian herbs
1 (16-ounce) can chopped
  tomatoes
6 shakes Tabasco sauce
1 beef bouillon cube
2–3 pounds ham with bone
Salt and pepper to taste

Rinse the beans under running water and remove any off color beans and dirt. Bring beans to a boil in cold water; reduce heat to low and simmer, uncovered for 2 minutes. Remove any floaters. Set aside to cool for 1 hour. Drain the beans and then proceed with the recipe.

Heat olive oil in large fry pan and stir-fry the garlic and onion until softened. Then in a large, heavy pot, pour the beans, sautéed vegetables, carrot, herbs, tomatoes, Tabasco sauce, and a bouillon cube. Add ham bone and water to cover the beans with at least 2 inches extra water over the top of the beans. Bring to a boil, then skim off the foam and partially cover the pan, setting the heat at low-simmer. Cook for 6–8 hours. Remove ham and cut into 1/2-inch cubes. Return to pot. Add salt and pepper to taste.

Note: This dish can be made in the crockpot, though the beans never become as soft as when cooked over the range. You will need to cook in a crockpot for a minimum of 10 hours on LOW.

Alaska Cooking: Featuring Skagway

SALADS

Alaskans have evolved into the "flyingest" people in the nation. With well over 10,000 registered pilots, roughly one in every 58 Alaskans has a license to fly. It's no wonder, since many towns and cities here are not accessible by road.

Chicken Fruit Salad

2 cups halved green grapes
1/2 cantaloupe (balls or cubes)
2 cups cubed watermelon
1/2 honeydew melon, cubed
2 kiwi fruit, sliced
1 apple, cut in chunks (dipped in lemon juice)
1 pear, cut in chunks (dipped in lemon juice)
1 banana, sliced (dipped in lemon juice)

1/2 pineapple, cut in cubes
Other fruit as desired or in season
3 cups cubed leftover chicken breasts or turkey, cooked and skin removed
Romaine lettuce leaves
Dressing
Toasted coconut*
Toasted almonds*

Toss fruits together and gently add chicken. Place in serving dishes on top of romaine lettuce leaf. Drizzle with Dressing. Sprinkle with toasted coconut and almonds.

DRESSING:
1 tablespoon mayonnaise   1/2 cup honey

Blend together until mixture looks clear.

*To toast coconut and almonds, place on cookie sheet in 350° oven and stir occasionally until golden brown and crispy (few minutes).

What's Cookin' in the Kenai Peninsula

Baked King Crab Salad

2 tablespoons chopped onion
1 cup chopped celery
1 green pepper, chopped
2 cups crabmeat
³/₄ cup mayonnaise
¹/₂ teaspoon salt

Pepper to taste
1 teaspoon Worcestershire sauce
¹/₂ cup buttered bread crumbs or
   small croutons
Lemon slices for garnish
Lettuce for garnish

Combine all ingredients, except crumbs and garnish. Place in 2-quart casserole and top with crumbs or small croutons. Bake at 350° for 20 minutes. Serve with lemon slices on a bed of lettuce.

Alaska's Cooking Volume II

Antipasto Alaska Crab Salad

2 pounds Alaska crab clusters
   (King, Snow or Dungeness)
   or split
   legs, thawed, if necessary
2 cups sliced fresh mushrooms
1 small cucumber, thinly sliced
1 (6-ounce) jar marinated
   artichoke hearts

3 tablespoons lemon juice
1 clove garlic, crushed
¹/₄ teaspoon oregano
1 tomato, cut into wedges
¹/₄ pound sliced Swiss cheese, cut
   into triangles
Lettuce

Steam crab 5 minutes and cool. Combine mushrooms and cucumber slices. Drain artichoke hearts, reserving liquid. Combine liquid with lemon juice, garlic, and oregano. Pour over mushrooms and cucumbers; toss lightly. Cover and refrigerate for 2 hours. Arrange crab, mushrooms, cucumbers, artichoke hearts, tomato wedges, and cheese triangles on 4 lettuce-lined salad plates. Drizzle with remaining marinade to serve. Serves 4.

License to Cook Alaska Style

Haines is best known for the wilderness recreation that it offers—Glacier Bay National Park is only 20 miles away. Haines is home to the largest gathering of Bald Eagles in the world. Over 3,000 bald eagles descend upon the Chilkat River, usually around mid-November. The citizens of Haines celebrate their arrival with the Alaska Bald Eagle Festival each year.

Alaska Trapper's Salad

1 medium head cabbage, shredded
1 (6-ounce) can shrimp with
  liquid
1 small onion, minced

1 tablespoon sugar
2 tablespoons vinegar
2 or 3 tablespoons mayonnaise
½ teaspoon salt and pepper

Combine all ingredients well. Let stand several hours or overnight.

We're Cookin' Now

Shrimp Mandarin Salad

1 (4-ounce) can cocktail shrimp
1 (11-ounce) can Mandarin
  oranges
½ cup sour cream
1 tablespoon oil and vinegar
  dressing

1 cup sliced celery
1 cup chopped onion
½ cup cashew nuts
Shredded lettuce

Chill shrimp and Mandarin segments in the cans. Drain. Rinse shrimp in cold water; blot dry. Soften sour cream with dressing; combine with shrimp, fruit, celery, onion, and cashews. Serve on shredded lettuce.

Methodist Pie

Because of the tilt of the earth, a summer's day in Alaska can last as long as 20 hours. Giant vegetables (such as those in the photo shown on opposite page taken at the Alaska State Fair) are common in Alaska thanks to the extremely long days in summer. Current records at the State Fair: Broccoli 39.50 pounds; Cabbage 105.60 pounds; Celery 49.10 pounds; Mushroom 25.30 pounds; Pumpkin 347.01 pounds; Squash 303.05 pounds; Sunflower (tallest) 16.75 feet.

Shrimp Medley

DRESSING:

1/4 cup mayonnaise
1/4 cup sour cream
1 teaspoon chili sauce

1 tablespoon lemon juice
1/8 teaspoon Worcestershire sauce
1 teaspoon grated horseradish

Combine all ingredients and mix until smooth. Set aside.

SALAD:

Leaf lettuce
1 large seedless orange, peeled,
  sliced, and cut in quarters
1 cup purple grapes, sliced in half
  and seeded
1 small can white asparagus tips

3/4 pound cooked shrimp, shelled
  and deveined
4 cooked crab claws for garnish
Whole purple grapes for garnish
Orange slices for garnish

Arrange lettuce on four plates. Arrange orange sections, grape halves, asparagus, and shrimp on lettuce. Pour Dressing over shrimp on plates. Garnish each plate with crab claws, grapes, and orange slices. Serves 4.

Alaska Shrimp & Crab Recipes

GARY TYLER

Editor Gwen McKee and husband Barney are amazed by the giant vegetables at the Alaska State Fair.

Ling Cod Salad Niçoise

2 medium yellow onions
1 pound Ling Cod fillets (red snapper or halibut can be used)
1 teaspoon dried rosemary
$1/2$ teaspoon salt
$1/2$ teaspoon pepper

$1/2$ pound green beans
4 small Yukon Gold potatoes
2–3 large tomatoes
4 hard-boiled eggs
3 cups loose leaf lettuce
$1/2$ cup brine-cured black olives

DRESSING:
3 tablespoons lemon juice
1 teaspoon dried oregano

$1/2$ cup olive oil
Salt and pepper to taste

Preheat oven to 400°. Peel and chop the onions. Arrange half the onions on a greased baking sheet; top with Ling Cod fillets, rosemary, salt and pepper, and finally the remaining onion. Bake in preheated oven until cooked through, about 10 minutes, depending on thickness of the fish. Set aside to cool.

Bring a large pot of salted water to a rolling boil, then drop in the green beans and cook them just until tender, 2–4 minutes. Immediately plunge the cooked beans into a bowl of ice water to set the color. Pour off all except 1 inch of water and put in the potatoes to steam, covered with a lid. The potatoes should take about 20 minutes to cook. Cool and slice the potatoes. Remove the strings from the cold beans. Cut the tomatoes and peeled eggs into wedges.

Stir the Dressing ingredients together. Break the cold fish into 1-inch chunks and toss with the onions and 2 tablespoons of the Dressing.

In separate bowls toss the potatoes and beans with a drizzle of the Dressing. Toss lettuce with the remaining Dressing. Line the plates with lettuce, then arrange various ingredients in strips on top of the lettuce, topping it all with the olives, tomatoes, and eggs. Serves 4–6.

Alaska Cooking: Featuring Skagway

Back Country Wild Rice Smoked Salmon Salad

$^1/_2$ cup wild rice
1 cup brown rice
3 cups plus 2 tablespoons water
1 teaspoon salt
1 yellow bell pepper, chopped

1 red pepper, chopped
1 pound smoked Chinook salmon, cubed
$^1/_2$ cup chopped walnuts
Lettuce leaves

DRESSING:

2 tablespoons red wine vinegar
$^1/_2$ teaspoon salt
$^1/_4$ teaspoon black pepper
$^1/_4$ teaspoon marjoram

1 teaspoon soy sauce
$^1/_2$ teaspoon grated lemon peel
4 green onions, chopped
1 large clove garlic, minced

Rinse the rice under running water. Bring the salted water to boil in medium saucepan. Add rice and stir. Reduce heat to low, cover and simmer until the rice is plump and tender, 35–45 minutes. If any liquid remains, drain it off. Cool slightly in a large bowl. Stir together the Dressing ingredients and toss the Dressing together with the rice. Chill. Add peppers, salmon, and walnuts and serve in lettuce cups. Serves 4–6 people.

Alaska Cooking: Featuring Skagway

Salmon Seashell Salad

3 cups seashell pasta, cooked,
  drained, and cooled
1 (8-ounce) can salmon, drained
  and dark pieces removed
1/2 cup chopped onion

1/2 cup chopped celery
1/4 cup chopped dill pickle
1/4 cup sliced black olives
2 tablespoons chopped fresh
  parsley or 1 tablespoon dry

Place shells in large mixing bowl, toss with salmon, onion, celery, pickle, olives, and parsley.

DRESSING:
1 cup mayonnaise
1/2 cup sour cream
1/2 cup buttermilk or milk

1/2 teaspoon garlic salt
1 teaspoon lemon juice
1/4 teaspoon cayenne

Mix until well blended and pour over salad ingredients. You may have to add more milk or mayonnaise if too dry.

Grannie Annie's Cookin' Fish from Cold Alaskan Waters

Salmon Salad

1 1/2 cups cooked salmon
1 cup sliced celery
1/4 cup sliced, stuffed olives
  (optional)
2 hard-cooked eggs

1/2 teaspoon minced onion
1/2 cup mayonnaise
1/4 cup French dressing
Salt and lemon juice to taste
Lettuce leaves

Combine all ingredients. Refrigerate. Serve on lettuce leaf.

A Taste of Sitka, Alaska

The Mendenhall Glacier in Juneau stretches 12 miles and reaches 1 1/2 miles across the Mendenhall Valley, with ice 400-800 feet deep. The glacier started retreating in the mid-1700s because its annual rate of melt began to exceed its annual total accumulation. The ice is retreating at a rate of 100 to 150 feet a year. At this rate, the glacier would take several centuries to completely disappear.

Dilled Slaw

1 small head cabbage, shredded
1 stalk celery, thinly sliced
2 green peppers, thinly sliced
1 red pepper, thinly sliced
1 small onion, chopped
³/₄ cup sugar

1 cup vinegar
1 teaspoon dry mustard
2 teaspoons dill seeds
1 teaspoon salt
³/₄ cup salad oil

Combine vegetables in a large mixing bowl. Sprinkle with sugar, tossing well. Heat vinegar, mustard, dill seeds, and salt to boiling. Remove from heat. Pour over cabbage mixture. Evenly drizzle oil over the mixture. Toss well to blend. Cover and refrigerate for at least 1 hour.

Alaska Connections Cookbook III

Broccoli-Cauliflower Salad

1 head broccoli
1 head cauliflower
2 carrots
4 radishes

1 cucumber or zucchini
1 small can sliced black olives
Cherry tomatoes and sliced
   almonds (optional garnish)

DRESSING:
1 cup oil
6 tablespoons red wine vinegar
2 teaspoons salt

¹/₂ teaspoon pepper
¹/₂ teaspoon dry mustard
Minced garlic

Cut up fresh vegetables. Add sliced black olives. Mix Dressing ingredients well. Pour Dressing over vegetables. Marinate overnight. Just before serving, add cherry tomatoes and sliced almonds, if desired.

A Taste of Sitka, Alaska

Pine Nut Salad

Cool, crisp and green—an excellent year-around salad.

¹/₄ cup pine nuts
2 cloves garlic
1 cup water
¹/₄ teaspoon salt
1 teaspoon Dijon mustard
2 tablespoons white wine vinegar
¹/₂ cup virgin olive oil

1 large head romaine lettuce, torn
    into pieces
Freshly ground black pepper to
    taste
¹/₄ cup coarsely shredded
    Parmesan cheese

Toast pine nuts under broiler until golden brown; watch carefully. Set aside. In small saucepan, boil garlic in water for 10 minutes; drain. In large salad bowl, mash garlic and salt to a paste. Whisk in mustard and vinegar. Add oil in a stream, whisking dressing until oil is emulsified. Add romaine; toss well and season with pepper. Sprinkle Parmesan and pine nuts over salad and serve. (Pine nuts are also sold under the name piñion nuts.)

Moose in the Pot Cookbook

Blue Cheese-Pear-Walnut Salad

1 Bartlett pear, cored and sliced
    lengthwise in thin strips
³/₄ cup crumbled blue cheese
³/₄ cup walnut halves, toasted
8 large romaine leaves, torn
¹/₄ cup olive oil

¹/₄ cup cider vinegar
3 cloves garlic, minced
5 large basil leaves, minced
1 teaspoon salt
1 tablespoon honey

Mix the pear, cheese, walnuts, and romaine in a medium-sized salad bowl. To make the dressing, stir the oil, vinegar, garlic, basil, salt, and honey in a small bowl with a wire whisk. Toss the dressing with the salad just before serving. Yields 4 servings.

A Taste of Kodiak

Blue Cheese Salad with Glazed Pecans

Variety of greens
Blue cheese dressing
Red grapes, halved
Small chunks of blue cheese

Glazed Pecan Bits
Smoked salmon or shrimp
  (optional)

Tear greens into a bowl. Add dressing to taste. Sprinkle on top the red grapes, blue cheese hunks, and Pecan Bits. Add salmon or shrimp, if desired.

GLAZED PECAN BITS:
1 1/2 cups finely chopped pecans
1/2 cup sugar

2 tablespoons butter
1/2 teaspoon vanilla

Line a baking sheet with foil. Butter the foil. Set aside. In a skillet, combine nuts, sugar, butter, and vanilla. Cook over medium heat, shaking occasionally till sugar melts. Do not stir. Turn heat to low. Cook till sugar is brown. Pour nut mixture on baking sheet. Cool completely. Break into small pieces. Add to salad. Can be stored tightly covered. Makes about 12 servings.

Be Our Guest

Roquefort or Bleu Cheese Dressing

1 cup mayonnaise
1 cup sour cream
1 (4-ounce) package Roquefort or
  Bleu cheese, crumbled

1/2 teaspoon garlic powder
1/2 teaspoon salt
3 tablespoons lemon juice
1/4 cup buttermilk

Blend together mayonnaise and sour cream with crumbled cheese. Add spices and lemon juice, mixing until fairly smooth, yet leaving a few cheese clumps. Thin with buttermilk. Let season in the refrigerator several hours or overnight before serving. Makes 2 1/2 cups.

Note: Powdered buttermilk can be used instead of fresh in this recipe.

33 Days Hath September

Editor's Extra: "Blue" cheese is sometimes called "Bleu" cheese, the latter being the French import variety.

Christmas Cranberry Whip Salad

1 (8¼-ounce) can crushed
  pineapple, drained, reserve
  syrup
Water
1 (3-ounce) package raspberry
  gelatin

1 (16-ounce) can whole cranberry
  sauce
1 teaspoon orange peel
1 (11-ounce) can Mandarin
  oranges, drained
1 cup whipping cream, whipped

To reserved pineapple syrup, add boiling water to make 1 cup. Dissolve gelatin. Stir in cranberry sauce and orange peel; chill until partially set. Fold in orange sections and pineapple. Fold in whipped cream. Chill until set. Makes 8–10 servings.

Alaska Women in Timber Cookbook

Frosted Cranberry Salad

1 (8½-ounce) can crushed
  pineapple
1 (1-pound) can whole cranberry
  sauce
2 (3-ounce) packages raspberry
  flavor gelatin

1 (8-ounce) package cream cheese,
  softened
2 tablespoons salad dressing
  (Miracle Whip or Ranch-type)
1 cup heavy cream, whipped
1 peeled and chopped tart apple

Drain pineapple and cranberry sauce, reserving liquid. Add enough water to make 2 cups liquid. Bring to boil. Dissolve gelatin in hot liquid. Chill until partially set. Beat softened cream cheese and salad dressing together until fluffy. Gradually beat in gelatin. Fold this mixture into whipped cream. Set aside 1½ cups of this mixture for topping. Add drained fruit and apple to cheese mixture. Pour into 12x17½x2-inch glass dish. Refrigerate until surface sets, about 20 minutes. Frost with reserved topping. Refrigerate several hours. May freeze for a few days; remove to refrigerator 1 hour before serving. Serves 12.

Our Cherished Recipes

Strawberry Surprise Salad

2 large packages strawberry
  Jell-O, divided
1 cup cold water, divided
1 large can crushed pineapple in
  heavy syrup, undrained, divided

2 cups hot water, divided
2 (16-ounce) packages sliced
  frozen strawberries, undrained,
  divided
1 large carton sour cream

Using 2 bowls, mix all ingredients, except sour cream, divided between the 2 bowls. After mixing pour 1 bowl of mixture into a large square pan. Refrigerate until firm; leave other bowl of mixture sitting out. When refrigerated Jell-O mixture has gotten firm, spread sour cream on top, then gently pour the remaining Jell-O mixture on top. Refrigerate until firm.

Our Cherished Recipes Volume II

Fireweed Salad

Early in the season the fireweed stems break easier than later on, so I just snap them off. Later I use a knife and clip them against my thumb. Use only the tops, for they will be tender even on a mature plant.

I generally collect a batch of fireweed and dip it in the lake in front of my cabin. You might call it washing, but the real reason is to get a little water on them to dilute the vinegar.

I bunch the fireweed in one hand and use a sharp knife to cross-cut it into short lengths (easier and faster than chopping in a bowl). Then I score an onion and dice it finely onto the cut fireweed. Chopped dry onion works about as well. Add some finely diced raw potato, some carrots, pickle, or whatever. Then, using a fork and a sharp knife, I chop the bowl contents again. Next add some sugar (be generous), salt, black pepper, a little chili powder, and some garlic powder or garlic salt. Add enough vinegar so that you have some juice in the bowl at the last serving. Mix up the salad and taste it for seasoning. Make any necessary adjustments at this point.

Now I add some Cheddar cheese diced finely and a bit of chopped lunch meat and mix again. Sprinkle on a dash of paprika for color. Often as not, I sprinkle on some brown sugar after everything else is in.

Alaska Magazine's Cabin Cookbook

VEGETABLES

Juneau is filled with geographical extremes. This view of the wharf emphasizes the way the mountains abruptly begin at the shoreline.

Sweet Potato Soufflé

2 cups mashed sweet potatoes
1/2 stick butter
1/2 teaspoon salt
2 eggs

3/4 cup sugar
2 tablespoons flour
2 teaspoons vanilla

Mash sweet potatoes with butter; add salt, eggs, sugar, flour, and vanilla. Mix well and put in 8x8-inch baking pan.

TOPPING:
1/4 stick butter
1/4 cup brown sugar

1/2 cup chopped nuts

Mix all ingredients together well. Top sweet potato mixture with Topping mixture. Bake for 25 minutes at 350°.

Ladies of Harley Cookbook

Sinful Spuds

8 medium potatoes
1 bay leaf
1 can cream of chicken soup
1/4 cup margarine, melted
1 1/2 cups sour cream
1 1/2 teaspoons salt and pepper

1 onion, finely chopped
1 1/2 cups grated cheese, Velveeta
   or Cheddar, divided
1/2 cup crushed potato chips for
   topping

Cook potatoes in salted water with bay leaf; drain and refrigerate. When cold, peel and slice thinly. Put potatoes in a greased 9x13-inch baking pan. Mix soup, margarine, sour cream, salt, pepper, onion, and 1 cup grated cheese; pour over potatoes. Bake at 350° for 35 minutes. Sprinkle with 1/2 cup grated cheese and crushed potato chips. Bake a few minutes more.

Alaska Women in Timber Cookbook

Alaska accounts for over 40% of the world's remaining temperate rainforests and the largest remaining intact forest tracts. Just 12% of Alaska rainforests have been clear-cut to date.

New Potatoes in Broth

Oh, you have to do this! I could make a meal out of this. Go dig up those new red potatoes, scrub, and don't you dare take the peel off!

1 can chicken broth
1 onion, chopped
1 cup fresh parsley or ¹/₂ cup
  dried
1 teaspoon minced garlic
¹/₂ teaspoon pepper

1 teaspoon lemon juice
About 12–15 new potatoes
2 tablespoons cornstarch (optional)
¹/₄ cup water (optional)
Salt and pepper

Bring broth, onion, parsley, garlic, pepper, and lemon juice to boil in large deep saucepan. Slip potatoes into broth, cover, and put directly on wood stove and let cook until the rest of your dinner is done. Thicken the broth, if you like, with cornstarch and water. Add salt and pepper to taste.

Grannie Annie's Cookin' on the Wood Stove

Swiss Scalloped Potatoes

1¹/₂ cups shredded Swiss cheese,
  divided
¹/₂ cup sliced green onions
2 tablespoons butter
2 tablespoons flour
1 teaspoon salt
Pepper

1 cup milk
1 cup sour cream
6–7 cups, cooked, peeled, thinly
  sliced (about 4 large) potatoes
¹/₄ cup fine bread crumbs
¹/₄ cup butter, melted

In a small bowl, toss together 1 cup Swiss cheese and onions; set aside. In quart saucepan, melt 2 tablespoons butter; stir in flour, salt, and pepper. Gradually stir in milk. Cook over medium heat, stirring constantly, until thickened. Remove from heat; stir in sour cream.

In a shallow, buttered baking dish, layer ¹/₃ of potatoes, ¹/₂ Swiss cheese mixture, and ¹/₂ of sour cream mixture. Repeat, making the top layer with last ¹/₃ of potatoes.

Combine ¹/₂ cup Swiss cheese, bread crumbs, and melted butter. Sprinkle over top of casserole. Bake at 350° for 30–35 minutes.

Simply the Best Recipes

Green Beans, Garlic and Pine Nuts

1¹/₂ pounds green beans, trimmed　　**2 tablespoons olive oil**
¹/₂ cup pine nuts　　　　　　　　**Pepper**
4 cloves garlic, minced or pressed

Cook beans in a pot of boiling water about 5 minutes until tender crisp. Drain and place beans in cold water to cool. Drain well. Toast pine nuts in a skillet over medium heat, being careful not to burn. Remove and set aside. Sauté garlic in olive oil in a skillet over medium heat for 1 minute. Add green beans and sauté until heated through, about 5 minutes or longer. Toss in pine nuts. Season with pepper. Yields 6 servings.

Note: Crumbled feta cheese can be added, if desired.

Drop the Hook, Let's Eat

Esta's Onion Patties

I don't want to say that these will cause riots, but I have seen unsightly human behavior when "just cooked" onion patties were placed within arms' reach.

³/₄ cup flour　　　　　　　　**¹/₂ cup powdered milk**
2 teaspoons baking powder　　**Cold water**
2 tablespoons sugar　　　　　**2¹/₂ cups chopped onions**
¹/₂ teaspoon salt　　　　　　　**Cooking oil**
1 tablespoon cornmeal

Mix together the first 6 ingredients. Stir in enough cold water to form thick batter. Stir in onions and drop by the teaspoon into hot deep oil. Flatten patties slightly as you turn them. Fry to a golden brown. Drain on paper towels.

Recipes From the Paris of the Pacific—Sitka, Alaska

Alaska joined the Union on January 3, 1959, as the 49th state. (Hawaii, the 50th state, joined the United States on August 21, 1959.) Alaska's nickname is "The Last Frontier," and its slogan is "North to the Future."

Zucchini Fritters

½ cup flour
1 cup shredded zucchini
½ teaspoon baking soda
½ teaspoon salt

¼ teaspoon pepper
2 eggs, separated
Vegetable oil
Salt to taste

In a small bowl mix the flour, zucchini, baking soda, salt, pepper, and egg yolks. In another bowl beat the egg whites until stiff; fold into zucchini mixture. Drop by heaping teaspoonfuls into hot vegetable oil and brown on both sides. Salt to taste. Makes 1 dozen.

33 Days Hath September

Tasty Whipped Squash

5 pounds Hubbard or butternut
  squash
2 tablespoons margarine
2 tablespoons brown sugar
⅓ cup golden raisins
½ teaspoon salt
¼ teaspoon nutmeg

⅛ teaspoon pepper
1 tablespoon margarine
1 tablespoon brown sugar
1 tablespoon light corn syrup
2 tablespoons pecans, finely
  chopped

Cut squash in halves lengthwise and remove seeds. Place cut-side-down in shallow baking pan; add ½ inch water. Cover and bake at 400° for 40–50 minutes or until tender. Drain, scoop out pulp, and discard shell.

Combine squash pulp, margarine, and brown sugar in a large bowl; beat with electric mixer until smooth. Spoon squash mixture into large saucepan; cook over medium heat 5 minutes, stirring often. Spoon squash into serving dish and keep warm. Combine remaining ingredients in a small saucepan; cook over medium heat until sugar dissolves, stirring constantly. Pour over squash. Serves 6–8.

Alaska Connections Cookbook III

Medium-Famous Orca Jones Vegetable Mess

Tim Jones, who is a charter boat skipper, says this is a good one-dish meal for a small stove. It is also great warmed up and added to. If some is left over, it's fine for breakfast.

Take one potato for each person you expect to feed, slice for frying, and put in a big frying pan with butter. Add a sliced onion, chives, and pepper. Cook until the potatoes are soft, but not hard-fried. Any number of seasonings can now be added. When potatoes are ready, throw in a vegetable. I like fresh broccoli for this, with cauliflower as second choice, but just about any vegetable will do. The broccoli, though, adds a nice green touch.

Cover and cook until the vegetable is warmed through, stirring once in a while. Keep the vegetable crisp. Once cooked, put slices of cheese on top. I like to use Tillamook medium Cheddar. Cover the pan again. Let the cheese melt down through the whole mess and serve. It's a good rib-sticking complement to any meat and leaves a lot of room to put in whatever you might have lying around as leftovers. Leftover game or fish can be cut into bite-size pieces and added, too.

Alaska Magazine's Cabin Cookbook

Stuffed Green Chiles

¹/₄ cup minced onion	1 can whole green chiles
1 clove garlic, minced	¹/₄ cup sliced olives
1 tablespoon butter or margarine	1 medium tomato, diced
1 can refried beans	1 cup shredded Cheddar cheese

Cook onion and garlic in butter until soft. Mix in beans. Fill chiles with beans. Place slit-side-down in 6x10-inch baking dish. Sprinkle with olives, tomatoes, and cheese. Bake in preheated oven, 350° for 35 minutes or until bubbly. Top with sour cream. Serves 4–6.

Tasty Treats from Tenakee Springs, Alaska

June's Boston Baked Beans

1 quart pinto beans (or small red)
3/4 pound cooked bacon
2 teaspoons salt, or to taste
1 1/2 tablespoons brown sugar

1/4 cup molasses
1/2 tablespoon dry mustard
Boiling water

Wash beans. Soak overnight in cold water; drain. Cover with water and simmer until skins just start to break. Test by taking a few beans on spoon and blowing on them. Skins will burst if sufficiently cooked. Drain beans. Chop bacon into large pieces and bury in beans. Put beans into bean crockery pot. Add sugar, molasses, and dry mustard. Add 1 cup boiling water and pour over beans; add more boiling water to cover beans. Cover bean pot; put in oven and bake slowly, 275°, for 6–8 hours. Add more water as needed.

We're Cookin' Now

Crispy Fried Carrots

3/4 cup cornmeal
3/4 cup all-purpose flour
1 teaspoon onion powder
1 teaspoon Old Bay Seasoning
1/2 teaspoon salt
1/2 teaspoon ground pepper
2 1/2 tablespoons chopped fresh
  parsley

1 egg white
2/3 cup buttermilk
1/2 teaspoon hot sauce
4 large carrots, scraped and cut
  into thin strips
Vegetable oil

Combine cornmeal, flour, onion powder, Old Bay Seasoning, salt, pepper, and chopped parsley. Set aside. Beat egg white until foamy. Stir in buttermilk, and hot sauce. Dip carrots into buttermilk mixture. Drain off excess mixture and dredge in cornmeal mixture. Pour oil to depth of 1 inch into a Dutch oven. Heat to 350°. Fry carrots 2 minutes or until lightly browned. Serve carrots immediately. Yields 4 servings.

Kay's Kitchen

Celery Custard

2 cups diced celery
2 small onions, chopped fine
2 cups milk

1 teaspoon salt
$^1/_8$ teaspoon pepper
4 eggs, slightly beaten

Cook celery and onions in milk, about 5 minutes, or until partially tender. Add salt and pepper and pour over eggs. Bake in 350° oven in buttered dish, which has been placed in a pan of water, for about 1 hour, or until firm.

Alaska Gold Rush Cook Book

Ranch Relish

$^1/_2$ cup vinegar
$^1/_2$ cup sugar
2 cups water
1 tablespoon pickling spice
2 (1-ounce) envelopes unflavored
  gelatin
$^1/_2$ cup cold water

$^1/_2$ cup white wine
1 (10-ounce) package frozen kernel
  corn
1 cup shredded cabbage
2 tablespoons chopped green onion
1 tablespoon chopped pimento

In saucepan combine first 4 ingredients; boil, then simmer for 5 minutes. Strain. Sprinkle gelatin over $^1/_2$ cup cold water. Stir to soften; add to hot vinegar mixture. Stir until gelatin is dissolved. Stir in wine. Refrigerate until mixture holds its shape, about 30–40 minutes. Stir in remaining ingredients and put in mold of your choice and refrigerate 4 hours or overnight.

Grannie Annie's Cookin' at the Homestead

PASTA, RICE, ETC.

PHOTO © BRIAN ALLEN, COURTESY OF FAIRBANKS CONVENTION & VISITORS BUREAU

This 18-foot bronze statue of the "Unknown First Family," stands in Golden Heart Park in Fairbanks. The statue is "dedicated to all families past, present and future, and to the indomitable spirit of the people of Alaska's interior."

Clam Spaghetti

¹/₂ pound bacon, cut in pieces,
  browned and drained
4 cloves garlic (or to taste),
  minced
1 onion, finely chopped
1 cup finely chopped celery
1 can cream of mushroom soup
1 (8-ounce) package cream cheese
1 (8-ounce) carton sour cream
1 small can sliced mushrooms,
  undrained
Ground clams (quantity to taste)
Cooked spaghetti

Sauté bacon, garlic, onion, and celery until tender. Add soup, cream cheese, sour cream, and mushrooms and simmer. Add clams 20 minutes before mixture is done. Serve over spaghetti noodles.

Pelican, Alaska: Alaskan Recipe Cookbook

Chicken Spaghetti

1 hen
1 teaspoon salt
2 stalks celery
1¹/₂ sticks butter
1 bell pepper, chopped
1 small onion, chopped
1 pod garlic, chopped
1 can mushroom pieces, drained
12 ounces spaghetti
1 can chopped Ro-Tel tomatoes
¹/₂–²/₃ pound Velveeta cheese
1 (16-ounce) can green peas and
  juice
Seasonings to taste

Boil hen with salt and celery until tender. Debone and cut chicken into bite-size pieces. Reserve broth. In butter, sauté bell pepper, onion, garlic, and mushrooms. Cook spaghetti in reserved broth. Mix all together in large casserole with tomatoes, cheese, and peas, then season to taste. Bake at 350° for 45 minutes.

Simply the Best Recipes

Halibut Fettuccine

1 (16-ounce) package fettuccine
1 pound halibut chunks
$^1/_4$ cup butter or margarine
1 clove garlic, minced
$^1/_4$ cup chopped green onions

1 cup whipping cream
$^1/_2$ cup dry vermouth
1 cup grated Parmesan cheese
$^1/_2$ cup chopped fresh parsley
$^1/_4$ teaspoon pepper

Cook fettuccine to desired doneness according to package directions; drain and rinse with hot water. Rinse and drain halibut chunks, making sure they are cut into small uniform pieces.

In a large saucepan, melt butter or margarine; add garlic, onions, and halibut. Sauté over medium heat for 3–4 minutes, stirring constantly. Add whipping cream and vermouth; cook until thoroughly heated, about 1 minute. Immediately stir in cooked fettuccine; toss to coat with sauce. Cook over medium heat for 3–5 minutes, or until mixture thickens slightly, stirring constantly. Remove from heat. Stir in cheese, parsley, and pepper; toss to coat. Serve immediately.

Just for the Halibut

Fettuccine Alfredo with Scallops

Goes great with white wine and French bread.

8 ounces uncooked egg noodles
3 quarts water, boiling
1/4 cup olive oil, divided
12 large scallops
2 cloves garlic, minced
1/2 teaspoon salt
1/2 teaspoon pepper
1/2 cup butter
1/2 cup heavy whipping cream
1 cup grated Parmesan cheese
2 tablespoons dried parsley flakes

Cook noodles in boiling water to which 1/8 cup olive oil is added. Drain when done and set aside. Heat remaining olive oil in a skillet; add the scallops, garlic, salt, and pepper. Cook until scallops are milky white halfway through, then turn and cook for another 3–5 minutes. Remove from heat and set aside.

Prepare the cheese sauce by melting butter in a saucepan over low heat; slowly add cream, stirring constantly, for 5 minutes. Add cheese and parsley and heat until cheese is melted. Add cheese sauce to the scallops in skillet; heat to thicken. Serve over noodles.

License to Cook Alaska Style

The gold rush brought more than miners and adventurers to the North. It also brought con men and thieves. Among them was Jefferson "Soapy" Smith, whose gang of over 100 men ruled Skagway in 1897 and 1898. He ran crooked gambling halls, freight companies that hauled nothing, telegraph offices that had no telegraph link, even an "army enlistment" tent where the victim's clothes and possessions were stolen while a "doctor" gave him a physical. His men met newcomers at the docks posing as clergymen, newspaper reporters, knowledgeable old-timers and freight company representatives. After sizing up a fellow with a fat wallet, they would direct him to one of Soapy's bogus businesses or mark him for a later robbery. Soapy met his end when he stole $2,800 in gold from a miner. The miner persuaded the citizens of Skagway to form a vigilante committee headed by Frank Reid, a civil engineer. Reid stood up to Soapy and shot him in the heart, but was fatally wounded himself in the shootout. Reid became a local hero.

Scallops and Fettuccine

3 tablespoons butter
2 tablespoons olive oil
2 red bell peppers, cored, seeded,
   and cut into thin strips
1 teaspoon minced garlic
1 tablespoon finely grated
   lemon zest
1/2 teaspoon crushed red pepper
1/2 cup chicken broth

1/4 cup dry white wine
2 tablespoons fresh lemon juice
1 pound sea scallops
3/4 cup chopped fresh parsley
12 ounces fettuccine, cooked
   al dente and drained
Freshly grated Parmesan cheese
   for garnish

In large skillet, melt butter over medium heat. Add olive oil, bell peppers, garlic, lemon zest, and crushed red pepper. Cook 2 minutes. Stir in chicken broth, wine, and lemon juice, and cook until reduced by half. Add scallops and cook 2 minutes or until opaque and thoroughly cooked. Sprinkle with parsley. Toss with hot fettuccine, garnish with Parmesan cheese and serve immediately. Makes 4 main dish servings.

A Taste of Kodiak

Shrimp Fettuccini

1 onion, chopped
1 small bell pepper, chopped
1 stick celery, chopped
1 stick butter
1 tablespoon parsley
1 clove garlic, chopped
1 pound shrimp, peeled and
   deveined

1/2 pint half-and-half
3/4 pound Velveeta cheese
1/8 cup flour
1 pound egg noodles
Jalapeños to taste
Salt, pepper, Konriko or Tony
   Chachere's seasoning

Sauté vegetables in butter; add parsley, garlic, and shrimp. Add half-and-half, cheese, and flour. Lower fire and cook for 30 minutes. Boil noodles and add to shrimp mixture. Add chopped jalapeño peppers and seasonings to taste. Pour into casserole dish. Bake at 350° for 25 minutes.

Simply the Best Recipes

Salmon Linguine

2 tablespoons butter
2 chicken bouillon cubes, in
  1/2 cup hot water
3 tablespoons dill weed
1 pound salmon, sliced in chunks

1 pint whipping cream (or less)
Cornstarch
Linguine noodles (12 ounces)
1/8 cup ReaLemon

Melt butter in large pan on medium-high heat. Add chicken bouillon/water mixture in pan with butter. Add dill weed. (I know it seems like way too much, but don't worry, it's the perfect amount!) Add salmon chunks and sauté until all salmon is cooked.

Pour up to 1 pint of whipping cream. Start with small amount at first. Reduce the liquid to thick consistency. Use cornstarch to thicken, if necessary. Cook linguine as directed on package. After water boils, add ReaLemon. Serve salmon sauce on top of linguine immediately!

Recipes to the Rescue

An old mining cabin on Lost Lake Trail stands testament to early 1920s mining claims.

Pasta with Salmon Cream Sauce

12 ounces fresh or dried cappellini, linguini, spaghettini, or other thin pasta

¹/₄ pound (1 stick) unsalted butter, divided

1 cup fresh shelled petite peas

1 cup heavy (whipping) cream

2 cups (about 12 ounces) flaked cooked salmon

1 cup freshly grated Parmesan cheese, preferably Parmigiano Reggiano, divided

Salt

Freshly ground white pepper

Freshly grated nutmeg

¹/₄ cup minced fresh parsley, preferably flat-leaf Italian type

Cook the pasta in 4 quarts boiling water until al dente, about 12 minutes for dried and 2 minutes for fresh. Meanwhile, melt 2 tablespoons of the butter in a sauté pan or skillet over medium heat. Add the peas and sauté until crisp-tender, about 3 minutes for fresh peas and 1 minute for thawed. Add remaining 6 tablespoons butter and the cream; reduce the heat to low and cook, stirring occasionally, until the butter melts. Add the salmon, ¹/₂ cup Parmesan, and salt, pepper, and nutmeg to taste. Simmer until the cheese melts and salmon is heated through, about 2 minutes; do not allow to boil.

Drain the pasta and place it in a heated bowl. Pour the sauce over the pasta. Add the parsley and gently toss to mix well. Serve immediately and pass the remaining ¹/₂ cup Parmesan cheese at the table. Serves 3 or 4 as a main course, or 6 as a starter.

A Taste of Kodiak

This old mining cabin (opposite page) is found along Lost Lake Trail, a seven-mile-long trail with an elevation gain of 1,820 feet. The trail was constructed by miners in the early 1920s to provide access to mining claims in the area and eventually became popular for hiking. In 1954, it was incorporated into the National Forest trail system. The trail head is located in a gravel pit at Mile 5 Seward Highway (just outside of town). The trail ends at Lost Lake which is two miles above the timberline.

Smoked Salmon Lasagne

¹/₂ medium onion, chopped
¹/₄ cup margarine, divided
¹/₄ cup flour
2 cups milk
2 cups smoked salmon, crumbled
¹/₄ teaspoon pepper, or to taste
1 pint cottage cheese

1 tablespoon dried parsley
1 tablespoon Worcestershire sauce
¹/₄ cup grated Parmesan cheese
9–12 lasagne noodles, uncooked
  (yes, uncooked)
¹/₂–³/₄ pound grated mozzarella
  cheese

Sauté the onion in ¹/₂ the margarine. Cook until onions are soft. Add remaining margarine, then blend in the flour and gradually add milk to make a sauce. Add smoked salmon and pepper. In a bowl, stir together cottage cheese, parsley, Worcestershire sauce, and Parmesan cheese.

In a greased, 9x13x2-inch casserole dish, layer creamed fish mixture, cottage cheese mixture, uncooked lasagne. Then add mozzarella cheese. Repeat, ending with creamed fish mixture. Bake in a 350° oven for 45 minutes covered, and an additional 15 minutes uncovered.

Panhandle Pat's Fifty Years

Alaska's state flag was designed by Benny Benson, a seventh-grader who entered his design in a territorial flag contest in 1926. On May 2, 1927, the Alaska Legislature adopted his design as the official flag. As for the design, the blue background is for the sky and the state flower, the Forget-me-not, which is blue. The North Star is for the future of the state of Alaska, the northernmost of the Union. The dipper is for the Great Bear, symbolizing strength.

Uncle Jack's Jambalaya

1 onion, chopped
2 tablespoons margarine or butter
1 green pepper, coarsely chopped
1 pound cooked reindeer sausage
links ($\frac{1}{2}$-inch slices)
1 pound fresh or frozen Alaska
spotted prawns, peeled*
1 ($10\frac{3}{4}$-ounce) can condensed
chicken broth
1 (6-ounce) can tomato paste

1 (16-ounce) can tomatoes,
undrained, cut up
$\frac{3}{4}$ cup uncooked rice
2 teaspoons sugar
1 teaspoon thyme leaves
2 cloves garlic, finely chopped
$\frac{1}{8}$ teaspoon cayenne pepper
$\frac{1}{8}$ teaspoon fresh-ground pepper
1 bay leaf

In a 5-quart pan or Dutch oven, sauté onion in margarine until tender, about 3 minutes. Stir in everything else and blend well. Simmer, covered, $\frac{1}{2}$ hour, stirring occasionally. Remove bay leaf. Serves 8. Delicious!

*If prawns are fresh, add last 15 minutes of cooking.

Alaska Connections Cookbook III

Shrimp Fried Rice

1 cup rice
1 cup water
2 eggs
1 onion, diced
2 garlic cloves, diced
1 teaspoon fresh ginger, grated

3–4 slices bacon or ham, chopped
1 pound fresh (small) shrimp
5 tablespoons soy sauce
3 tablespoons picante sauce
4 tablespoons cooking oil

Half-cook rice using 1 cup water and set aside. Scramble eggs and set aside. In a large frying pan, fry onion, garlic, ginger, and bacon or ham bits until golden. Add shrimp and cook 2–4 minutes. Add cooked rice, eggs, soy sauce, picante sauce, and oil; stir-fry until rice fries lightly in its own sauce, about 10–15 minutes.

Tasty Treats from Tenakee Springs, Alaska

Company Rice

I have often served this side dish with a baked salmon for company dinner. But it's a good everyday dish, as well. It starts with my old stand-by rice mixture.

1 package Uncle Ben's Long-Grain and Wild Rice	2 medium onions, peeled and sliced
3 tablespoons butter (or olive oil)	1 cup craisins (dried cranberries)
2 teaspoons brown sugar	1 teaspoon dried orange peel

Cook rice according to package directions. Keep warm. Meanwhile, in a large, nonstick skillet, melt butter; add brown sugar and onions. Cook until onions are translucent; stirring frequently. Slowly continue to cook onions, 10–15 minutes, until golden brown. Add craisins and orange peel; stir and cover. Cook slowly, another 10 minutes or so. Fold the onion mixture into the rice mixture; serve with baked salmon or pork tenderloin. Yields 6–8 servings.

Welcome Home

Deep Dish Salmon Pizza

1 (7³/₄-ounce) can salmon
1 (8-ounce) package refrigerated
    crescent rolls
¹/₃ cup tomato sauce
¹/₂ teaspoon salt
¹/₈ teaspoon pepper
¹/₄ teaspoon garlic powder

¹/₂ teaspoon oregano
¹/₄ cup grated Parmesan cheese
1 green pepper, sliced
1 tomato, sliced
1 cup shredded Monterey Jack
    cheese

Drain salmon and flake. Press crescent roll dough on bottom and sides of 9-inch-square baking pan. Bake at 400° for 7 minutes. Remove from oven and spread with tomato sauce. Sprinkle with salt, pepper, garlic powder, oregano, and Parmesan cheese. Top with salmon, green pepper, and tomato. Sprinkle with Monterey Jack cheese. Bake at 425° for 15 minutes. Serves 4.

Salmon Recipes

Pizza Buns

A favorite for lots of company. Serve with chips and a salad. Everyone loves these.

1 pound bacon
1 cup chopped onion
2 pounds hamburger
1 cup cut-up pepperoni
2 cups shredded mozzarella
    cheese

1 can cream of mushroom soup
1 can tomato soup
1 small can sliced mushrooms,
    drained
Hamburger buns

Brown bacon, drain, and crumble. Sauté onion in 1 tablespoon bacon drippings. Brown hamburger in same pan. Drain and add pepperoni, cheese, soups, and mushrooms. Heat through. Spread mixture on hamburger bun halves and broil until browned. Serve immediately.

Literary Tastes

Cassy's Calzones

DOUGH:

1¹/₂ teaspoons dry yeast
1 tablespoon honey or sugar
1 cup warm water

1¹/₂ cups whole wheat flour
1¹/₂ cups white flour
¹/₂ teaspoon salt

Mix the first 3 ingredients together and allow to sponge for 5–10 minutes. Add flour and salt. Knead for 5–10 minutes. Let rise until double. Punch down and divide into 6 rounds. Roll the rounds out into 6-inch circles about ¹/₄ inch thick. Place ¹/₂–³/₄ cup of desired Calzone Filling on half of the circle. Fold over and wet edges with water. Pinch edges together to seal dough crescents. Prick each Calzone with a fork. Place on oiled cookie sheet and bake at 450° for 15–20 minutes. Makes 6 servings.

PIZZA FILLING:

Salami
Cheese

Thick tomato sauce

Slice salami and cheese. Mix with thick tomato sauce.

CHICKEN POT PIE FILLING:

Cooked chicken
Cooked vegetables

Chicken broth
Cornstarch

Mix cooked chicken and cooked vegetables and chicken broth; thicken with cornstarch to desired consistency.

SWISS CHEESE AND HAM FILLING:

Swiss cheese

Ham chunks

Mix cheese and chunked ham together.

BBQ BEEF FILLING:

Cooked roast beef, sliced
BBQ sauce

American cheese

Mix roast beef, BBQ sauce, and American cheese.

Sharing Our Best

Pilgrim Sandwich

This is a knife-and-fork sandwich.

Butter as needed
8 slices French bread, cut on an
  angle
2 cups Thousand Island dressing

8 or more slices, thinly sliced
  turkey
8 slices, processed Swiss cheese

Butter one side of 4 pieces of bread. Place on grill, butter-side-down. Cover with Thousand Island dressing. Lay 2 slices of cheese on each piece of bread in such a way as to cover the dressing. After bread is grilled, place in oven to finish melting the cheese.

Meanwhile, butter remaining 4 pieces of bread. Place on grill. Cover each with Thousand Island dressing. Cover each piece with 2 turkey slices, or more if desired. Lightly coat turkey with thousand island dressing. Grill until heated through. Remove from grill. Place the pieces with the melted cheese on top of the turkey, cheese-side-up.

Kay's Kitchen

During the Gold Rush Era, a "Tent City" sprang up in the wilderness at the mouth of Ship Creek where Anchorage is now located and soon swelled to a population of over 2,000. On July 9, 1915, the Anchorage townsite auction was held, and over 600 lots in a fixed grid were sold for a total of approximately $150,000. Although the area had been known by various names, in this same year the U.S. Post Office formalized the use of the name "Anchorage," and despite some protests, the name stuck. Voters had previously chosen "Alaska City."

Fiddlehead Fern Quiche

1 cup fresh or frozen fiddleheads
9 slices thick bacon, crisply fried
  and crumbled
1/2 cup minced onion
1 cup shredded Swiss cheese
1 (9-inch) unbaked pie shell

4 egg yolks
1 teaspoon salt
1/2 teaspoon sugar
1/2 teaspoon cayenne pepper
2 cups whipping cream or
  half-and-half

Sprinkle fiddlehead fern, bacon, onion, and cheese in pastry-lined pie pan. Beat egg yolks lightly; add salt, sugar, and cayenne pepper; pour in cream. Bake 10 minutes at 450°; reduce temperature to 300° and bake 30 minutes longer, or until toothpick stuck into quiche comes out clean.

Let's Taste Alaska

Smoked Salmon Quiche

1 cup smoked salmon, canned or
  fresh from the smoker
1/2 cup chopped green or yellow
  onion
1/4 cup chopped green and red
  pepper
1–2 cups shredded cheese,
  Cheddar, Swiss, Monterey Jack
  or combination

1 cup Bisquick
2 cups milk
4 eggs
1/4 teaspoon garlic salt
1/4 teaspoon cracked pepper
Sprinkle of cayenne pepper

Oil a large 10-inch deep-dish pie plate. Sprinkle bottom of pan with salmon, onion, peppers, and cheese. In a large bowl combine Bisquick, milk, eggs, garlic salt, cracked pepper, and cayenne. Mix and pour over the smoked salmon/cheese in the pie plate. Bake in hot (400°) oven for 35 minutes or until a knife inserted comes out clean. Let rest for 10 minutes. Cut in wedges and serve with toasted sourdough bread.

Variation: Add canned green chiles or grated zucchini or both in bottom of pan.

Grannie Annie's Cookin' Fish from Cold Alaskan Waters

Broccoli Salmon Quiche

1 (9-inch) pie crust
2 cups fresh broccoli, cut in
   florets
1 (16-ounce) can salmon
   (or leftover cooked salmon,
   if available)

1 cup shredded Swiss cheese
$1/4$ cup chopped, fresh chives
5 eggs, beaten
1 cup heavy whipping cream
$1/4$ teaspoon cayenne red pepper
1 teaspoon dried dill weed

Preheat oven to 350°. Prepare bottom of 9-inch deep pie dish by spraying with nonstick cooking spray. Line with pie pastry. Cover bottom of dish with broccoli florets, chunks of salmon, and sprinkle with cheese and chives. Set aside. In medium bowl, beat eggs, whipping cream, cayenne, and dill until thoroughly combined. Bake in preheated oven for 1 hour, or until crust and eggs are lightly browned, and quiche is puffy in center. Yields 6 servings.

Alaska's Gourmet Breakfasts

Halibut Quiche

1 (9-inch) unbaked pastry shell
3 eggs
$1/4$ teaspoon nutmeg
$1/2$ teaspoon salt
$1/8$ teaspoon white pepper
1 teaspoon dill weed

1 cup milk
$1/2$ pound cooked halibut, flaked
2 tablespoons finely chopped onion
1 cup shredded Swiss cheese
$1/4$ cup finely shredded Parmesan
   cheese

Bake pastry shell in 450° oven for 7–8 minutes, till lightly browned and cooked. Turn oven down to 350°. Remove pie shell from oven.

Break eggs into medium bowl. Add spices and milk and beat lightly. Distribute halibut over bottom of pie shell, then add onion and Swiss cheese; pour egg mixture over all. Sprinkle top with Parmesan cheese. Bake at 350° until knife inserted comes out clean, approximately 45 minutes.

Recipe from Chocolate Drop B&B, Homer
Favorite Recipes from Alaska's Bed and Breakfasts

Crepes à la Bette

CREPES:

2¼ cups flour
¾ teaspoon salt
½ teaspoon baking powder
3 cups milk

3 eggs
2 tablespoons butter or margarine, melted

Mix flour, salt, and baking powder. Stir in milk, eggs, and butter or margarine. Beat until smooth. Pour scant ¼ cup of batter into hot skillet, immediately rotating skillet so that batter covers skillet bottom. Cook until top is dry and bottom is light brown; turn and cook other side until light brown; cool.

1½ pounds halibut chunks
2 fresh lemons, wedged
1 small package frozen peas, thawed
½ cup sliced mushrooms

½ cup chopped scallions
⅓ cup sliced almonds
2 teaspoons lemon pepper
¼ teaspoon white pepper
1½ cups grated mozzarella cheese

Place halibut chunks in a shallow baking dish and liberally squeeze lemon over all. Let marinate for about 1 hour. Meanwhile place thawed peas, mushrooms, scallions, sliced almonds, lemon pepper, and white pepper in a large mixing bowl. Prepare Sauce.

Drain halibut, place in bowl with mushrooms and scallions; add about ⅓ of Sauce mixture to the halibut mixture and mix together; spoon into Crepes. Place seam-side-down in a baking dish, pour remaining Sauce over all, and cover with mozzarella cheese. Bake for 40 minutes in 375° oven, then place under broiler to brown cheese. Serve with fresh fruit compote.

SAUCE:

6 tablespoons butter or margarine
¼ cup flour
2 cups half-and-half
⅓ cup sparkling white wine

1 tablespoon lemon juice
½ teaspoon salt
1 cup grated Jack cheese

Melt butter or margarine in saucepan; add flour and stir until smooth and bubbly. Add half-and-half; cook, stirring constantly, until sauce starts to thicken. Then add wine, lemon juice, salt, and Jack cheese; continue to cook just until cheese is melted; remove from heat.

Just for the Halibut

Chugach Chiles

Fresh fruit and muffins make a nice accompaniment.

2 (7-ounce) cans whole green chiles
Cheddar or Pepper Jack cheese, sliced into ¹/₂-inch-wide strips
8 large eggs
2 cups milk
¹/₂ cup all-purpose flour
¹/₄ teaspoon salt (optional)
¹/₄ cup Parmesan cheese
Prepared salsa

Slit chiles longways, wash, and pat dry on paper towel. Stuff each with 1 (¹/₂-inch-wide) slice of cheese and lay in a single layer in a greased 2¹/₂-quart baking dish. Mix eggs, milk, flour, Parmesan, and salt in a blender and pour over chiles. Bake at 350° for 1 hour, or until top is lightly browned and a toothpick inserted in the center comes out clean. Serve with salsa. Serves 4.

Recipe from Southshore B&B, Wasilla
Favorite Recipes from Alaska's Bed and Breakfasts

Keemuk
Whale Blubber

Keemuk is chewy and gristly, not at all like other fats.

Cut into pieces for boiling. Cook in water until tender. Slice and eat—not too much, for it is rich.

To cook salted keemuk, soak for two days or more, changing water daily. Boil until tender. Slice and eat.

Eskimo Cookbook by Alexandra

Encompassing 1,955 square miles, Anchorage is nearly the size of the state of Delaware, stretching more than 50 miles from Portage Glacier to the head of Cook Inlet.

Rose Hip Catsup

1 quart Rose Hip Purée
2 cups vinegar
2 cups sugar
1 teaspoon onion powder
¹/₂ teaspoon black pepper
¹/₂ teaspoon dry mustard

¹/₂ teaspoon salt
Dash of cayenne
¹/₂ teaspoon ground cloves
¹/₂ teaspoon cinnamon
1 teaspoon garlic powder
   (optional)

Combine and cook about 50 minutes, until thick as desired (it will not be as thick as tomato catsup). Pour into sterilized jars. Add lids. Process 15 minutes in boiling water bath, or refrigerate.

ROSE HIP PURÉE:

The prickly rose grows everywhere in Alaska. The "hip" is the fruit of the plant, the part of the flower that's left on the bush after the petals drop.

Use soft, ripe rose hips (the riper they are, the sweeter they are). It takes about 4 cups rose hips to make 2 cups purée. Remove stalks and blossom ends. Rinse berries in cold water; put them into a pan and add enough water to almost cover. Bring to a boil and simmer 10–15 minutes.

Press through a sieve or strainer. All that does not go through the sieve is placed in the pan again. Add a little water, enough to almost cover; if you want a thicker purée, add slightly less water. This time heat, but do not boil. Press again one more time.

Tasty Treats from Tenakee Springs, Alaska

MEATS

The Alaska Legislature has recognized the Red Dog Saloon as the oldest man-made attraction in Juneau. The original saloon opened its swinging doors on December 23, 1949 and continues to preserve the memory of Alaska's early prospecting days.

Barbecued Moose on the Wood Stove

1 can tomato sauce or stewed
  tomatoes, or in a pinch, 1 can
  tomato soup
$^1/_4$ cup vinegar
3 tablespoons brown sugar
$^1/_2$ cup Worcestershire sauce

$^1/_2$ cup chopped onion
$^1/_2$ cup diced green pepper
2 tablespoons minced garlic
Salt and pepper to taste
1 (3- to 4-pound) moose roast

Mix all ingredients, except roast. In your trusty Dutch oven with lid, place roast and cover with mixture. Place lid on Dutch oven. Cook on the hottest place on the wood stove until it falls apart when you pierce it with a fork. Take 2 forks and pull the meat apart while still in the pot. Serve on toasted hoagie buns, sourdough bread, rice, or smashed potatoes.

Grannie Annie's Cookin' on the Wood Stove

Editor's Extra: Don't have any caribou or moose? Try any of these recipes with venison or beef.

Succulent Moose Roast

1 (3- to 6-pound) moose roast
Bacon fat
Flour
Salt to taste
Pepper to taste

Ginger to taste
1 onion, diced
Water
3–4 potatoes, quartered

Thaw roast, if frozen. Coat a broiling pan with bacon fat, then flour the bottom. Rub the roast with bacon fat, salt, pepper, and ginger. Place the roast in pan; cover with onion and add a bottom-full of water. Add quartered potatoes around roast. Bake covered at 350° for 2 hours and 25 minutes, or until done.

Moose in the Pot Cookbook

Moose Pot Roast

2 onions, chopped
4 tablespoons oil
4 tablespoons flour
1 teaspoon salt
1/4 teaspoon pepper
4-pound moose roast

2 cups canned tomatoes
1/3 cup vinegar
1 crushed bay leaf
2 teaspoons brown sugar
1 tablespoon pickling spices

Brown onions in oil. Combine flour, salt, and pepper. Rub mixture on moose roast and brown on all sides. Combine all other ingredients and add to moose. Cover and bake at 350° for about 3 hours. Check roast occasionally and maintain 1/4 inch water in roaster. Serves 6.

Moose & Caribou Recipes of Alaska

Moose Tips

4 pounds moose roast, cut in
2-inch cubes
Small amount of oil for sautéing
2 large white onions, sliced or
cut in 8ths
Water
1 cup red wine
1 tablespoon Kitchen Bouquet

1–2 pounds medium-size
mushrooms
1/4 cup cornstarch
1/2 cup cold water
2 teaspoons salt
1/2 teaspoon pepper
1 pound wide egg noodles,
prepared per package directions

Sear meat in hot frying pan until good color shows. Add onions after beef and sauté just until they sweat and become glossy. Put meat and onions in roasting pan. Add enough water to fry pan to deglaze, and add that to the roasting pan. Add wine and Kitchen Bouquet and enough water to come to the top of the meat cubes. Roast in oven for 1 hour at 350°, then add mushrooms. Cook another 1 1/2 hours or until tender. Mix cornstarch and cold water. Move roasting pan to top of stove and turn burner to medium-high. Mix cornstarch and water into juices of meat, stirring quickly and constantly until it thickens. Salt and pepper to taste. Serve over egg noodles.

Literary Tastes

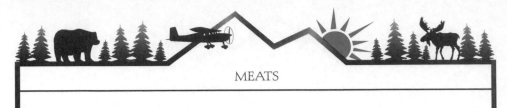

Moose with Oyster Sauce and Snow Peas

1 (10-ounce) moose backstrap
1 teaspoon dry sherry
2 teaspoons cornstarch in
   3 tablespoons water
1/2 teaspoon baking soda
1 tablespoon soy sauce
1 dash pepper
4 tablespoons cooking oil, divided
1 teaspoon sugar

1 1/2 tablespoons oyster-flavored
   sauce (found in gourmet section)
2 green onions, chopped
1 (6-ounce) package frozen or fresh
   snow peas (Oriental pea pods)
Lettuce
Scallions or white part of green
   onions, shredded
Cooked rice

Cut steak cross-grain into 1x1 1/2-inch pieces, very thinly, and marinate about 45 minutes in mixture of sherry, cornstarch, baking baking soda, soy sauce, pepper, and 2 tablespoons cooking oil.

Heat 2 tablespoons oil in wok or sauté pan. Add sugar and oyster sauce, then add steak and stir-fry until no red is visible in meat. Add green onions and snow peas; stir for a couple of more minutes till peas are tender but still crisp. On a serving plate, make a bed of lettuce. Transfer steak and peas, arranging nicely on the lettuce. Sprinkle with shredded scallions. Serve with hot steamed white rice.

Moose in the Pot Cookbook

The moose is Alaska's official state land mammal. The world's largest member of the deer family, the Alaska moose is the largest of all moose species. Males in prime condition weigh from 1,200 to 1,600 pounds. Adult females weigh 800 to 1,300 pounds. More people hunt moose than any other of Alaska's big game species.

Moose Teriyaki

MARINADE:

2 cups soy sauce
2 cups water
2 tablespoons Worcestershire
2 tablespoons lemon

1 teaspoon parsley
1 teaspoon pepper
1 teaspoon marjoram
1–2 pounds moose, cut into strips

Combine all ingredients, except moose, in bowl large enough to marinate moose strips. Marinate meat for 1/2 hour.

STIR-FRY:

1 onion, chopped
1 green pepper, chopped
1 cup sliced mushrooms

1 cup sliced water chestnuts
1 cup bamboo shoots
3 cups cooked rice

After meat has marinated for 1/2 hour, remove from marinade. Heat wok or large saucepan, and combine meat with onion, green pepper, mushrooms, water chestnuts, and bamboo shoots; stir-fry till meat is no longer pink and vegetables are tender-crisp. Serve over rice.

Moose in the Pot Cookbook

Moose Kabobs

MARINADE:

3 tablespoons soy sauce or
    teriyaki sauce
1 cup oil
2 teaspoons vinegar

2 teaspoons ketchup
6 crushed garlic cloves
1 (2- to 3-pound) moose roast

Mix sauce, oil, vinegar, ketchup, and garlic. Cut meat into bite-size pieces. Marinate meat for at least 15 minutes.

KABOBS:

10 cherry tomatoes
10 fresh mushrooms
1 onion, cut in chunks

1 green pepper, cut in chunks
1 zucchini, cut in wedges
10 pieces of cauliflower

Skewer veggies and meat in varying order. Grill on medium heat until done. Serve over rice.

Moose in the Pot Cookbook

Grilled Moose Steak

**4 boneless moose steaks, cut
 1¹/₂ inches thick
¹/₄ cup vegetable oil
¹/₂ teaspoon salt
¹/₂ teaspoon pepper**

**1 teaspoon Worcestershire sauce
1 teaspoon chili powder
1 tablespoon dry mustard
2 tablespoons beef broth**

Brush steak with oil. Sprinkle with salt and pepper. Combine remaining ingredients to make a thin paste. Place steaks on grill 4 inches above source of heat. Brush with paste and grill 4–5 minutes. Turn steaks with tongs to prevent piercing and brush with remaining paste. Grill to desired doneness. Serves 4.

Moose & Caribou Recipes of Alaska

Mesquite Moose Steaks

You'll want at least two moose steaks—cut about ³/₄ inch thick—for each person. We've never seen anyone eat fewer than two at a sitting. Dip the steaks in cooking oil and season with plenty of pepper, garlic powder, and a little salt. If the steaks are tough, use some meat tenderizer and no salt.

   To grill these steaks, you'll need a covered charcoal grill; the cover is important because the mesquite smoke penetrates the meat better if the smoke is trapped by a cover. Light the grill and wait until the coals are hot. Then toss on a few mesquite chips. Put the steaks on the grill, sear them quickly, and then put the cover on the grill. The steaks cook quickly (roughly 4–5 minutes). Make sure they don't overcook—it's best to leave them a bit rare.

Alaska Magazine's Cabin Cookbook

Magic Meat Pie with Ground Moose Meat

2 onions, diced
4 tablespoons shortening, divided
1 pound ground moose meat
  (or any other)
1 carrot, sliced
1 cup cooked peas
3 tablespoons flour

$1/2$ teaspoon salt
Dash of pepper
1 teaspoon Worcestershire sauce
$2^{1}/2$ cups boiling water
1 recipe baking powder biscuit
  dough

Sauté onions in 2 tablespoons shortening until yellow. Add ground meat and sauté until richly browned. Add carrots and peas. Turn into greased casserole. Melt remaining 2 tablespoons shortening. Add flour, salt and pepper; blend. Add Worcestershire sauce and water, stirring constantly and cooking until thickened. Pour $3/4$ cup gravy over mixture in baking dish. Reserve remaining gravy to serve with pie. Roll baking powder dough to fit casserole and prick with fork. Adjust dough over meat and seal edge. Bake in very hot oven, 450°, 25–30 minutes. Serves 6.

The Original Great Alaska Cookbook

Mooseburger Meat Loaf

2 pounds mooseburger
2 eggs
1 cup ground dry bread crumbs
1/2 cup diced celery or
   3 tablespoons dried celery tops
2 or 3 large onons, ground
2 1/2 cups evaporated milk
1 1/2 teaspoons salt

1/4 teaspoon pepper
2 cloves garlic, minced
2 teaspoons celery salt
1 teaspoon mustard
1/4 teaspoon sage or 1/8 teaspoon
   thyme
3 or 4 slices bacon

Combine meat with other ingredients except bacon, using enough milk so that the mixture is very soft. Place in a large deep pan, pressing down well. Since this is a completely unorthodox loaf, make no attempt to have it hold its shape. Lay strips of bacon across the top, cover and bake in a moderate, 350° oven for 2–2 1/2 hours. Uncover the last 1/2 hour to brown. For a Spanish flavor, omit the thyme and add 1/2 teaspoon cumin and 1 tablespoon chili powder. This loaf is delicious hot or cold. Makes grand sandwiches. Warm over by browning lightly in bacon drippings.

The Original Great Alaska Cookbook

LAUREN JONES

Caution! Moose crossing. Each year 500 to 1,000 moose are killed on Alaska's roads and railways. By law, all big game animals killed by motor vehicles belong to the State of Alaska, and anyone who kills one with their vehicle must report it to the local police or state troopers. Most areas of the state maintain a list of individuals and charities who will respond to the scene and salvage the meat for human consumption. As the police are informed an animal has been killed, the dispatcher calls the first person on the list. If that person cannot salvage the animal in a timely manner, the next person on the list is called, and so on. The main goal of the State is to get meat to the people who need it, and to make sure that the animal is salvaged before it spoils.

Alaskaladas

An Alaskan version of enchiladas.

1–2 pounds ground mooseburger, or 3 chicken breasts, cubed in small pieces
¹/₂ onion, chopped
1 tablespoon minced garlic
2 cans cream of mushroom soup
1 can stewed diced tomatoes
¹/₂ cup sour cream
1 (8-ounce) can chopped green chiles (do not drain)

1 cup cubed Mexican Velveeta
1 teaspoon garlic salt (or more)
¹/₂ teaspoon black pepper
1 teaspoon ground cumin
6–8 corn tortillas, divided
Mozzarella cheese
Additional garlic salt
Additional black pepper
Paprika

Brown meat (moose or chicken), onion, and garlic in saucepan. In a large bowl, place soup, tomatoes, sour cream, green chiles, and Velveeta. When meat is almost cooked through, stir in garlic salt, black pepper, and cumin. Add meat mixture to soup mixture and stir until well blended. Taste for more salt.

Soften tortillas in small amount of hot vegetable oil in cast-iron skillet. Drain on paper towels and place 3¹/₂–4 in oblong casserole dish. Spoon ¹/₂ the mixture onto the tortillas. Place the rest of the tortillas over mixture and spoon remaining mixture on top. Top with shredded mozzarella cheese. Sprinkle top with garlic salt, pepper, and paprika. Bake for 45 minutes to 1 hour, until bubbly and brown on top. Let set 15 minutes before serving with a nice green salad and a tall glass of cold limeade...lime sherbet for dessert or key lime pie.

Grannie Annie's Cookin' at the Homestead

Moose Jerky

2 pounds flank or other lean
   moose meat
1 cup soy sauce
¹/₄ cup vegetable oil

1 teaspoon garlic salt
1 teaspoon salt
2 teaspoons black pepper

Cut meat with the grain in very thin strips. Grasp meat, a strip at a time, with both hands and stretch lengthwise to tenderize.

Combine remaining ingredients in large bowl. Add meat strips and marinate 1 hour, stirring often. Drain, discarding marinade. Place strips directly on oven rack with a sheet of aluminum foil on a lower rack to catch drips. Bake at 175° for 10 hours with oven door slightly open. Serve as snacks. Yields ³/₄ pound.

Moose & Caribou Recipes of Alaska

Miner's Steak

¹/₄ cup flour
1 teaspoon salt
¹/₄ teaspoon pepper
1 teaspoon garlic salt
1¹/₂ pounds moose or caribou
   steak, cut into ¹/₂-inch strips
1 large onion, sliced
1 green pepper, sliced

1 (10-ounce) can mushrooms,
   drained
1 tablespoon molasses
3 tablespoons soy sauce
1 cup beef broth
1 (19-ounce) can tomatoes,
   chopped
Hot cooked noodles

Combine flour and spices in a plastic bag. Shake meat strips in flour mixture and place in a Dutch oven or roaster. Place onion, green pepper, and mushrooms over meat. Combine molasses, soy sauce, beef broth, and tomatoes; pour over meat and vegetables. Cover and bake at 325° for 2¹/₂–3 hours. Stir once or twice while baking. Serve over noodles.

Nome Centennial Cookbook 1898-1998

Caribou with Blue Cheese

6 caribou steaks
Salt and pepper
³/₄ cup butter, divided

1 cup mushrooms, sliced
2 teaspoons brandy
¹/₂ cup blue cheese

Broil steaks 8 minutes on each side. Sprinkle with salt and pepper. Heat ¹/₄ cup butter in small skillet over medium heat. Add sliced mushrooms and sauté for about 15 minutes. Stir in brandy and cook for 1 minute. Set aside.

Mash blue cheese and remaining ¹/₂ cup butter together until smooth. Spread cooked steak with cheese and butter mixture so it melts slightly. Garnish with mushrooms. Serves 6–8.

Moose & Caribou Recipes of Alaska

Caribou Pot Roast
with Sour Cream Sauce

Caribou shoulder roast
1 onion, sliced
2 carrots, sliced
1 small turnip, diced
2 stalks celery, sliced
¹/₄ cup oil
Salt and pepper

Thyme, pinch
1 bay leaf
4 juniper berries
1 lemon, sliced thin
1 cup red wine
1 cup beef broth
¹/₂ cup sour cream

In large pan, brown meat and vegetables in hot oil. Add spices, berries, lemon, wine, and broth. Cover and simmer over low flame for 2 hours. Remove meat. Strain sauce back into pan, pressing vegetables through sieve. Add sour cream to sauce and blend. Return meat to pan and simmer until tender.

Moose & Caribou Recipes of Alaska

Alaska has almost twice as many caribou as people. The human population numbers around 600,000, while there are over one million caribou in the state. The largest herd is the Western Arctic herd with almost half the total caribou in Alaska.

Stuffed Slices of Caribou or Moose

2 cups bread crumbs
6 tablespoons butter, divided
1 onion, minced or grated
2 tablespoons minced parsley
2 tablespoons diced boiled ham
4 egg yolks

2 tablespoons Parmesan cheese
Pinch thyme
Salt and pepper
2 pounds thinly sliced meat
Additional bread crumbs and
    butter for rolling

Make a stuffing by browning the bread crumbs in ¹/₂ the butter in a saucepan. In another pan sauté onion, parsley, and ham in remaining butter. Combine sautéed mixture with bread crumbs and add egg yolks, cheese, thyme, salt and pepper; mix well. Place about 1 tablespoon stuffing in each slice of meat, roll or turn in edges and skewer. Dip each skewered slice in melted butter, then in bread crumbs, and bake in 350° oven until done (20–25 minutes).

Alaska Gold Rush Cook Book

Spicy Meatballs

1 egg, beaten
2 tablespoons milk
³/₄ cup soft bread crumbs
2 tablespoons finely chopped
    onion
¹/₂ teaspoon ground sage

¹/₂ teaspoon salt
¹/₂ teaspoon garlic powder
1 pound caribou, ground
³/₄ cup barbecue sauce
¹/₃ cup orange marmalade
¹/₃ cup water

Combine egg, milk, bread crumbs, onion, sage, salt, and garlic powder. Add meat and mix well. Shape into 1-inch meatballs. Place in shallow baking pan and bake at 350° for 15–20 minutes. Drain.

Combine barbecue sauce, marmalade, and water. Heat to boiling. Pour over meatballs. Serve hot. Yields about 42 meatballs.

Moose & Caribou Recipes of Alaska

Caribou Enchiladas

1 pound caribou, ground
1 envelope taco seasoning
1 package medium-size flour
   tortillas, room temperature
1 (16-ounce) can refried beans
1 small onion, chopped

1 cup shredded sharp Cheddar
   cheese, divided
1 can cream of chicken or
   mushroom soup
$1/2$ soup can milk or plain yogurt

Brown meat until all pink color is gone. Pour off most of the fat and stir in the taco seasoning according to package directions. Simmer for 10–15 minutes. Meanwhile, spray a large casserole dish with cooking spray, or lightly oil it with vegetable oil.

Preheat oven to 350°. Lay tortillas out flat and fill each with a spoonful of beans and a spoonful of the meat mixture. (Spread beans around on the tortilla, then spread the meat on top.) Sprinkle onions and some of the cheese on top of the meat mixture. Roll the tortillas up by folding over the two sides, then roll from the bottom. Place in the casserole dish seam-side down. Stir together the soup and milk or yogurt. Use a whisk, or stir the mixture until it is smooth. Pour the sauce over the filled tortillas, sprinkle with remaining cheese and cover with foil. Bake for 30–45 minutes. Check at 30 minutes; remove foil for the last 5 minutes or so. Serve with a green salad.

Moose in the Pot Cookbook

The Alaska State Park System is the largest in the United States with more than 3.2 million acres of land and water. The largest state park in Alaska, and in the nation, is the Wood-Tikchik State Park, which comprises 1.6 million acres of wilderness.

Caribou Strips

MARINADE:

2 cups red cooking wine
2 cloves garlic

2 teaspoons soy sauce
1/2 teaspoon dry mustard

Combine all ingredients and add the caribou strips. Marinate in refrigerator for 8 hours or overnight.

2 pounds caribou strips,
approximately 1/2 x 2 1/2 inches
1 cup flour
2 teaspoons seasoned salt
1/2 teaspoon pepper

1/2 teaspoon tarragon
1/2 teaspoon garlic salt
1/4 cup olive oil
2 tablespoons butter

Mix flour and seasonings. Dredge drained caribou strips in the flour; sauté in oil and butter. Stir in a few strips at a time to complete browning. Serve with wooden toothpicks; dip in Sauce.

SAUCE:

1/4 cup barbecue sauce

1/4 cup apricot jam

Combine.

Nome Centennial Cookbook 1898-1998

Mexican Elk Steak

This is a favorite of hearty eaters served with a green salad and sopapillas. Fresh pineapple for dessert is refreshing.

2 pounds elk or venison, trimmed and cut into 1-inch cubes
4 tablespoons vegetable oil
2 onions, cut in rings
2 large green peppers, cut in strips
1 (1-pound, 12-ounce) can tomatoes
1 (6-ounce) can tomato paste
1 teaspoon chili powder
$^1/_2$ teaspoon paprika

1 (10-ounce) can mild enchilada sauce
1 clove garlic, minced
2 bay leaves
1 teaspoon ground cumin
$^1/_2$ teaspoon oregano
1 (7-ounce) can taco sauce
2 large potatoes, cubed
1 (7-ounce) can chopped green chiles

Brown meat in oil. Add onions and green peppers and simmer about 30 minutes. Add remaining ingredients and simmer slowly until meat is tender, about $1^1/_2$ hours. Yields 6 servings.

A Taste of Kodiak

Bear Tenderloins
with Blackberry Sauce

Be sure not to overcook wild game because of the low-fat content of the meat.

2 pounds bear meat tenderloin
$^1/_2$ cup butter
1 cup seedless blackberry jam

1 can beef broth, or 2 beef bouillon cubes in $1^1/_2$ cups hot water

In an ovenproof pan, brown tenderloin in butter on all sides (4–5 minutes). Transfer to 450° oven and bake, turning once, until a meat thermometer inserted in thickest part registers 150° (12–15 minutes). Cut to test; meat should no longer be pink in center of thickest part. Transfer meat to a warm platter and keep warm. Add jam and broth to drippings in pan; bring to a boil. Cook, stirring until reduced to about $^2/_3$ cup (about 8 minutes). Slice meat, stirring any juices into sauce. Spoon sauce over meat to serve. Serves 6.

License to Cook Alaska Style

Country Deer Steak

4 venison steaks	1 package dry onion soup mix
Salt and pepper to taste	1 cup water
Flour	1–2 teaspoons Worcestershire
Vegetable oil	sauce

Tenderize steaks, if necessary. Add salt and pepper; flour steaks. Brown in hot oil in a heavy large skillet with a lid that fits tightly. Add soup mix, water, and Worcestershire sauce. Simmer 1 hour until tender, adding water as needed; do not allow to go dry. This is great served with potatoes or rice.

Huna Heritage Foundation Cookbook

Tlingit Stir-Fry

1–2 pounds venison (lean beef,	1 onion, finely chopped
pork or fowl can be used also)	1 can clams and juice
1 small head cabbage, finely	1 large handful black seaweed
chopped	Cooked rice

Stir-fry the meat until done; set aside. In small frying pan, sauté the cabbage and onion until tender. Add clams with juice and seaweed. Stir until heated through. Add meat and when hot, serve over rice.

Note: You can add different chopped vegetables for variety, like celery, bok choy or green pea pods.

Huna Heritage Foundation Cookbook

Willow Meats

Inside of barkbirch there is something that is yellowish. That is called the meat of willows. They are very good to eat. People eat it with sugar and seal oil. First clean off the barkbirch from the meat of the willow. There is also soft green barkbirch inside of outside barkbirch. Never eat green stuff on willows. Often times, we use a knife to scrape off the barkbirch. I don't think they use oolo for scraping out the barkbirch.

Eskimo Cookbook

Editor's Note: The recipes in this cookbook are somewhat impractical to prepare but are fascinating to read. See the catalog section for a description of this unique cookbook.

Braised Venison

3 pounds venison
3 slices salt pork
Salt, pepper, and flour
$^1/_4$ cup fat
$^1/_4$ cup hot water

$^1/_2$ teaspoon vinegar
$^1/_2$ cup chopped celery
1 carrot, diced
1 tart apple, chopped
$^1/_2$ tablespoon lemon juice

Use the less tender cuts of venison for this method. Lard venison with salt pork and rub with salt, pepper, and flour. Sauté in hot fat until well browned, turning frequently. Add hot water with vinegar. Cover and cook until tender, about 2–2$^1/_2$ hours, adding more water as it evaporates. One-half hour before meat is done, add remaining ingredients. Cook until vegetables are tender. Serve with a tart jelly.

The Original Great Alaska Cookbook

Barbecued Venison Chops

Serve with hot buttered noodles and a green salad.

8 venison chops
Oil
1 teaspoon salt
$^1/_2$ teaspoon nutmeg
1 cup water

$^1/_2$ cup ketchup
1 teaspoon celery seed
$^1/_3$ cup vinegar
1 bay leaf

Brown chops in hot oil. Combine remaining ingredients; pour over chops in oven-proof baking dish. Bake at 325° for 1–1$^1/_2$ hours. Turn chops once. The liquid will bake into the chops leaving a nicely glazed covering on the meat.

Pelican, Alaska: Alaskan Recipe Cookbook

Caribou are the only member of the deer family in which both sexes grow antlers.

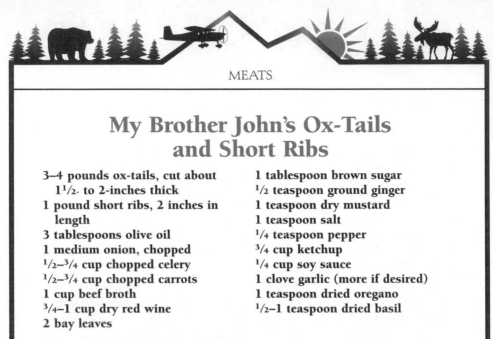

My Brother John's Ox-Tails and Short Ribs

3–4 pounds ox-tails, cut about
1½- to 2-inches thick
1 pound short ribs, 2 inches in
length
3 tablespoons olive oil
1 medium onion, chopped
½–¾ cup chopped celery
½–¾ cup chopped carrots
1 cup beef broth
¾–1 cup dry red wine
2 bay leaves

1 tablespoon brown sugar
½ teaspoon ground ginger
1 teaspoon dry mustard
1 teaspoon salt
¼ teaspoon pepper
¾ cup ketchup
¼ cup soy sauce
1 clove garlic (more if desired)
1 teaspoon dried oregano
½–1 teaspoon dried basil

Remove excess fat from ox-tails. Untrimmed short ribs are preferred over trimmed ones, which are drier. In a heavy skillet, heat olive oil and sauté meat lightly. Remove meat from pan and sauté onion, celery, and carrots for 5 minutes. Return meat to pan.

In a bowl, mix together beef broth, red wine, bay leaves, brown sugar, ginger, mustard, salt, pepper, ketchup, soy sauce, garlic, oregano, and basil. Pour over meat and vegetables. In pan with cover, place in 350° preheated oven. Cook for 3 hours, stirring occasionally. As sauce cooks down, add additional broth and wine as needed. Check in 1½ hours; the short ribs may cook sooner. If so, remove, and add them later. If needed, blend 1 tablespoon cornstarch with 1 or 2 tablespoons water; add mixture to sauce to thicken. Place in refrigerator and remove fat when solidified. Heat before serving. Good to serve with potatoes, as sauce makes good gravy.

Kay's Kitchen

Alaska has a year-round population of approximately 630,000 (plus over one million visitors each year). Anchorage has the majority of the permanent population with approximately 260,000 residents.

Roast Prime Rib

1 prime rib with ribs
  (approximately 8 pounds)
2 tablespoons Worcestershire
  sauce
1¹/₂ teaspoons garlic powder

1 teaspoon pepper
2 tablespoons salt
¹/₂ teaspoon white pepper
1¹/₂ teaspoons thyme leaves

Let roast sit, fat-side-up, at room temperature for 1 hour. Poke fat at 1-inch intervals with fork, being careful not to puncture meat. Rub top and side with Worcestershire sauce. Mix remaining seasonings and rub into fat. Place roast in large, shallow pan, fat-side-up. Let stand at room temperature 2 more hours.

Heat oven to 350°. Roast beef 1³/₄–2 hours, until internal temperature reaches 120°. Let stand in warm, draft-free area 30–40 minutes, until temperature reaches 130° (rare) or 140°. Serve with au jus gravy.

Alaska Women in Timber Cookbook

Editor's Extra: Au jus (oh-zhoo) is a French term describing meat served with its own natural juices.

Sweet & Sour Spareribs

2–3 pounds pork, beef, moose,
  or venison ribs
1 teaspoon ginger
1 cup packed brown sugar
4 tablespoons margarine

1 tablespoon cornstarch
1 cup cold water
¹/₄ cup vinegar
¹/₄ cup soy sauce
¹/₂ cup ketchup

Brown ribs in oven for 1 hour at 350°. Mix remaining ingredients in a saucepan over medium heat until it boils and thickens. Pour over browned ribs and continue to bake them another 1¹/₂ hours at 325°. Watch carefully so ribs and sauce don't burn. Cover, if needed. Serves 6.

Note: If there are leftovers, soak a pound of navy beans overnight and use ribs and sauce to flavor when cooking. Very good!

Literary Tastes

Stuffed Hamburger Patties

1½ pounds ground beef
16 thin slices pepperoni
4 large slices onion
4 large slices tomato

4 slices American or Swiss cheese
Garlic salt
Pepper to taste
Hamburger buns

Form 8 thin but large meat patties. Place 4 slices of pepperoni and 1 slice each, onion, tomato, and cheese between 2 patties. Completely seal the 2 patties by pinching the edges so that none of the stuffing ingredients can seep out. Cook in frying pan or grill, turning only once. Place on hamburger buns. Serves 4.

All-Alaska Women in Timber Cookbook

Halupki-Stuffed Cabbage Rolls

2 pounds lean hamburger
3 cups cooked rice
1½ tablespoons lemon juice
1 medium onion, minced
1 cup finely chopped celery,
    divided

1 teaspoon garlic salt
1 teaspoon salt
¼ teaspoon pepper
1 large head cabbage
1 can tomato soup
1 cup water

Combine meat, rice, juice, onion, ½ cup celery, garlic salt, salt, and pepper. Core cabbage and cover with boiling water until cabbage begins to wilt. Separate leaves; drain thoroughly. If leaves are very tough and will not bend, place in boiling water for a short time again. Place about ½ cup meat mixture on leaves and roll up securely. Place scraps of cabbage on bottom of baking pan. Sprinkle with remaining celery. Put cabbage rolls on top of this. Mix soup and water together and pour over cabbage rolls. Bake, covered, for 1 hour at 350° or until cabbage is tender.

What's Cookin' in the Kenai Peninsula

Pork Chops Bubba

6 big, thick pork chops (deboned)
White wine
Vinegar
Sugar
Dash of ginger

1 regular can sliced pears,
undrained
1 bunch scallions, chopped
1 tablespoon cornstarch

Cook pork chops in skillet about 5 minutes on each side; remove from skillet. Add a little bit of white wine, vinegar, and sugar to drippings; heat to caramelized stage. Add ginger, sliced pears, another splash of white wine, and chopped scallions. Cook all together until scallions are tender. Thicken sauce with cornstarch dissolved in a little water. Put pork chop on plate; pour pears and sauce around it. Serve with fluffy rice. Chow Down!

Ladies of Harley Cookbook

Cranberry Burgundy Glazed Ham

1 (10- to 14-pound) ham
Whole cloves
1 (16-ounce) can whole cranberry
sauce

1 cup brown sugar
½ cup burgundy
2 teaspoons prepared mustard

Place ham, fat-side-up in shallow pan. Score fat in diamond shape, stud with cloves. Bake in 325° oven for 2½–3 hours. In saucepan, stir together cranberry sauce, brown sugar, burgundy, and mustard, and simmer uncovered for 5 minutes. During last 30 minutes baking time for ham, spoon half of cranberry glaze over ham. Pass remaining as a sauce. Makes 2⅔ cups sauce. Makes about 20–38 servings of ham.

All-Alaska Women in Timber Cookbook

When America declared war on Japan in 1941, Alaska's strategic position was suddenly important. By the time Japan invaded the Aleutian Islands in 1943, more than 140,000 military personnel were stationed in Alaska. The Aleutian campaign, known as the "One Thousand Mile War," was the first battle fought on American soil since the Civil War.

Homemade Salami

5 pounds ground chuck or lean
  ground beef
$^1/_4$ cup Morton's Quick Cure Salt
  (do not substitute)
2 tablespoons liquid smoke
1 teaspoon garlic powder

1 teaspoon onion powder
2 tablespoons peppercorns or
  ground pepper
1 cup water
1 tablespoon mustard seed

Mix and refrigerate overnight the beef, salt, liquid smoke, garlic and onion powders, peppercorns, water, and mustard seed. Make into roll of desired size. Wrap each roll in foil, shiny-side-in. Punch holes in the bottom of the rolls. (It helps to punch the foil first before using it to wrap.) Place the rolls on rack in broiler pan. Bake at 250° for 2 hours. These rolls freeze quite well.

Kay's Kitchen

Mustard and Apple Jelly Sauce

1 jar apple jelly
1 jar mustard

Kielbasa, hot dogs, etc., sliced

Melt jelly and mustard in fondue pot. Add sliced meats and heat. Serve with fondue picks and crackers.

We're Cookin' Now

POULTRY

Tlingit natives carve totem poles in red cedar. These totem poles honor clan crests as well as ancestors, and also serve as reminders of people, legends, or events. House posts and pillars, like this one in Haines, are part of the house decorations inside and outside.

Pepperoni Chicken

4 ounces pepperoni, divided
8 boneless, skinless chicken
  breast halves
1 (26-ounce) jar chunky
  spaghetti sauce
1 green pepper, chopped

3–4 mushrooms, sliced
1 medium onion, chopped
1 can medium black olives, sliced
8 ounces shredded mozzarella
  cheese
1 large package spaghetti, cooked

Spray 9x13-inch dish with cooking spray. Place ½ pepperoni in pan. Place chicken in pan on top of pepperoni. In bowl, mix sauce, green pepper, mushrooms, onion, and black olives. Spread mixture over chicken. Sprinkle evenly with cheese and dot with remaining pepperoni. Bake at 350°, uncovered, for 45 minutes to an hour. Serve with cooked spaghetti.

Simply the Best Recipes

50 Clove Garlic Chicken

Slow roasting the garlic mellows and sweetens it.

2 whole chickens
50 whole cloves unpeeled garlic
1 pound carrots

2 stalks celery
2 tablespoons cooking sherry
½ teaspoon nutmeg

Cut up, skin, and trim fat from chicken. Separate garlic cloves. Cut carrots lengthwise and then into 3-inch pieces. In a 3-quart casserole, lay celery stalks followed by alternating layers of chicken, garlic, and carrots. Drizzle on sherry. Sprinkle with nutmeg. Cover tightly with heavy foil. Bake at 375° for 90 minutes. Spoon garlic cloves into a side dish, and spread on warm sourdough French bread. Serve with a tossed salad to 8 people.

Be Our Guest

The Denali Fault is one of the longest continental faults in the world, stretching for over 700 miles across Alaska, slicing the rugged Alaska Range and climbing the north face of Mount McKinley. The Denali Fault rivals California's San Andreas Fault in size.

Chicken Tacos

2 boneless and skinless chicken
  breasts
Salt and freshly ground pepper
2 tablespoons olive oil
2 medium tomatoes, cut into
  ½-inch dice
1 medium onion, finely chopped

1 garlic clove, finely chopped
4 bay leaves
12 small soft corn tortillas
2 cups vegetable oil
Sour cream
Guacamole
Salsa

Season the chicken fillets with salt and pepper to taste. Place in a small skillet and add just enough water to cover. Over moderately-high heat, bring to a boil. Reduce heat to moderately low and simmer, covered, until firm to the touch, about 5 minutes. Cool, then shred into long, thin strips.

Heat olive oil in a medium sauté pan or skillet over moderately-high heat. Add tomatoes, onion, garlic, and bay leaves. Reduce heat to medium and cook until onions are softened, 7–10 minutes.

Add chicken and simmer, partially covered, for 15 minutes. Remove from heat and discard the bay leaves. Place about 1 table-spoon chicken mixture in center of each tortilla. Roll and secure with a toothpick.

In a moderately-large skillet, heat vegetable oil to 375°. Working with only a few tacos at a time, fry them until golden brown, about 5 minutes, turning frequently. Do not overcrowd the pan or the tacos will not brown. Drain on paper towels. To serve, cut the tacos in half and place on a large ceramic serving platter, accompanied by bowls of sour cream, guacamole and salsa.

Alaska Connections Cookbook III

Hibachi-Style Teriyaki Chicken

1 cup soy sauce
1 cup chicken stock
$^1/_2$ cup brown sugar
1 cup mirin or sake

2 tablespoons grated onion
2 cloves garlic, minced
2 pounds chicken pieces

Put soy sauce, chicken stock, and brown sugar in a saucepan.
Dissolve sugar over low heat. Add mirin or sake, onion, and garlic.
Cook and stir 5 minutes over low heat. Cool sauce. Pour over
chicken and refrigerate 5 hours or overnight. Turn occasionally.
Cook over coals, brushing on marinade while you cook. Or cook in
oven at 350° for about 45 minutes in sauce. Turn chicken once.

A Taste of Sitka, Alaska

Almond Chicken Stir-fry

2 skinned, boneless chicken
  breasts
2 tablespoons soy sauce, divided
2 tablespoons oil
1 tablespoon water
1 teaspoon brown sugar

1 teaspoon cornstarch
$^1/_2$ teaspoon vinegar
2 dashes garlic salt
$^1/_8$ teaspoon ground ginger
$^1/_4$ pound sliced mushrooms
$^1/_2$ cup toasted almond slices

Cut chicken in strips or cubes and toss with 1 tablespoon soy sauce.
Heat oil in 10-inch skillet and stir-fry chicken. In a cup, mix 1 tablespoon soy sauce, water, brown sugar, cornstarch, and vinegar. Add
garlic salt and ginger. Add mushrooms to meat and stir-fry 2–3 minutes. Stir in soy sauce mixture. Cook and stir until sauce thickens,
then add almonds. Makes 4 servings.

Our Cherished Recipes

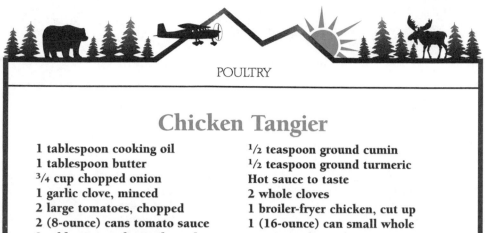

Chicken Tangier

1 tablespoon cooking oil
1 tablespoon butter
³/₄ cup chopped onion
1 garlic clove, minced
2 large tomatoes, chopped
2 (8-ounce) cans tomato sauce
2 tablespoons chopped parsley
1 teaspoon salt
¹/₂ teaspoon ground cinnamon
¹/₂ teaspoon ground ginger
¹/₂ teaspoon ground cumin
¹/₂ teaspoon ground turmeric
Hot sauce to taste
2 whole cloves
1 broiler-fryer chicken, cut up
1 (16-ounce) can small whole onions, drained
¹/₃ cup sliced almonds
¹/₃ cup golden raisins

Put oil and butter into Dutch oven and heat. Add chopped onion and garlic. Cook, stirring occasionally, about 5 minutes, or until onion is soft. Add tomatoes, tomato sauce, parsley, salt, cinnamon, ginger, cumin, turmeric, hot sauce, and cloves. Stir to mix well. Add chicken pieces in a single layer to sauce. Bring to a boil, reduce heat to low, and cook covered for 45 minutes. Uncover and cook 15 minutes longer, or until sauce is slightly thickened and fork can be inserted into chicken with ease. Add whole onions, stir gently, and cook 5 minutes longer; remove cloves. To serve, pour sauce over chicken and sprinkle with almonds and raisins. Serves 4.

A Taste of Kodiak

Chicken Fricassee Hollandaise

1 (3-pound) frying chicken
2 leeks
2 sprigs of parsley
1 bay leaf
2 whole cloves
1 sprig thyme
1 blade mace
1 carrot, sliced
1 onion, sliced
1 quart boiling water
1 teaspoon salt
$1/2$ teaspoon pepper
4 tablespoons butter
4 tablespoons flour
3 cups chicken broth
1 can mushrooms, sliced
2 egg yolks, beaten
$1/2$ cup cream
Juice of $1/2$ lemon, strained
Chopped parsley

Cut and wash chicken, then place in kettle; make a bouquet (with cheesecloth), tying together leeks, parsley, bay leaf, cloves, thyme, and mace; add to chicken. Add carrot, onion, water, and seasoning. Cover and bring to boil. Simmer 40 minutes. Remove chicken to serving dish. Keep warm.

Melt butter in saucepan; add flour and blend. Gradually add chicken broth, then mushrooms; bring to boil; simmer 10 minutes. Combine egg yolks and cream; stir in lemon juice; stir this mixture into broth. Pour sauce over chicken; sprinkle with chopped parsley.

The Original Great Alaska Cookbook

Mom's Chicken Tetrazzini

1 (7-ounce) package thin spaghetti
2 (8-ounce) cans sliced
  mushrooms, drained
$1/2$ cup butter
2 cups sour cream
4 double chicken breasts, cut in
  strips or cubes
2 cans cream of chicken soup
1 cup shredded fresh Parmesan
  cheese

Cook and drain spaghetti. Sauté mushrooms in butter. Mix all ingredients, except cheese, together; put into casserole. Sprinkle cheese on top. Bake, uncovered, for 40 minutes at 350°.

Recipes From the Paris of the Pacific—Sitka, Alaska

Duck with Orange in Casserole

2 young ducks	1 glass currant jelly
6 small carrots, sliced	$^1/_4$ cup red wine
2 cups peas, shelled	1 teaspoon salt
3 onions, sliced	$^1/_8$ teaspoon pepper
1 cup lima beans	$^1/_4$ teaspoon paprika
6 slices bacon	Mashed potatoes
1 cup water	Parsley
4 temple oranges, rind and juice*	4 slices bacon, partially cooked

Cut ducklings as for serving. Place rack in roaster, add combination of vegetables and a cup of water.

Brown portions of duck in frying pan and lay them over the vegetables. Cover roaster and cook for 1 hour at 375°. Make a brown gravy from juices in roaster using 2 tablespoons flour, well-browned, and the juice of the oranges and their zested rind, the currant jelly, and red wine. Add salt, pepper, and paprika. (May be seasoned more highly.) Into individual casseroles, put portions of the vegetables, placing pieces of duck on top. Add to each casserole part of the sauce. Top with rosettes of mashed potatoes and sprinkle more of orange peel and chopped parsley.

Put a slice of partially cooked bacon on top of the potato, then place the casseroles into a 475° oven. Bake long enough to finish cooking the bacon and to make sure that everything has blended and the gravy is sizzling hot.

*Temple oranges are best, but others will do. When making a substitution, add about 2 teaspoons orange marmalade for more zip. One large casserole may be substituted for the individual ones.

The Original Great Alaska Cookbook

Skagway and Haines are the only two cities in Southeast Alaska that are accessible by road, air and ferry.

Duck Surprise

Sometimes it is difficult to know just what to do with the ducks one has bagged. If you keep this recipe in mind, you will have no trouble deciding how to prepare them.

1 cup salad oil	1 sprig rosemary
¹/₂ cup vinegar	1 tablespoon celery seeds
¹/₄ cup soy sauce	Salt and pepper to taste
6 cloves garlic, crushed	2–3 ducks

Simmer all ingredients except ducks together for 10 minutes. Cut your ducks in half and baste with the mixture. Grill over an open flame. Bake some potatoes to go with these and toss a green salad. Sourdough French bread is mighty good with it, too.

Alaska Magazine's Cabin Cookbook

Grouse/Ptarmigan Fajitas

¹/₄ cup olive oil	3 cloves garlic, minced
4 breasts of grouse or ptarmigan, sliced	¹/₂ teaspoon black pepper
1 red bell pepper, sliced	¹/₂ teaspoon salt
1 green bell pepper, sliced	¹/₄ cup red wine
10–15 fresh mushrooms, sliced	10–15 soft tortilla wraps

Heat olive oil and stir-fry, on high heat for 5 minutes, all ingredients, except wine and tortilla wraps. Add wine and fry another 5 minutes. Place onto tortilla wraps and fold. Serves 2–3.

License to Cook Alaska Style

Found in Alpine tundra and extreme northern mountain valleys, the willow ptarmigan is the Alaska state bird. Unlike most other state birds, it is not against the law to hunt them. Other states that allow hunting of their state bird include: California (California quail), Pennsylvania (ruffed grouse), and South Dakota (ring-necked pheasant).

SEAFOOD

PHOTO BY LAUREN JONES

This 175-pound Halibut is small in size compared to the largest ever recorded for the northern Pacific—it was caught near Petersburg, Alaska, and weighed in at a whopping 495-pounds!

Crab-Topped Muffins

¹/₂ cup Tanner (Snow) crab
1¹/₂ tablespoons finely chopped
  celery
2 tablespoons finely chopped
  onion
Dash hot pepper sauce

1 teaspoon Worcestershire sauce
¹/₂ cup mayonnaise
Grated cheese (about ¹/₂ cup)
6 Sourdough English Muffin
  halves*
Cheddar cheese

Mix all ingredients except muffin halves and Cheddar cheese for topping. Allow to stand 30–45 minutes so flavors blend. Keeps well refrigerated, provided crab is fresh. Toast muffin halves until crisp. Butter. Place heaping spoonful of crab mixture on centers. Top with thin wedge, approximately ¹/₂ x 2, sharp Cheddar cheese, press down slightly, and broil 4–5 minutes or until cheese is bubbly.

*See page 44 for Sourdough English Muffin recipe, or you may use store-bought English muffins.

A Cook's Tour of Alaska

Crab Dogs

1 can crabmeat or fresh crab
1 (8-ounce) package cream cheese,
  softened
1 small jar pimento cheese

Dash of garlic salt
1 tablespoon mayonnaise
1 package hot dog buns

Mix together all except buns. Hollow out hot dog buns; add mixture in them. Wrap in foil. Bake at 400° for 10–15 minutes.

Alaska Connections Cookbook III

Crab Puffs

1 small loaf white bread	1 quart mayonnaise
2 cups shredded crabmeat	Splash of milk
1 bunch green onions, finely chopped	

Remove crust from bread; cut into very small chunks. Combine crab, green onions, and mayonnaise. Fold into bread; add enough milk to make the consistency of thick dip. Set aside while making Puffs.

PUFFS:

2 cups water	2 cups flour
1 cup butter or margarine	8 eggs

Heat oven to 400°. Heat water and margarine to rolling boil; stir in flour. Stir vigorously over low heat until mixture forms a ball (and pulls away from sides of pan). Remove from heat. Beat eggs until smooth; add to mixture. Drop dough by teaspoonfuls on ungreased cookie sheet. Bake until puffed and golden, about 15 minutes. Cool away from drafts (puffs will collapse). Poke a small hole into the side of each puff. Remove any filaments of soft dough. Start with 2 cups crab filling in a ZipLoc bag; cut a small hole in the corner of bag and pipe into Puffs.

Pelican, Alaska: Alaskan Recipe Cookbook

Editor's Extra: This makes alot! But is easy to halve for a small luncheon. Add peppered seasoning to the filling if you like a little extra zip.

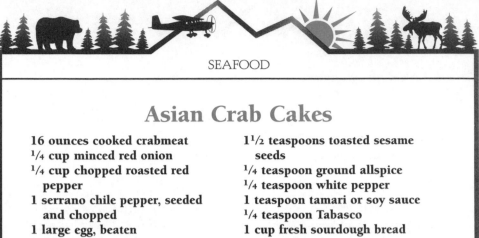

Asian Crab Cakes

16 ounces cooked crabmeat
$^1/_4$ cup minced red onion
$^1/_4$ cup chopped roasted red
  pepper
1 serrano chile pepper, seeded
  and chopped
1 large egg, beaten
1 teaspoon chopped fresh
  cilantro

$1^1/_2$ teaspoons toasted sesame
  seeds
$^1/_4$ teaspoon ground allspice
$^1/_4$ teaspoon white pepper
1 teaspoon tamari or soy sauce
$^1/_4$ teaspoon Tabasco
1 cup fresh sourdough bread
  crumbs
Canola oil for frying

Mix everything except oil. Shape into small $^1/_4$-inch-thick patties.
Heat enough oil in skillet to cover bottom over medium setting.
Cook patties until golden brown, about 5 minutes per side. Drain
on paper towels and transfer to dish in which Spicy Sauce has been
prepared. Add more oil and cook remaining batch of patties until
done. Yields 16 crab cakes.

SPICY SAUCE:

$^1/_2$ cup rice vinegar
3 tablespoons honey
2 tablespoons fresh lime juice
2 tablespoons water
2 teaspoons chopped roasted red
  pepper

2 cloves garlic, minced or pressed
1 teaspoon chopped fresh cilantro
1 teaspoon toasted sesame seeds
$^1/_4$ cup grated, seeded, and peeled
  cucumber

Combine vinegar, honey, lime juice, and water and stir until honey
is dissolved. Add remaining ingredients. Let stand at room temperature about 30 minutes to blend flavors. Serve crab cakes topped
with sauce.

Drop the Hook, Let's Eat

In Alaska, there are three commercial king crab species including Blue king
crabs, Golden king crabs and Red king crabs, which are the commercial
"king" of Alaska's crabs. Since statehood in 1959, U.S. fishers have harvested nearly 2 billion pounds of Red king crab worth $1.6 billion from Alaska
waters. Record statewide harvest and value for Red king crabs was 183 million
pounds and $235 million during the 1966-67 and 1978-79 seasons, respectively.

Tenakee Inlet Crab Cakes

2 tablespoons chopped onion
2 tablespoons butter
1 pound crabmeat, flaked
1 egg, beaten
$^1/_2$ teaspoon powdered mustard
$^1/_2$ teaspoon salt
$^1/_2$ teaspoon garlic powder

Dash of black pepper
Dash of cayenne pepper
$^1/_2$ cup cracker meal or crushed
   cornflakes
Parsley (approximately 2
   tablespoons)
Lemon wedges for garnish

Cook onion in butter until tender. Combine all ingredients, except crumbs and parsley. Shape into 6 cakes and roll in crumbs; place cakes in a heavy frying pan with $^1/_8$ inch of oil, hot but not smoking. Fry at moderate heat. Brown on one side, then turn carefully to brown other side, approximately 6 minutes. Drain. Garnish with lemon wedges. Serves 6.

Tasty Treats from Tenakee Springs, Alaska

Swiss and Crab Pie

4 ounces natural shredded Swiss
   cheese
1 (9-inch) unbaked pastry shell
1 (7$^1/_2$-ounce) can crabmeat,
   drained
2 green onions, sliced (with tops)
3 eggs, beaten

1 cup light cream
$^1/_2$ teaspoon salt
$^1/_2$ teaspoon grated lemon peel
$^1/_4$ teaspoon dry mustard
Dash ground mace
$^1/_4$ cup sliced almonds

Arrange cheese evenly over bottom of pastry shell. Top with crabmeat; sprinkle with green onions. Combine eggs, cream, salt, lemon peel, dry mustard, and mace. Pour evenly over crabmeat. Top with sliced almonds. Bake in slow 325° oven for about 45 minutes or until set. Remove from oven and let stand 10 minutes before serving. Makes 6 servings.

All-Alaska Women in Timber Cookbook

Dungeness Crab Quesadilla

Make these for dinner served with salsa, green salad, and apple slices.

Spray cooking oil
$^1/_2$ cup finely chopped onion
$^1/_2$ cup finely chopped red bell
 pepper
$^1/_4$ cup cream cheese
$^1/_4$ cup diced jalapeño chiles
$^1/_4$ cup mayonnaise

2 teaspoons lemon juice
1 teaspoon each, salt and pepper
1 pound Dungeness crabmeat
10 flour tortillas
1 cup diced tomatoes
1 cup shredded Monterey Jack
 cheese

Preheat oven to 350°. Coat skillet with oil. Sauté onion and bell peppers for 2 minutes. Add cream cheese and jalapeño chiles. Remove from heat and stir. Mix mayonnaise, lemon juice, salt and pepper into pan with onion/cheese mixture. Gently fold in crabmeat. Spread crab mixture on half of each tortilla. Sprinkle with tomatoes and cheese. Fold tortilla in half and press firmly to seal. Coat underside of tortilla with cooking spray and place on cookie sheet. Bake 6–8 minutes. Cut in wedges.

Note: You may substitute cooked, flaked halibut or salad shrimp.

Wild Alaska Seafood—Twice a Week

LAUREN JONES

Famous, extra windy and ferociously cold Thompson Pass is near Valdez. The reflector posts are used instead of electric road lights. They also mark the road when the snow becomes so high that it is not possible to see the road. Snowfall extremes in Alaska are all credited to a station at Thompson Pass. The record measurements are: for one month in February, 1953: 298 inches; and in one 24-hour period in December, 1955: 62 inches.

Dilled Shrimp

1½ cups mayonnaise
⅓ cup lemon juice
¼ cup sugar
½ cup sour cream
1 large red onion, sliced

2 tablespoons fresh dill weed
¼ teaspoon salt
2 tablespoons capers (optional)
2 pounds cooked, peeled shrimp

Mix all together. Let set at least 4 hours or overnight.

Recipes From the Paris of the Pacific—Sitka, Alaska

Shrimp Curry

⅓ cup butter
½ cup chopped onion
1 clove garlic, mashed
1 teaspoon salt
1 tablespoon curry powder
1 tablespoon flour
1 tablespoon granular chicken
  bouillon

2 cups yogurt
4 cups cooked shrimp
Toppings: chutney, raisins, nuts,
  coconut, bacon, banana,
  pineapple chunks, hard-boiled
  eggs

Heat butter in skillet; sauté onion and garlic until soft and lightly browned. Combine salt, curry, flour, and chicken bouillon. Stir into onion and garlic mixture. Cook 2–3 minutes, stirring constantly. Stir in yogurt and shrimp. Cook over low heat, stirring occasionally, until bubbly and heated through. Serve with small side dishes of toppings.

We're Cookin' Now

Russian explorers were the first Europeans to set foot in Alaska in 1741. They established the first non-native settlement in 1784. The Russian czar started trade with Alaska in the mid-18th century and commissioned the Russian America Company in 1799 as the exclusive trading agent. In colonial days, trade was based on furs, chiefly sea otter and seal pelts.

Creamed Shrimp
with Wine on Toast

1 pound raw shrimp, shelled and
   deveined
Flour
$^1/_4$ cup finely chopped onion
$^1/_4$ cup butter

1 cup dry white wine
1 cup whipping cream
$^1/_4$ teaspoon salt
Pepper to taste
Toast

Coat shrimp with flour. Sauté shrimp and onion in butter for 2–3 minutes. Remove mixture from pan. Add wine, cream, salt, and pepper. Cook stirring constantly until thickened and smooth. Return shrimp to pan and heat thoroughly. Serve on toast. Serves 4.

Alaska Shrimp & Crab Recipes

Poached Spot Prawns

1 quart water
1 small onion, sliced
1 teaspoon Old Bay Seasoning

$^1/_2$ teaspoon salt
$1^1/_2$ pounds spot prawns, unpeeled

Boil water, onions, and seasonings in a 4-quart saucepan. Add prawns. Cover and simmer for 3 minutes. Drain and cool. Remove shells and serve hot or cold. Use in any recipe calling for cooked prawns or shrimp.

COCKTAIL SAUCE:
1 (8-ounce) can tomato sauce
1 tablespoon chili sauce
$^1/_4$ teaspoon each oregano, thyme,
   basil

$^1/_4$ teaspoon garlic powder
$^1/_4$ teaspoon Tabasco
$^1/_2$ teaspoon sugar

Combine all ingredients in a small saucepan. Simmer for 10 minutes, stirring occasionally. Serve hot or cold. Makes about 1 cup.

Wild Alaska Seafood—Twice a Week

Shrimp Tetrazzini

8 ounces thin spaghetti, cooked
2 medium-size onions, halved and
   sliced
1 teaspoon minced garlic
1 pound mushrooms, sliced
4–6 tablespoons margarine or oil
2 pounds shrimp, cleaned and
   deveined

$^{1}/_{2}$ cup real mayonnaise
$^{1}/_{2}$ cup grated Parmesan or
   Cheddar cheese
$^{1}/_{2}$ cup flour
1 teaspoon salt
4 cups milk
$^{1}/_{2}$ cup cooking sherry

Hold cooked spaghetti in hot water. Sauté onions, garlic, and mushrooms in margarine or oil until onions wilt. Remove with slotted spoon to bowl. Add shrimp to pan and cook, stir for 5 minutes. Remove to bowl with onion mixture. Add mayonnaise to skillet. Heat slowly; add flour and salt. Stir well to blend and cook to just bubbly. Gradually stir in milk and sherry. Boil 1 minute.

Toss creamed mixture with drained spaghetti. Layer spaghetti, then onion-shrimp mixture in greased 3-quart casserole. Sprinkle top with cheese. Cover; bake at 350° for 30 minutes. Remove lid and continue baking 7–10 minutes.

A Cook's Tour of Alaska

At a length of 13,300 feet (or 5 miles), the Anton Anderson Memorial Tunnel on the Portage Glacier Highway is the longest highway tunnel in North America. The tunnel is also the longest tunnel that accommodates both rail and highway use. Two sophisticated computer systems ensure that trains and cars are never in the tunnel at the same time.

Selawik Stuffed Salmon

1 teaspoon white pepper
¾ teaspoon cayenne or red
  pepper
¾ teaspoon black pepper
1 teaspoon salt
½ teaspoon onion powder
¼ teaspoon dried thyme
Dash of dried oregano
1 stick margarine
1 cup finely chopped onions
½ cup finely chopped celery
½ cup finely chopped green bell
  pepper
½ cup finely chopped green
  onions

1½ teaspoons minced garlic
½ pound peeled shrimp, chopped
  (or use 2 cans small shrimp)
½ pound crabmeat (canned,
  good quality, lump crabmeat)
1 cup fine bread crumbs
4 tablespoons butter
1 egg, well beaten
3 tablespoons grated Parmesan
  cheese
1 whole (10–15 pound) sockeye or
  silver salmon
Lemon pepper

Thoroughly combine white, cayenne, and black peppers, salt, onion powder, thyme, and oregano in a small bowl. Melt 1 stick margarine in skillet over medium-high heat; when half melted, add onions, celery, bell pepper, green onions, and garlic. Sauté about 5 minutes, stirring occasionally. Add shrimp and crabmeat; mix well. If using fresh shrimp and crab, cook 5–7 minutes, stirring occasionally. Add bread crumbs; stir well, then add butter and continue cooking until butter melts. Remove from heat and cool slightly. Combine egg with Parmesan cheese; add to mixture in skillet and mix well. Transfer to bowl, cover and chill in refrigerator.

Meanwhile, season inside of cleaned, whole fish with lemon pepper and seasoning mixture. When ready to bake, stuff inside of fish with stuffing mix and bake at 375° for 45–60 minutes or until done. Time depends on size and thickness of fish. Serves 6–8.

Recipe from Wood River Lodge
Best Recipes of Alaska's Fishing Lodges

Salmon Stuffed with Crab and Shrimp

1 (6-pound) salmon, a nice little
   silver, or a roast cut from a
   king
1/2 pound cooked crabmeat,
   chopped
1/2 pound raw shrimp, chopped
1/2 cup butter, melted

2 tablespoons chopped parsley
1/2 cup chicken broth
1/2 cup chopped celery
1/4 cup chopped onion
1/2–1 cup fine bread crumbs
Salt and pepper to taste

Remove scales, fins, head and tail. Using a very sharp filet knife, peel back the skin, beginning at the belly and working towards the backbone. Leave 1/8- to 1/4-inch meat attached to the skin. Do to both sides, so that skin is completely released from the backbone. Set skin aside. Filet the meat from the backbone. Discard the bones and cut the fish into 1-inch cubes. Place the cubes in a large mixing bowl.

Mix remaining ingredients well with the salmon cubes. Add more stock, if too dry. Lay the reserved skin out flat. Mound the salmon mixture onto one half of the skin in an even thickness. Fold the other half of the skin over the filling. If you have used a small salmon rather than a roast, it will again look like a fish. Soak a piece of long cotton twine in a little cooking oil. Wrap around the fish in several places and tie. Cover lightly with foil. Bake at 325° for 1 hour or more until done. Remove wrap before serving. Serves 8–10.

Methodist Pie

During the frenzy of the gold rush, Alaska's salmon commercial fishing industry was born. By 1900, more than 50 salmon canneries were operating between Ketchikan (kech´i-kan) and Bristol Bay.

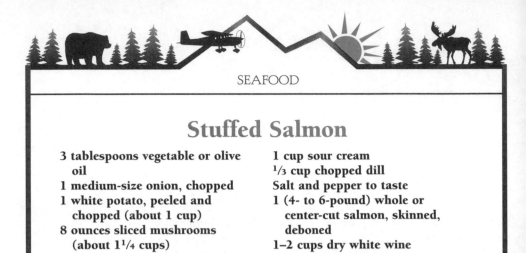

Stuffed Salmon

3 tablespoons vegetable or olive
  oil
1 medium-size onion, chopped
1 white potato, peeled and
  chopped (about 1 cup)
8 ounces sliced mushrooms
  (about 1¼ cups)

1 cup sour cream
⅓ cup chopped dill
Salt and pepper to taste
1 (4- to 6-pound) whole or
  center-cut salmon, skinned,
  deboned
1–2 cups dry white wine

To make stuffing, heat 3 tablespoons oil in large skillet, over moderately high heat. Add onion and potatoes and sauté, turning often, until golden brown and potatoes are nearly done. Add mushrooms and sauté until soft. If mixture is too dry, add more oil. Remove from heat and stir in sour cream, dill, salt and pepper to taste. Cool to room temperature.

Place salmon in center of heavy foil. Open salmon out; sprinkle with salt and pepper. Spread stuffing over half the fish; fold other half over to enclose stuffing. Preheat oven to 350°. To determine cooking time, measure the thickness of the fish at its thickest point, and allow 10 minutes per measured inch. Transfer salmon to shallow roasting pan. Bend edges of foil up to hold enough wine to reach 1 inch up the sides of fish, then fold foil over to seal. Bake fish as directed; it is done when the flesh flakes with the tip of a sharp knife. Remove from pan, open foil, and cool slightly. Remove fish to platter. Serves 6.

License to Cook Alaska Style

Seal's Bare Feet
(Seal Flippers)

Put the seal's bare feet into a cooking pan. Cover them with blubber and keep in a hot place until the fur comes off. Then it is time to eat the seal's bare feet. You can cook them or eat them without cooking.

Eskimo Cookbook

Stuffing for Salmon

2 cups bread crumbs
1 cup grated carrots
1 cup chopped onions, sautéed
   in butter
1/2 cup parsley, chopped
1 cup fresh mushrooms, sliced

1 egg
1 1/2 tablespoons lemon juice
1 clove garlic, chopped
2 teaspoons salt
1/4 teaspoon marjoram
1/2 teaspoon pepper

Mix lightly and stuff a 6–8 pound salmon. Bake for 1–1 1/2 hours at 350°.

Pioneers of Alaska Auxiliary #8

Salmon Marinade

This marinade is great for marinating any type seafood and vegetables for kabobs.

1/2 cup olive or vegetable oil
1/4 cup light soy sauce
2 tablespoons cider or wine
   vinegar
1 tablespoon Dijon mustard

2 tablespoons chopped green
   onion
1 clove garlic, minced
1/2 teaspoon lemon pepper
2 pounds salmon steaks

Combine all ingredients except fish. Marinate fish at least 6 hours. Grill on medium heat till cooked.

Grilling tips: Place fish steaks on top of tin foil when grilling.

To keep food from sticking to your grill's grate and help make for easier clean-up, rub the grate with vegetable oil, or spray with nonstick cooking spray before barbecuing.

If using wooden skewers, soak them in water 20–30 minutes before adding food for kabobs to prevent skewers from burning.

Recipes to the Rescue

Grilled Cedar Planked King Salmon

Southeast Alaskan natives long ago discovered the wonderful flavors that result when smoking and cooking seafood with wood. Cedar or alder are traditional favorites.

Grilling plank	¹/₂ teaspoon each salt and pepper
2 king salmon steaks	Juice of 1 fresh lemon
1 tablespoon olive oil	

Soak plank for at least 30 minutes. Lightly coat salmon with olive oil. Sprinkle both sides with salt and pepper. Place salmon on grilling plank and set on grill over indirect heat. Grill for approximately 20 minutes or until internal temperature reaches 145°.

Tip: Cover salmon with the grill lid or make a foil lid which will trap in and surround the salmon with more smoke.

Wild Alaska Seafood—Twice a Week

Grilled Citrus Salmon

Juice from 1 lemon	2 teaspoons soy sauce
Juice from 1 lime	¹/₃ cup oil (not olive)
Juice from 1 orange	¹/₂ teaspoon crushed hot pepper
2 teaspoons chopped, fresh ginger	flakes
2 cloves garlic, chopped	Salmon fillets (no fat, no skin)
1 tablespoon honey	Grilled fruit slices for garnish

Mix all ingredients except salmon. Marinate salmon in mixture in fridge 45 minutes. Grill salmon. Baste lightly with extra marinade. Garnish with grilled fruit slices.

Recipes From the Paris of the Pacific—Sitka, Alaska

Gail's Hot-Buttered Rum Grilled Salmon

Best when done on an outdoor grill, but can be broiled in an oven. This is a terrific and easy summer entrée and is delicious with a Caesar salad, grilled corn-on-the-cob, and garlic bread sticks.

1 large salmon fillet (skin on)   **¹/₂ cup butter**
Salt and pepper to taste   **1 cup brown sugar**
Dijon or other spicy mustard   **¹/₂ cup dark rum**

Line the top of a grill with greased foil before you begin. Salt and pepper the salmon fillet to taste, then spread on a thin layer of the mustard. When grill is hot, place salmon fillet, skin-side-up, on the greased foil, and cook for about 5 minutes. While the salmon is cooking, melt the butter in a saucepan and mix in brown sugar and rum. The sauce should be of a thick paste consistency. (Add a little more brown sugar, if necessary.) Turn fillet over, spread with a little more mustard, and baste with the butter mixture. Cook and baste for about 5 minutes more or until salmon is flaky, but not dry. Be sure not to overcook.

License to Cook Alaska Style

Sesame Salmon and Hunan Noodles

6–8 ounces dried oriental noodles
(such as Chuka Soba)
4 tablespoons sesame oil, divided
1/2 cup soy sauce, divided
1 tablespoon hot chili oil
2 tablespoons rice wine vinegar
1 tablespoon sugar
1 tablespoon plus 1 teaspoon
peeled, minced fresh gingerroot,
divided
2 tablespoons sliced green onions

1/3 cup fresh peas, thawed frozen
peas, or snow peas, cut in thirds
1/3 cup shredded carrots
1/3 cup sliced fresh mushrooms
1/3 cup thinly sliced red bell pepper
3–4 tablespoons fresh lemon juice
Freshly ground pepper
4 (4-ounce) salmon fillets
Mixed salad greens, rinsed and
dried

Cook noodles according to package directions. Drain well. Place in a large bowl and toss with 2 tablespoons sesame oil. In a small bowl, combine 1/4 cup soy sauce, hot chili oil, vinegar, sugar, and 1 teaspoon ginger. Stir until well blended and add to noodles. Toss to blend. Add green onions, peas, carrots, mushrooms, and bell pepper. Toss and chill for 2 hours.

In a shallow glass bowl, combine lemon juice, remaining 1/4 cup of soy sauce, remaining 2 tablespoons sesame oil, and remaining 1 tablespoon ginger, and pepper to taste. Add salmon and turn to coat. Cover tightly with plastic wrap and chill for 2 hours.

Preheat grill to medium-high. Discard marinade. Grill salmon for 4–5 minutes each side.

Place salad greens on serving plate and top with noodle mixture and salmon. Serve immediately, or chill and serve cold. Makes 4 servings.

Be Our Guest

A 97-pound, 4-ounce giant king salmon caught in the Kenai (kE´-nI) River was the largest ever caught in Alaska. The giant king salmon, significant to the state's commercial salmon fishery, is the Alaska state fish.

Pecan-Crusted Salmon

1 1/2 cups dry bread crumbs
1/2 cup crushed pecans
2 teaspoons garlic powder
6 (6-ounce) salmon fillets, about
  3/4 inch thick

6 teaspoons stoneground mustard
Pepper

Preheat oven to 425°. In a small bowl, combine bread crumbs, pecans, and garlic powder together. Place salmon fillets in a lightly oiled, oblong baking dish. Spread 1 teaspoon mustard on each fillet. Evenly sprinkle bread crumb mixture over each salmon fillet and season with pepper. Bake 10–15 minutes, depending on the thickness, until salmon is slightly opaque and topping is lightly browned. Transfer to a platter and serve. Yields 6 servings.

Drop the Hook, Let's Eat

Barbecued Salmon

1/4 cup olive oil
1/4 cup butter
1/4 cup lemon or lime juice
1 large clove garlic, minced
1/4 teaspoon each salt and pepper

1/4 teaspoon Worcestershire sauce
1/4 teaspoon crushed thyme or
  tarragon
1/8 teaspoon cayenne pepper
6 salmon steaks

Combine all ingredients, except steaks; mix well. Brush mixture on both sides of steaks. Grill steaks over charcoal, allowing 10 minutes per inch of thickness of salmon. Brush steaks frequently with sauce, turning steaks once during cooking. Before removing steaks from cooking grill, brush steaks thoroughly. Serves 6.

Salmon Recipes

Salmon and Mushrooms

4 salmon steaks, ³/₄ inch thick
¹/₂ teaspoon salt, divided
1 small onion, chopped
1 stalk celery, chopped
¹/₄ cup butter

3 cups cubed bread
3 cups sliced, fresh mushrooms
2 tablespoons chopped parsley
1 tablespoon lemon juice
¹/₄ cup cream

Preheat oven to 350°. In a greased, shallow baking pan, arrange salmon steaks and season with ¹/₄ teaspoon salt. In a large skillet, sauté onion and celery in butter until tender. Add bread, mushrooms, parsley, ¹/₄ teaspoon salt, and lemon juice; mix well. Spoon stuffing on top of salmon steaks. Drizzle cream over top. Bake for 25–30 minutes. Serves 4.

Salmon Recipes

Salmon Sticks

When you're tired of salmon, these are still a treat. And they are so easy!

2 pounds salmon
1 cup flour
³/₄ cup cornmeal
Garlic salt to taste
Onion salt to taste

Black pepper to taste
Cayenne pepper to taste
Paprika to taste
2 eggs

Cut salmon into sticks about ¹/₂ inch thick. Combine flour, cornmeal and spices to taste (Mrs. Dash is a good substitute for the spices listed). In separate bowl, beat the eggs. Dip salmon sticks in egg and drain briefly. Roll sticks in flour/cornmeal/spice mixture. Fry in deep fat 90 seconds to 2 minutes at 350° or until golden brown. Be careful not to overcook. Serve with tartar sauce.

Sharing Our Best

Baleek

Smoked Salmon

Baleek is "Number One" on my list. Try it with afternoon tea, fresh bread, and baleek sliced very thinly. Great!

Clean and split fish, leaving tail and part of bone intact. Place salmon into a barrel with salt brine overnight, or until as salty as desired. Remove from brine; place on racks and let dry in the open air until a thin film forms on the surface. Place salmon on racks in the smokehouse high enough over-head so you can walk under them. Don't put the salmon too close together. Air should circulate freely around them. Smoke with a low smoldering fire for 2–3 weeks. It isn't necessary to smoke every day. After the first 5 or 6 days of smoking, skip a day or 2 and then resume smoking. Store in a cool, dry place.

Eskimo Cookbook by Alexandra

LAUREN JONES

The boat harbour in Valdez is a photographer's dream on such a clear day. A boat tour to experience the beauty of Prince William Sound is highly recommended. On days when the weather is fairly dreary, the boat tours are not as spectacular as when the sun is out, but the beauty is still astounding, and the wildlife viewing is often better.

Smoked Salmon and Eggs in Puff Pastry

1/2 (17 1/4-ounce) package frozen
    puff pastry (1 sheet)
8 eggs
1/2 cup skim milk
1/4 teaspoon salt
1/4 teaspoon pepper
1 tablespoon butter or margarine
1/2 (8-ounce) tub cream cheese
    with chives and onion

1/2 teaspoon dried dill weed
3 ounces thinly sliced smoked
    salmon (lox-style)
1/3 cup shredded mozzarella cheese
1 egg, slightly beaten
1 tablespoon water

Thaw puff pastry according to package directions. Lightly grease a baking sheet; set aside. In mixing bowl, beat together eggs, milk, salt, and pepper. In a large skillet, melt butter. Over medium heat, pour in egg mixture. Cook without stirring until mixture begins to set on the bottom and around edge. Using a spatula or a large spoon, lift and fold the partially cooked eggs so the uncooked portion flows underneath. Continue cooking over medium heat for 2 minutes or until eggs are just set. Remove from heat. Dot with cream cheese and sprinkle with dill weed. Stir gently until combined. Set aside.

Unfold pastry on a lightly floured surface. Roll into a 17x12-inch rectangle. Place on baking sheet (short sides may extend over side of sheet). Arrange the smoked salmon crosswise down the center 1/3 of the pastry, to within 1 inch of the top and bottom of pastry. Spoon scrambled eggs over salmon. Sprinkle eggs with the shredded mozzarella cheese. Combine beaten egg with water. Brush edges of pastry with egg mixture. Fold 1 short side of pastry over filling. Fold the remaining short side over top. Seal top and ends well and brush top of pastry with egg mixture. Top with about 10–12 puff pastry stars, if desired, and brush with egg mixture. Bake in a 375° oven for 25 minutes or until pastry is a golden brown. Makes 6 servings.

Note: You may cover and chill unbaked pastry up to 24 hours. Uncover. Bake in 375° oven for 35–40 minutes or until pastry is golden brown, and filling is hot.

Kay's Kitchen

Pirok
Salmon Pie

Cook 2 cups of rice and a dab of rock salt in 4 cups water for 45 minutes. Fillet salmon and set aside. Make pastry using 4 cups flour to 1 cup lard, a pinch of salt, and enough cold water to hold dough together.

    Roll half the dough and line a baking pan. Put a layer of rice on the bottom, using half the rice. Put a layer of salmon sprinkled with wild onion. Cover the salmon with the remaining rice. Roll the rest of the dough and cover the dish, cutting off excess dough. Seal edges. Make slits on top. Bake an hour. One of my favorites.

Eskimo Cookbook by Alexandra

Perok

1 large package carrots, grated
1 medium cabbage, shredded
1 large onion, chopped
3 medium stalks celery, chopped
1 large rutabaga, chopped
1 stick butter
Salt and pepper to taste

1 (10- to 12-pound) salmon,
   skinned, boned, and filleted
Pie crust for top and bottom of
   10x15x2-inch pan
1 cup rice, cooked, divided
4 or 5 hard-boiled eggs, chopped

Preheat oven to 350°. Cook carrots, cabbage, onion, celery, and rutabaga in butter until done. Set aside. Salt and pepper salmon to taste. Line greased 10x15x2-inch pan with pie crust. Place a thin layer of rice on the bottom, then a layer of ½ the cooked vegetables, filleted fish, layer of eggs, other ½ of the vegetables; another layer of rice, then the top crust. Bake approximately 1 hour.

A Taste of Kodiak

Annie's Salmon Patties

Make extra of these so you can have a fish sandwich the next day on a toasted bun with lettuce, tomato, thin slice of onion, cheese, dill pickle, mayonnaise, ketchup, or tartar sauce.

1 pint salmon (remove dark pieces but leave bones and liquid)	1¹/₂ tablespoons lemon juice
2¹/₂ cups very dry mashed potatoes	¹/₂ teaspoon lemon pepper
	¹/₂ teaspoon garlic salt
¹/₄ cup diced onion	4–6 shakes of hot sauce
¹/₄ cup diced celery	1 egg
¹/₄ cup diced green pepper	1 tablespoon mayonnaise
	¹/₂ cup fine cracker crumbs

Mash the salmon into the potatoes. Add remaining ingredients. Form into patties (if mixture does not hold its shape, add a few more cracker crumbs to the mixture). Let set a few minutes and then form patties. If too dry, add another egg or a small amount of milk.

COATING:

1 or 2 sleeves of crackers, crushed fine   ¹/₂ cup plain, fine bread crumbs

Place 1 cup cracker crumbs and bread crumbs in a large plastic bag. Place patties in the cracker crumbs inside the bag. Pat down and turn over bag very carefully and pat crumbs into patty. Remove to a cracker-crumb-sprinkled cookie sheet. Refrigerate for 2 hours. (At this point, you can freeze the patties for 3 months; thaw in fridge before using.) Fry in ¹/₂ inch vegetable oil in a large cast-iron skillet, 2 at a time. Remove to warm platter. Makes about 6 patties.

Grannie Annie's Cookin' Fish from Cold Alaskan Waters

Alaska is so big it has its own time zone: Alaska Standard Time (AST). Alaska Standard Time is one hour behind Pacific Standard Time and four hours behind Eastern Standard Time. So, if it's 4:00 p.m. in New York, and 1:00 p.m. in California, it's noon in Alaska. The Aleutian Islands west of Umak Island is on Hawaii-Aleutian Time which is an hour earlier than Alaskan time. The state once had four time zones but in 1983 they were consolidated into two in order to improve business and communication.

Alaska Salmon Nuggets

1 tablespoon finely minced celery	$1/4$ teaspoon salt
1 tablespoon finely minced onion	$1/8$ teaspoon pepper
1 tablespoon butter, melted	1 teaspoon Worcestershire sauce
$1^1/2$ cups cooked, flaked salmon (or canned salmon)	1 egg, well beaten
	$1/4$ pound processed cheese
$1/2$ cup cooked, mashed potatoes	1 cup finely sifted bread crumbs

Colorlessly fry celery and onions in butter over low heat until they turn clear. Place fish and potatoes in a bowl and mash them. Add celery, onion, salt, pepper, Worcestershire sauce, and egg. Mix thoroughly. Roll the mixture into balls the size of walnuts. Cut cheese into $1/4$-inch cubes. Roll these in palms of hands until round. Push 1 piece of cheese into the center of each fish ball and reshape by rolling in hands again. Roll in sifted bread crumbs. Fry in deep fat, 375°, until golden brown.

The Original Great Alaska Cookbook

Salmon Burgers

1 ($15^1/2$-ounce) can Alaska pink salmon	$1/2$ cup fresh whole-wheat bread crumbs
1 egg	1 tablespoon lemon juice
$1/2$ cup chopped onion	$1/2$ teaspoon crushed rosemary
$1/2$ cup finely chopped green pepper	$1/8$ teaspoon pepper
	Your choice of toppings
1 teaspoon grated lemon peel	Toasted hamburger buns

Drain salmon; reserve 2 tablespoons liquid; flake. Combine salmon, egg, onion, green pepper, lemon peel, bread crumbs, reserved liquid, lemon juice, and seasonings; mix well. Form into 4 or 5 patties. Pan-fry in lightly oiled skillet about 5 minutes (lightly browned); turn halfway through cooking time.

Top with your choice of toppings, such as tomato, pickle, onion, cheese, mustard, relish, ketchup, mayonnaise, tartar sauce, thousand island dressing and lettuce. Serve on toasted hamburger buns.

Huna Heritage Foundation Cookbook

Salmon Loaf with Shrimp Sauce

2 (1-pound) cans salmon, drained,
  reserve liquid
$^1/_4$ cup finely minced onion
$^1/_4$ cup chopped, fresh parsley
$^1/_4$ cup lemon juice
$^1/_2$ teaspoon salt
$^1/_2$ teaspoon pepper

$^1/_2$ teaspoon crushed thyme leaves
2 cups coarse cracker crumbs
$^1/_4$ cups milk or more, divided
4 eggs, well beaten
$^1/_4$ cup butter or margarine, melted
1 (10.5-ounce) can condensed
  cream of shrimp soup

Flake salmon in bowl. Add onion, parsley, lemon juice, salt, pepper, thyme, and cracker crumbs. Mix lightly. Add enough milk to reserved liquid to make 1 cup. Add liquid, eggs, and butter to salmon; mix lightly. Spoon mixture into greased $8^1/_4$x$4^1/_2$x3-inch glass baking dish. Bake in 350° oven 1 hour or until loaf is set in center. Remove from baking dish onto serving platter.

Combine soup and $^1/_4$ cup milk in saucepan; heat well. Serve with loaf. Makes 8 servings.

Alaska's Cooking Volume II

Baked Salmon with Cucumber Dill Sauce

1 (15½-ounce) can salmon, drained and flaked
1 medium-size onion, chopped
1 small, sweet green pepper, halved, seeded and chopped
½ cup chopped celery
½ cup plain, dry bread crumbs
¼ cup plain yogurt
¼ cup mayonnaise
1 egg, slightly beaten
¼ teaspoon pepper
Cucumber Dill Sauce
Dill sprigs (optional)

Preheat oven to 325°. Generously grease 4 (6-ounce) custard cups. Combine salmon, onion, green pepper, celery, bread crumbs, yogurt, mayonnaise, egg, and pepper in bowl. Stir until well blended. Divide mixture evenly among prepared custard cups; pack well. Arrange on small cookie sheet. Bake for 30 minutes or until salmon mixture begins to pull away from sides of cups. To unmold, run small knife around edge of each cup. Invert onto serving dish. Spoon Cucumber Dill Sauce over tops. Garnish with sprigs of dill, if you wish. Serves 4.

CUCUMBER DILL SAUCE:
½ cup mayonnaise
¼ cup sour cream
¾ cup finely chopped, seeded cucumber
¼ cup finely chopped onion
¼ cup plain yogurt
1 tablespoon chopped fresh dill or 1 teaspoon dillweed

Stir ingredients together in saucepan. Heat over very low heat just until warmed through. Serve over Baked Salmon cups.

Salmon Recipes

The meaning of the word "Eskimo" is dependent on the context in which it appears. "Eskimo" may mean "one who speaks another language," or "one who is from another country," or "one who has an unusual behavior," or "one who eats raw meat."

Wine Poached Halibut

4 tablespoons butter or margarine,
  divided
1/2 pound mushrooms, chopped
Salt and pepper to taste
Dash of sugar

1/2 cup dry white wine
1 1/2 pounds halibut fillets, divided
2 tablespoons flour
1/2 cup light cream
Dash of nutmeg

In a small saucepan, melt 2 tablespoons butter. Add mushrooms and sauté 2 minutes. Season with salt and pepper and sprinkle with sugar.

Butter a large oval skillet. Pour in wine and add 1/2 of the fillets; cover with mushrooms and top with remaining fillets. Cut waxed paper to fit pan; butter one side of waxed paper and fit buttered side down over fillets. Heat to boiling. Lower heat to medium and cook for 5 minutes.

In medium saucepan, melt remaining butter. Add flour and cook on low for 3 minutes, or until smooth and bubbly. Slowly add cream and nutmeg, stirring constantly until thickened.

Place cooked fillets on oven-proof platter. Strain poaching liquid into sauce. Stir and cook 3 minutes longer. Spoon sauce over fillets and brown under broiler; serve immediately.

Just for the Halibut

Lemon Pepper Halibut

This is an excellent way to enjoy fresh halibut; it allows the delicious flavor to remain unmasked.

1 pound halibut fillets
1 1/2 tablespoons butter
2 teaspoons seasoned salt

1 tablespoon lemon pepper
1 teaspoon garlic salt

Place halibut fillets in a glass baking dish, dot with butter, sprinkle seasoned salt, lemon pepper, and garlic salt over top, and place in microwave. Cook on HIGH for about 4 minutes per inch of thickness, or until fish flakes easily.

Just for the Halibut

Creamy Deep Fried Halibut

Needs no sauce; tastes delicious alone.

1 pound halibut chunks
1¹/₂ cups prepared ranch salad
  dressing

1 cup dehydrated potato flakes
Salt to taste

Dip halibut into ranch dressing, then roll into potato flakes, and deep fry until golden brown. Remove halibut from frying pan, drain, and salt to taste.

Just for the Halibut

Sesame Halibut

2 tablespoons orange juice
1 tablespoon ketchup
1 tablespoon soy sauce
¹/₂ tablespoon lemon juice

¹/₂ teaspoon sesame oil
¹/₂ tablespoon brown sugar
1 pound halibut fillets
1 tablespoon sesame seed, toasted

Combine orange juice, ketchup, soy sauce, lemon juice, oil, and brown sugar. Pour over halibut. Let set for 2 hours, turning once. Remove fish and reserve marinade. Coat pan with butter cooking spray. Put fish on pan and broil 5 minutes on each side (depends on how done you like fish). Heat leftover marinade and pour over fish. Top with sesame seed.

A Taste of Sitka, Alaska

Halibut Stuffed with Alaskan Crab

CAPER BUTTER:

¹/₄ pound butter, softened	2 tablespoons lemon juice
2 tablespoons chopped capers	1 teaspoon chopped, fresh dill
1 tablespoon chopped shallots	1 teaspoon Dijon mustard

Mix butter with capers, shallots, lemon juice, dill, and mustard. Set aside.

STUFFING AND HALIBUT:

2 slices bacon, chopped fine	Salt to taste
1 tablespoon butter	Pepper to taste
2 stalks celery, diced	1 teaspoon chopped fresh thyme
¹/₄ cup dried onion	1 teaspoon chopped fresh parsley
¹/₂ cup sliced mushrooms	1 egg
¹/₄ pound crabmeat, flaked	1 pound halibut fillet or steak

Sauté bacon in butter until brown. Add celery, onion, and mushrooms. When tender, add crab, salt, pepper, and herbs. Remove from heat and mix in egg. Set aside to cool. Cut a pocket in halibut and stuff with crab mixture. Grill until halibut flakes. Top with Caper Butter. Serves 2.

Alaska Shrimp & Crab Recipes

Grilled Halibut with Mango Relish

MANGO RELISH:

1 mango, peeled, seeded and diced

1/4 cup seeded and chopped cucumber

2 tablespoons chopped red onion

1/4 cup chopped fresh cilantro

1 jalapeño, seeded and minced

1 clove garlic, minced or pressed

1 teaspoon grated lime peel

2 tablespoons fresh lime juice

1 tablespoon olive oil

1 tablespoon honey

Combine mango, cucumber, red onion, cilantro, jalapeño, and garlic. Whisk together lime peel and juice, olive oil, and honey in a small bowl. Add to the mango mixture and stir well. Refrigerate until ready to use.

2 tablespoons tamari or soy sauce

1 tablespoon dry sherry

1 tablespoon olive oil

1 teaspoon grated lime peel

1 tablespoon fresh lime juice

1/4 teaspoon cinnamon

1 clove garlic, minced or pressed

2 1/2 pounds halibut fillets, 1 inch thick

Combine tamari, sherry, oil, lime peel and juice, cinnamon, and garlic in an oblong dish. Chill and marinate halibut fillets for 1 hour.

Generously oil grill prior to preheating (unless you are using a separate hinged wire grill). When coals are hot, place fillets on grill; cook for 5–7 minutes on one side before carefully turning. Cook another 3–5 minutes or more depending on thickness, until fish easily flakes with a fork. Baste with marinade on each side. Transfer to a platter and spread Mango Relish on top before serving. Yields 6 servings.

Drop the Hook, Let's Eat

Grilled Halibut

1 pound halibut fillets	1/2 cup sour cream
2 tablespoons soy sauce	1/2 cup fine cornflakes
1 teaspoon lemon juice	2 tablespoons sesame seeds,
Salt and pepper	toasted

Brush halibut with a mixture of soy sauce, lemon juice, salt and pepper. Coat both sides of halibut with sour cream. Combine cornflakes and sesame seeds; roll fillets in the mixture. Place fillets in a wire basket and broil over medium coals for 10 minutes; burn only once. Serves 4.

Alaskan Halibut Recipes

Valdez Halibut

1 teaspoon minced onion	2 tablespoons chili powder
1 garlic clove, minced	1/2 teaspoon sugar
1/2 cup olive oil, divided	10 green olives, sliced
2 cups tomato sauce	8 halibut steaks
2 peppercorns, ground	3 potatoes, boiled and diced
2 whole cloves	4 slices bread, sautéed and cut in
1/8 teaspoon ground cinnamon	strips

Sauté onion and garlic in 1/2 the oil. Add tomato sauce and spices, and cook for 20 minutes. Add sugar and olives. Sauté the steaks in the rest of the oil until halibut flakes. When halibut is done, add to the sauce with the potatoes. Garnish with bread sticks. Serves 8.

Alaskan Halibut Recipes

 Valdez is a busy seaport, shipping oil from the Trans-Alaska Pipeline to the west coast of the United States, and now to the Orient. Approximately 640 oil tankers and 70 cruise ships dock in Valdez every year.

Halibut Almandine

Flour
Salt and pepper
2 pounds halibut fillets
1/2 cup butter, melted, divided

1 can peaches, drained
1/2 cup blanched almonds
2 tablespoons lemon juice

Season flour with salt and pepper to taste. Dip halibut in butter, then in seasoned flour. Place halibut fillets in a greased baking pan and pour 1/2 the remaining butter over them. Bake at 350° for 20–25 minutes, or until fillets flake.

Sauté peaches and almonds in remaining butter. Add lemon juice. Spoon a peach and some juice over each fillet. Serves 4.

Alaskan Halibut Recipes

Teriyaki Halibut

1/4 cup soy sauce
1/4 cup reserved pineapple juice
2 teaspoons vegetable oil
1/4 teaspoon garlic
1/4 teaspoon ginger

1/2 teaspoon sugar
1 1/2 pounds halibut fillets
1 (15-ounce) can pineapple chunks,
   drained (reserve juice)

Combine all ingredients except halibut and pineapple. Mix well. Pour over halibut; let stand for 20 minutes. Remove halibut. Place halibut on broiler rack (or barbecue). Broil 5 minutes on each side for thin fillets, longer if thick. Fish should flake when cooked. Cover with pineapple last few minutes.

Simply the Best Recipes

Icy Strait BBQ Halibut

Dale has a reputation for guiding anglers to barn-door-size halibut of 100–200 pounds. A fish this size will yield anywhere from 60–140 pounds of boneless, white fillets that more and more people are preferring over steak. This is enough halibut for a block party barbeque when you return home. Dale says if you use this recipe, "Be certain you've saved a few fillets for yourself, because there won't be any leftovers."

5 pounds halibut fillets
2 sticks butter
2 onions, sliced
2 tomatoes, diced
2 tablespoons pressed garlic
1 lemon
6 tablespoons fine white wine, divided

3 tablespoons grated Parmesan cheese
1 cup fresh mushrooms
2 tablespoons butter
Dash of garlic powder

Cut the fillets into serving portions and place on a piece of heavy-duty foil, large enough to fold it over the top and seal so that the juices from the fish can steam the fillets white cooking. Slice butter. Place butter slices, along with sliced onions, tomatoes, and garlic on top of fillets. Squeeze the juice of a lemon over the top. Sprinkle with 5 tablespoons wine and Parmesan cheese.

Seal foil over fish and place in preheated barbecue grill. (Dale likes to add a few green sticks of alder to the hot coals just before putting the fish on.)

Let the fish simmer over the coals for about 10–12 minutes, then open seal on foil to allow a touch of the unique alder-smoke flavor to seep into the fillet. Cook with foil open for another 8–10 minutes.

This is the most critical time, because the cook must test the fillet to make sure it is perfect for those who have gathered to savor the moment. The key is to not overcook; let the fish cook just until it loses its shiny translucence and is white throughout.

While fish is cooking on the grill, prepare fresh mushrooms, sautéing them in 2 tablespoons butter. Add a dash of garlic powder and a tablespoon of wine. Top fish with lightly sautéed mushrooms.

Note: Have the rest of the meal preparation completed, because you need to serve this immediately, hot and steaming. Serves 10–12.

Best Recipes of Alaska's Fishing Lodges

Baked Halibut Supreme

1 cup white wine
1 teaspoon salt
1 pound halibut fillets or steaks
5 slices dry bread, crumbled,
  divided

1 cup mayonnaise
1/2 cup sour cream
1/4 cup chopped onion
Paprika

Mix wine and salt; marinate fish for 1 hour or all day, if possible. Drain fish; dry with paper towels. Dip both sides of fish into bread crumbs (reserving some for top); place in buttered baking dish. Mix mayonnaise, sour cream, and onion, and spread over halibut. Sprinkle with remaining crumbs and paprika. Bake at 500° for 20 minutes or until fish flakes with fork.

Alaska's Cooking Volume II

Halibut Olympia

2 pounds halibut fillets
3/4 cup chopped green onions,
  divided
1 cup sour cream

1 cup mayonnaise
3/4 cup freshly grated Parmesan
  cheese

Pat halibut fillets dry. Place 1/2 the green onions on the bottom of baking dish. Place halibut on top of the onions and sprinkle the other 1/2 of onions over fillets. Mix together sour cream, mayonnaise, and cheese; spread evenly over halibut and onions. Bake at 400° for 15–20 minutes or until fish easily flakes.

Just for the Halibut

Alaska has more than 100,000 glaciers covering approximately 30,000 square miles of land—5% of the state. The longest glacier in Alaska is Bering Glacier at more than 100 miles long. The largest glacier is the Malaspina Glacier at 850 square miles. A glacier is a perennial accumulation of ice, snow, water, rock and sediment that moves under the influence of gravity. The density of ice causes it to absorb all light and reflect only blue, thus giving glaciers their blue/white appearance.

Tomie's Golden Halibut

1½ pounds halibut fillets
Seasoned bread crumbs
½ cup mayonnaise
1½ teaspoons lemon juice
½ cup low-fat yogurt

1 egg white, beaten stiff
¼ cup chopped green onion
¼ cup sliced almonds
Dash paprika

Preheat oven to 400°. Dip fillets in crumbs and place in a greased baking dish. Combine in a bowl the mayonnaise and lemon juice; add yogurt and blend well. Fold in egg white. Sprinkle fillets with onions and spoon mayonnaise mixture on top. Sprinkle with almonds and paprika. Bake for 20 minutes or until halibut flakes. Serves 4.

Alaskan Halibut Recipes

Great Halibut Baked in Foil

1 teaspoon chopped green onion
1½ cups soft bread crumbs
1 egg, well beaten
2 tablespoons butter, divided

2 pounds halibut fillets
½ cup condensed asparagus soup
8 large mushroom caps, fresh or
   canned

Mix together onion and crumbs. Add egg and 1 tablespoon melted butter. Spread on fillets, then roll them up and fasten with a toothpick. Place each fillet on a greased square of aluminum foil large enough to wrap completely. Spoon asparagus soup over each fillet. Top with a mushroom cap and a dot of butter. Fold foil around each fillet. Bake at 400° for 25–30 minutes. Serves 4.

Alaskan Halibut Recipes

Today Alaska Natives represent approximately 16% of Alaska's residents and are a significant segment of the population in over 200 rural villages and communities. Many Alaska Natives have retained their customs, languages, hunting and fishing practices and ways of living since "the creation times." Alaska's Native people are divided into 11 distinct cultures, speaking 20 different languages.

Halibut Parmesan

3 tablespoons each flour and
  yellow cornmeal
1/2 teaspoon each garlic salt and
  dry mustard
1/4 teaspoon each dry rosemary
  leaves and pepper
3 tablespoons milk

2 1/2 pounds halibut fillets
3 tablespoons butter, melted
Paprika
1/4–1/3 cup grated Parmesan
  cheese, divided
Lemon wedges

Mix flour, cornmeal, garlic salt, mustard, rosemary, and pepper. Dip fish in milk; drain briefly, then roll in coating mixture to cover evenly. Arrange fish in baking dish and cover with melted butter. Sprinkle fish lightly with paprika and 1/2 the grated Parmesan cheese. Bake at 350° until fish flakes easily.

Halfway through baking time, turn fish over; sprinkle lightly with paprika and the remaining Parmesan cheese. Garnish with lemon wedges. Serves 4.

Alaskan Halibut Recipes

Broiled Halibut
with Mushrooms and Sour Cream

2 pounds halibut fillets	1 cup sliced mushrooms
Juice of 2 limes	2 green onions, sliced
Salt and pepper to taste	1 cup sour cream
3 tablespoons butter, divided	

Place halibut in a shallow dish. Squeeze on lime juice. Season with salt and pepper, and let fish marinate for 1 hour, turning occasionally. Place halibut on hot, oiled broiler pan. Dot fish with 1 tablespoon butter. Cook 3 inches under broiler for 10–15 minutes, until it barely flakes. Don't turn. Baste while cooking.

Sauté mushrooms and onions in remaining 2 tablespoons butter until tender. When fish is almost cooked, heat sour cream in mushroom and onions. Serve halibut with sauce. Serves 4.

Alaskan Halibut Recipes

Broiled Halibut Skewers
with Pesto Sauce

2 pounds halibut, cut into 1-inch cubes	1 green bell pepper, cut into chunks
1 red bell pepper, cut into chunks	1/2 pound fresh mushrooms

Arrange halibut, peppers, and mushrooms alternately on skewers.

PESTO SAUCE:

1/2 cup olive oil	2 garlic cloves
1/2 cup parsley leaves	1 teaspoon dried basil
1/4 cup lemon juice	

Combine Sauce ingredients in food processor and process until parsley and garlic are finely chopped. Brush halibut with Pesto Sauce. Broil 8–10 minutes, basting occasionally with sauce and turning skewers for even cooking. Serves 6–8.

License to Cook Alaska Style

Happy Halibut

¹/₄ cup soy sauce
¹/₂ cup dry white wine
1–2 tablespoons maple syrup or
   1 tablespoon dark Karo syrup
1 large clove garlic, minced
1 tablespoon fresh ginger, shaved
   thin, or 1 teaspoon ground ginger

1 tablespoon toasted sesame oil
   (the vital ingredient)
Halibut fillets (from single serving
   up to 5 pounds), filleted and in
   serving-size pieces

Mix the first 6 ingredients for marinade. Store unused portion in refrigerator. To use, marinate as much halibut as you need for meal by placing fish in zip-top plastic bag with enough marinade to coat all fish. Expel air and seal bag. Marinate for ¹/₂ hour minimum, up to 4 hours maximum, turning occasionally so all surfaces are exposed to marinade. Choose the most convenient cooking method.

Bake: Place fish in lightly greased dish and bake in 400° oven for 20 minutes, until fish flakes nicely. Spoon marinade over fish part way through cooking.

Barbeque grill: On hot grill, cook fish until it flakes easily, brushing throughout cooking with marinade. Do not overcook.

Microwave: Place fish in microwave dish and cover tightly with plastic wrap. Microwave on HIGH for 3 minutes; turn dish ¹/₄ turn and microwave until fish flakes easily (2–4 minutes).

For a sauce to serve with the fish, mix pan juices. Add more marinade if needed with cornstarch and cold water. Bring to a boil and serve over fish. For a single serving, as little as 1 teaspoon cornstarch will thicken the sauce. If you are making 1–2 cups of sauce for a larger serving, you will need 2 tablespoons of cornstarch and 2 tablespoons cold water to add to the pan juices and marinade.

Pioneers of Alaska Auxiliary #8

Alaska has 6,640 miles of coastline (longer than that of all of the rest of the lower 48 states) and, including islands, 33,904 miles of shoreline.

Baked Halibut with Coconut and Cashews

1 cup fresh, grated coconut
$1/3$ cup vegetable oil, divided
1 large onion, finely chopped
2 cloves garlic, finely chopped
2 cans mild green chiles, chopped
$1/2$ teaspoon salt
1 teaspoon curry powder
2 tablespoons chopped unsalted cashews
1 pound halibut fillets, finely chopped
1 tablespoon lemon juice
2 eggs, lightly beaten

Sauté coconut in 1 tablespoon oil until lightly browned. Sauté onion in remaining oil until tender but not browned. Add garlic, chiles, salt, and curry powder, and cook, stirring, 2 minutes. Add coconut, nuts, and halibut. Cook 2 minutes. Cool slightly. Mix lemon juice with eggs and add to skillet. Divide halibut mixture among 6 oiled (7-inch) squares of aluminum foil. Wrap tightly and place on a baking sheet. Bake at 375° for 20 minutes. Serves 6.

Alaskan Halibut Recipes

Halibut Caddy Ganty

3 pounds halibut fillets, cut into serving-size pieces
Dry white wine
Fine, dry bread crumbs
Paprika to taste
2 cups sour cream
$1/2$ cup mayonnaise
1 onion, chopped fine

Place halibut pieces into a bowl. Cover the halibut with dry white wine. Place waxed paper over the bowl and refrigerate for 2 hours. When halibut is marinated, drain fillets and pat them as dry as possible between 2 towels. Roll the fillets in bread crumbs and place in a single layer in a baking dish. Mix together sour cream, mayonnaise, and onion. Spread this sauce over the halibut, smoothing it out to the edges of the pan. Sprinkle with paprika and bake at 500° for 15–20 minutes, or until light brown and bubbly. Serve at once.

Welcome Home

Halibut Enchiladas

4 ounces cream cheese, softened
1/4 cup sour cream
1/4 cup mayonnaise or more
1 small can sliced black olives
1 small can chopped Ortega
  peppers
1/2 medium onion, chopped

1 1/2 cups flaked, baked halibut
  fillet (or more)
1 1/2 cans enchilada sauce (hot or
  regular), divided
1 package flour or corn tortillas
2 cups grated cheese, divided

Cream cheese, sour cream, and mayonnaise. Add olives, peppers, onion, and halibut; mix well. Place 1 spoonful of enchilada sauce on each tortilla and enough filling to make a good sized enchilada. Put some cheese in each tortilla. Roll up and place in greased 9x13-inch pan, with 1/2 remaining enchilada sauce on bottom. Put remaining cheese over the top of the enchiladas and pour the remaining sauce over the entire casserole. Bake at 350° for 45 minutes or until heated through and cheese is melted.

Pelican, Alaska: Alaskan Recipe Cookbook

Halibut Enchiladas

1 can chopped green chiles
1 onion, finely chopped
1 pint sour cream
2 cups cooked and flaked halibut
2 cups grated Cheddar cheese,
  divided

Salt and pepper to taste
1 dozen flour tortillas
1 can tomato sauce
2 cups mild enchilada sauce

Mix chiles, onion, sour cream, halibut, and 1 1/2 cups cheese together; season to taste. Fill tortillas with mixture; place in greased baking pan. Mix tomato sauce and enchilada sauce. Pour over top of enchiladas. Garnish with remaining Cheddar cheese. Bake at 375° for 15–20 minutes, until heated throughout.

Methodist Pie

South Pelican Tacos

TORTILLAS:

4 cups flour
2 teaspoons salt
6 tablespoons Crisco

1–1¹/₄ cups lukewarm water, divided

Combine flour and salt, work in Crisco, stir in 1 cup of water, then form a ball. If necessary use rest of water to clean bowl clear of dough. Knead dough on a lightly floured board. Shape into biscuit-size balls and let stand 15 minutes. Roll out as thin as possible. Bake on a hot ungreased griddle or skillet for 2 minutes on one side; turn and cook other side till you think it's done. Set aside.

Halibut pieces
Oil
Seasoning
Lettuce

Tomatoes
Onion
John's Pico de Gallo

Quick-fry parts of halibut in oil with your choice of hot seasoning. Set on warmer. Chop lettuce, tomatoes and onion; set aside. Place a tortilla in your hand. Put some halibut on tortilla; garnish with lettuce, tomato, and onion, then top with John's Pico de Gallo—WOW. Then roll your way to the promised land!

JOHN'S PICO DE GALLO:

2 tomatoes, finely chopped
¹/₂ cup finely chopped onion

¹/₂ cup finely chopped jalapeños
1 lime

Combine tomatoes, onion, and jalapeños; squeeze lime over all. Mix well; better the next day.

Pelican, Alaska: Alaskan Recipe Cookbook

There are no pelicans in Alaska, however two pelicans proudly grace the entrance to Juneau's Federal Building. In 1980, Juneau ordered two bald eagle sculptures to place in front of the federal building. When the shipment arrived, two bronze pelicans were delivered instead. The eagles were sent to Florida's capitol, and Florida officials decided to keep them.

South of the Border Halibut

1 cup boiling water
$^1/_2$ cup margarine
1 (8-ounce) package cream
  cheese
1 can green chiles, diced

1 teaspoon cumin
$^1/_2$ teaspoon cilantro
2 pounds halibut fillets
Salt and pepper to taste
$^1/_2$ cup white wine

When water comes to a boil in saucepan, reduce heat and add margarine and cream cheese. Stir until blended as a white sauce. Add green chiles, cumin, and cilantro. Place halibut in baking dish. Season to taste. Pour wine over and bake 25–30 minutes at 375° or until flaky. Pour excess liquid off the halibut. Add white sauce on top and serve.

A Taste of Sitka, Alaska

Scallop Pie

6 large mushrooms, sliced
$^1/_4$ cup butter, divided
3 green onions, chopped
3 tablespoons flour
1 teaspoon curry powder
$1^1/_2$ cups milk
$^1/_4$ cup cooking sherry
12 small whole onions, boiled

2 tablespoons sliced red or green
  bell pepper
$^1/_2$ pound large sea scallops, sliced
  in half lengthwise
Garlic salt
Fresh cracked pepper
Puff or regular pastry

Heat oven to 425°. In saucepan, sauté mushrooms in $^1/_8$ cup butter; add green onions. Blend in flour and curry powder. Add milk; cook until thick, stirring steadily. Remove from heat. Add sherry, whole onions, bell pepper, and drained and dried scallops. Season to taste with garlic salt and cracked pepper; stir to blend. Divide between 4 individual baking dishes or 1 (10-inch) pie plate; dot with remaining butter. Top with pastry. Bake 20–25 minutes. Allow to cool 10 minutes before serving.

A Cook's Tour of Alaska

Oodook

Sea Urchin

These are eaten on the beach. Break in half and scoop out the roe. Rinse in sea water and eat. Sometimes roe was used in place of eggs. Place roe (6 of them) in a bowl and beat well. Add enough flour to make a medium-thick batter. Add 1–2 teaspoons baking powder and salt to taste. Drop into a hot pan to which lard has been added. Fry like pancakes. These will be at least ¾ inch thick. When golden brown, eat with any berry jam or jelly. Blueberry jam goes well with this.

Eskimo Cookbook by Alexandra

Cod a la Filo

Many of our winter family outings were to hand jig for cod. It seemed that the colder, windier and rainier, the better the cod catch. Hand-jigging for fish is a lost art. A successful "jig" is a combination of the flick of the wrist and pull of the lower arm, resulting in a cod fish wiggling with every pull. In the early 1970s, I won my first microwave oven with "hand-jigged" cod.

4 (4-ounce) cod fillets, boneless and skinless
Salt and pepper to taste (optional)
½ cup butter
1 teaspoon bouquet garni
2 cloves garlic, finely minced
1 cup vegetables, finely chopped (mix mushrooms, celery, carrots, and onions)
1 cup grated, sharp Cheddar cheese
12 sheets filo dough

Preheat oven to 350°. Lay cod on paper towels and pat very dry. Season with salt and pepper. Melt butter in a small saucepan; add Bouquet Garni and garlic. Keep warm on low heat. For each fillet, use 3 sheets of filo dough. Brush each layer with melted butter. Place cod in middle end of each filo layer. Spoon ¼ of vegetables over fish and sprinkle with cheese. Fold sides of filo over fish and roll as in egg roll. Seal dough with melted butter. Place seam-side-down on cookie sheet. Bake for 30 minutes.

Wild Alaska Seafood—Twice a Week

Editor's Extra: Bouquet garni is a "bunch of herbs," usually being the trio of parsley, thyme, and bay leaf, sometimes tied in a cheesecloth.

Codfish in Tomato Sauce

1 pound salt codfish
1 quart stewed tomatoes
2 medium-size onions
2 whole cloves
¼ teaspoon celery salt

2 tablespoons butter or margarine
4 tablespoons flour
½ teaspoon salt
¼ teaspoon pepper

Cover fish with boiling water and cook until tender; drain and separate into small pieces. Combine tomatoes, onions (sliced thin and browned), cloves and celery salt. Cook 10 minutes, then strain. Melt butter; add flour gradually, stirring constantly, and cook until the mixture bubbles. Add the strained tomato mixture gradually and cook until the sauce is of a smooth consistency. Season with salt and pepper. Add the codfish and serve on slices of buttered toast.

Alaska Gold Rush Cook Book

Mami

Clams

Cockels and butter clams are called "mami." Cockels are used for steaming and silianka (chowder). They have a stronger clam flavor.

To steam: Wash cockels thoroughly. Place in a pan with a little water and bake until shells open. To eat: Dip into bear fat. Don't eat too many.

To make silianka: Peel 3 medium potatoes; wash, cube and cook in enough water to cover potatoes—about 2 inches for 5 minutes. Add diced salt pork and minced wild onion. Clean and shuck enough clams to measure 4 cups when minced. Add to cooked potatoes and cook until tender. Add salt to taste. Salted wild onion can be used here. Watch the salt when using them.

To fry butter clams: Shuck clams. Clean thoroughly and wash in several waters. Roll in flour. Heat pan. Add lard and fry clams until golden. They are delicious. To make silianka: Follow cockel recipe. Don't be surprised at the flavor. It will be delicate compared to cockels.

Eskimo Cookbook by Alexandra

Grandpa's Scalloped Clams and Potatoes

6 cups thinly sliced potatoes
$^1/_3$ cup flour
$^1/_2$ cup chopped onion
$1^1/_2$ teaspoons salt or to taste
$^1/_8$ teaspoon pepper
$^1/_2$ teaspoon granulated onion or powdered onion

$1^1/_2$ cups chopped razor or other clams
1 cup water
1 cup evaporated milk
1 tablespoon butter or margarine

Dust potatoes with flour. Mix remaining ingredients (including all the flour) together, except milk and butter. Place in greased $2^1/_2$-quart casserole dish with cover. Pour milk on top and dot with butter. Cook in 350° oven $1^1/_4$ hours, covered, and 15 minutes, uncovered, or until potatoes are almost done.

Note: May use clam nectar in place of milk and/or water.

What's Cookin' in the Kenai Peninsula

Seafood Casserole

2 hard-boiled eggs, sliced
$^1/_2$ cup chopped onions, or
  1 tablespoon flakes
1 cup sliced green pepper
$^2/_3$ cup slivered almonds
1 cup chopped celery
$1^1/_2$ cups milk
$1–1^1/_2$ cups cooked crab, shrimp, tuna, or halibut

1 cup mushroom soup
$^1/_2$ cup sliced mushrooms
$^1/_3$ cup chopped fresh parsley, or
  1 tablespoon dried
3 tablespoons white wine
$1^1/_4$ cups mayonnaise
1 cup instant rice
1 cup bread crumbs
2 tablespoons butter, melted

Set egg slices aside. Mix remaining ingredients, except bread crumbs and butter. Gently stir in egg slices. Pour into greased casserole dish. Mix bread crumbs with butter and sprinkle on top; bake for 1 hour at 350°.

Our Cherished Recipes Volume II

CAKES

This Russian church in Juneau provides a valuable link to the past. The most lasting legacy of the Russian era is the Russian Orthodox religion.

Crazy Chocolate Cake

3 cups flour
2 cups sugar
$^1/_2$ teaspoon salt
2 teaspoons baking soda

5 heaping tablespoons cocoa
$^3/_4$ cup cooking oil
2 tablespoons vinegar
2 cups cold water

Mix all ingredients together. Bake in greased and floured 9x13-inch pan (or 2 round cake pans) at 350° for 35–40 minutes.

We're Cookin' Now

Zucchini Chocolate Cake

2 cups shredded or sliced zucchini
$^1/_2$ cup water
1 teaspoon salt, divided
2 cups flour
1 teaspoon baking soda
1 teaspoon baking powder
1 teaspoon cinnamon
$^1/_2$ teaspoon nutmeg

4 tablespoons cocoa
3 large eggs
2 cups sugar
$^1/_2$ cup oil
$^3/_4$ cup buttermilk
1 teaspoon vanilla
1 teaspoon orange peel
1 cup chopped pecans or walnuts

Preheat oven to 350°. Grease and flour 9x13-inch pan. Cook zucchini 10 minutes with water and $^1/_2$ teaspoon salt; drain and mash. Sift dry ingredients, including remaining salt. Beat eggs until light. Beat in sugar and oil. Combine zucchini and buttermilk. Stir flour mixture into eggs, alternating with buttermilk/zucchini. Stir in vanilla, orange peel, and nuts. Pour into prepared pan. Bake for 40–50 minutes.

Our Cherished Recipes

Ken's Mayonnaise Cake

4 cups flour
2 cups sugar
²/₃ cup cocoa
2 teaspoons baking soda
2 cups mayonnaise

2 cups hot water
2 teaspoons vanilla
1 cup chopped nuts
1 cup raisins

Preheat oven to 350°. Sift together the flour, sugar, cocoa, and baking soda. Add mayonnaise, hot water, vanilla, nuts, and raisins. Grease and flour a Bundt pan or 9x13-inch pan. Pour into prepared pan. Bake 1 hour (a little less for 9x13-inch pan).

Recipes From the Paris of the Pacific—Sitka, Alaska

Earthquake Cake

1 cup chopped pecans
1 cup coconut
1 German chocolate cake mix
1 (8-ounce) package cream cheese, softened

1 stick butter or margarine, softened
1 pound powdered sugar
1 teaspoon vanilla

Spray bottom of 9x13-inch pan with nonstick cooking spray. Sprinkle pecans and coconut on bottom of pan. Mix cake according to directions on box; pour in pan. Mix cream cheese, butter, powdered sugar, and vanilla. Drop by spoonfuls onto cake. Bake at 350° for 50 minutes. Cake will crack open when done.

Simply the Best Recipes

Approximately 11% of the world's earthquakes, and 52% of all earthquakes in the United States have occurred in Alaska. Alaska has more earthquake activity than any other region in North America. Three of the six largest earthquakes in the world and seven of the ten largest in the United States occurred in Alaska.

Kulich

Kulich (koo-lihch) is a tall cylindrical Russian Easter cake consumed on Easter Sunday to break the Lenten Fast and used for 40 days after Easter.

2 packages RapidRise yeast
³/₄ cup lukewarm water
4 cups evaporated milk,
   undiluted
4 cups sugar, divided
16 cups flour, divided
1 tablespoon cardamom*
1¹/₂ cups butter

2 tablespoons salt
1 tablespoon vanilla
1 tablespoon grated orange peel
1 tablespoon grated lemon peel
9 eggs
3 cups raisins (white or dark)
1 cup chopped walnuts

Dissolve yeast in the lukewarm water. Set aside. Scald and cool to lukewarm the 4 cups milk. Add yeast and 1 cup sugar, 4 cups flour and cardamom to the lukewarm milk. Mix into a smooth sponge and set in a warm place for approximately 2 hours. When sponge is done resting, melt and warm the butter. Stir remaining 3 cups sugar, salt, vanilla, and zests into the butter and add to the sponge. Gradually work in the remaining 12 cups flour until the dough is smooth and elastic. Knead for 5 minutes.

Add raisins and nuts and knead another 5 minutes. Place in greased bowl, and oil or butter dough to prevent crust from forming. Let rise until double in bulk. Roll into various-sized balls and place in greased various-sized metal cans you have saved (coffee cans, fruit cans, etc). Oil the top of dough. Bake in a 350° oven. Baking time will vary, depending on size of cans. When dough is done, remove from pan and butter the crust. Place on baking rack to cool.

*You may substitute almond or lemon extract for cardamom.

What's Cookin' in the Kenai Peninsula

Potato Caramel Cake

2 cups light brown sugar
4 eggs, separated
²/₃ cup shortening
¹/₂ cup sweet milk
3 squares chocolate, melted
1 cup hot potatoes, riced
2 cups pastry flour, divided

¹/₂ teaspoon salt
2 teaspoons baking powder
1 teaspoon cloves
1 teaspoon cinnamon
1 teaspoon nutmeg
1 cup chopped nuts

Cream together the light brown sugar, egg yolks, and shortening. Add milk, melted chocolate (beaten in while hot), and hot riced potatoes. Reserve ¹/₄ cup flour for nuts. Add remaining flour, salt, baking powder, and spices sifted together; fold in the floured nuts. Beat egg whites until stiff; fold into mixture. Pour into 3 greased and floured layer cake pans, and bake at 350° for 25 minutes. Make Filling.

FILLING:
1 cup thin cream
1¹/₂ cups butter

2 cups brown sugar
1 teaspoon vanilla

Cook cream, butter, and sugar together until it forms a soft ball in cold water; remove from heat, add vanilla, and beat until creamy. When cool, spread between cake layers and on top.

Alaska Gold Rush Cook Book

Salmonberry Upside-Down Cake

³/4 cup (1¹/2 sticks) unsalted
   butter, divided
¹/2 cup firmly packed brown
   sugar
¹/2 pound salmonberries
1 cup sugar

2 large eggs, room temperature
2 teaspoons vanilla extract
1 cup all-purpose flour
1 teaspoon baking powder
1 teaspoon salt
¹/2 cup sour cream

Heat oven to 350°. In a 2-quart saucepan, melt ¹/4 cup (¹/2 stick) butter and brown sugar over medium-low heat, stirring to combine. Pour into a 9x2-inch round cake pan. Tilt the pan to spread the brown sugar mixture evenly. Arrange salmonberries in pan; 1 layer only. Set aside.

Melt remaining ¹/2 cup (1 stick) butter. In a medium bowl, combine butter, sugar, eggs, and vanilla. With a mixer, beat at high speed until smooth, about 2 minutes. Reduce speed to low and add the flour, baking powder, and salt, mixing just until combined. Scrape down the sides of the bowl and mix for 15 seconds. Add sour cream and mix until combined.

Pour batter over the top of fruit in cake pan. Smooth gently. Bake cake until lightly brown and center of the cake is clean when a cake tester is inserted, about 1 hour. Cool on wire rack exactly 5 minutes. Place a cake stand or serving plate onto the cake pan and turn the cake upside-down onto the cake stand. Carefully lift the cake pan straight up and away. Let cool 10 minutes. Serve warm or room temperature. Enjoy!

A Taste of Kodiak

Editor's Extra: Salmonberries are raspberry-like but light orange when ripe. Traditionally they were called salmonberries by Alaska Natives because they look like salmon eggs. Raspberries would work in this recipe.

Jane's Tootie Fruity Upside-Down Cake

Our daughter-in-law, Jane, wanted to add to the Fourth of July picnic table with her favorite berry up-side down cake. In checking out the yard for berries, she was unable to find an ample supply of any one kind of berry or fruit so, using her imagination, she made the best combination of fruit you could dream of or ask for or want. Absolutely delicious!

1 cup each: blueberries, raspberries, thimble berries, red huckleberries and rhubarb
1 small package Jell-O (raspberry or strawberry)

1 cup sugar
3 cups miniature marshmallows
1 package yellow cake mix, prepared according to package directions

In a large, greased 9x13x2-inch pan, dump the combined berries. Sprinkle with dry Jell-O and sugar, then add the marshmallows. Top all of this with the prepared cake mix. Bake in 350° oven until cake is done, about 45 minutes. Remove from heat and invert on larger sheet pan (cookie sheet). Cool.

Panhandle Pat's Fifty Years

Anchorage is known as the City of Lights in the Winter and City of Flowers in the Summer. The Anchorage Chamber of Commerce sponsors the City of Lights program, a 19-year-old winter project that encourages businesses and residents to decorate with lights to help brighten and beautify the community from October through March. The City of Flowers name comes naturally—with increased hours of daylight during summer months, Anchorage is literally awash in blossoms during the summer.

Pound Cake with Rum Sauce

1 cup Crisco
2 cups sugar
7 eggs
2 teaspoons rum flavoring or
  vanilla extract

2 cups flour
$^1/_2$ teaspoon salt

Blend Crisco and sugar; add eggs, 2 at a time, and blend well after each addition. Mix rum or vanilla in with the last egg. In separate bowl, mix flour and salt; fold in to mixture by hand. Bake in a greased 10-inch tube pan for 50 minutes at 350°.

RUM SAUCE:

2 tablespoons cornstarch
1 cup sugar
2 cups water

1 tablespoon rum flavoring
1 tablespoon butter or margarine

In a small saucepan, mix together cornstarch with sugar. Add water. Heat, bringing to a boil, and stir constantly. Add flavoring and butter.

Variations: For Vanilla Sauce, omit rum flavor and replace with vanilla (excellent on hot, fresh chocolate cake). For Lemon Sauce, replace rum flavor with juice of 1 lemon. For Nutmeg Sauce, reduce vanilla to 1 teaspoon and add 1 teaspoon nutmeg.

33 Days Hath September

The Best Rhubarb Cake

All rhubarb cakes are good, but this is the best!!!

¹/₄ cup shortening
¹/₄ cup vegetable oil
1¹/₂ cups brown sugar
1 egg
1 teaspoon vanilla
1 teaspoon baking soda
¹/₄ teaspoon salt

1 cup buttermilk or sour milk
  (1 teaspoon vinegar in a cup of
  milk)
2 cups flour
1¹/₂–2 cups diced rhubarb
1 cup chopped walnuts (optional)

Cream shortening and oil with brown sugar. Add egg and vanilla. Cream until very fluffy. While this is mixing; combine baking soda, salt, and flour in a separate bowl. Alternate buttermilk and flour mixture into the creamy mixture; mix slowly until fully incorporated. Stop mixer and fold in rhubarb and nuts, if using. Pour into a greased 9x13-inch cake pan and sprinkle with Topping. Bake in 350° oven for 45 minutes.

TOPPING:

¹/₄ cup brown sugar
¹/₄ cup white sugar

1 teaspoon cinnamon

Mix with a fork and sprinkle on top of the unbaked cake.

Variation: Instead of rhubarb, you may substitute same amount of chopped apples, dried apricots, peaches, etc.

Grannie Annie's Cookin' at the Homestead

Birch Syrup is a truly unique flavor from Alaska's forests—and quite rare. Produced by collecting the sap from the paper birch tree and evaporating it to syrup, an average of 100 gallons of sap is needed to make one gallon of birch syrup (maple syrup averages 40:1). Total 2001 commercial production in Alaska was just over 1,000 gallons. Because it does not harm the tree to tap it every other year, birch syrup production promotes sustainable use of Alaska's forest resources. Birch syrup is not produced in significant quantities anywhere else in the world.

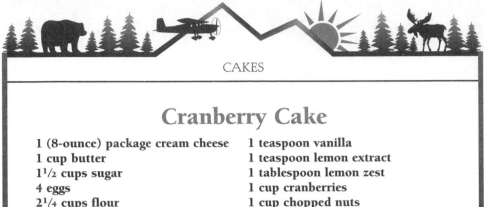

Cranberry Cake

1 (8-ounce) package cream cheese
1 cup butter
1½ cups sugar
4 eggs
2¼ cups flour
1½ teaspoons baking powder

1 teaspoon vanilla
1 teaspoon lemon extract
1 tablespoon lemon zest
1 cup cranberries
1 cup chopped nuts
Powdered sugar

Cream cheese, butter, and sugar until light and fluffy. Add eggs, one at a time, mixing after each addition. Stir in flour and baking powder. Add flavorings. Stir in (by hand) the cranberries and nuts. Bake in a 9x13-inch greased and floured pan in 350° oven for about an hour or until toothpick comes out clean. When cool, sprinkle with powdered sugar.

Pioneers of Alaska Auxiliary #8

During the Alaska State Fair lumberjacks participate in a speed climbing contest.

LAUREN JONES

Blueberry Sugar Plum Fantasy Cake

4 eggs
$^1/_2$ cup white sugar
$^1/_2$ cup brown sugar
$^1/_2$ cup vegetable oil
$^1/_2$ cup butter, melted
1 tablespoon vanilla
1 tablespoon lemon juice
1 teaspoon nutmeg
1 teaspoon grated lemon peel
$^1/_2$ teaspoon salt
$^1/_2$ teaspoon ground cardamom

1 teaspoon baking powder
1 teaspoon baking soda
$2^1/_2$ cups flour, divided
1 cup chopped walnuts or pecans
1 cup Mandarin orange slices,
   drained and chopped
1 cup semi-dried blueberries (the
   sugar plums)
Apricot jelly
Cream cheese frosting

In a large bowl, beat together the eggs, sugars, oil, butter, vanilla, lemon juice, nutmeg, lemon peel, salt, and ground cardamom. Combine baking powder, baking soda, and 2 cups flour, and mix with the egg mixture.

Toss walnuts, Mandarins, and blueberries with $^1/_2$ cup flour. Fold into batter. Adjust mixture with flour or liquids to make a thick, but pourable batter.

Bake at 325° in a well-greased and floured Bundt pan for approximately 1 hour. Place a serving plate over finished cake. Let stand 5 minutes, then turn upside down. Cake should release easily if done, while hot. Brush generously with apricot jelly and cool. At this point, the cake can be aged a few days.

Frost with a cream cheese frosting, a five-year-old's imagination, and lots of gumdrops, jellybeans, and TLC.

The Best of the Blueberry Bash, 1994-2002

Palmer, located in the center of the lush farmlands of the Matanuska Valley, is home of the Alaska State Fair. The 11-day fair attracts visitors from all over Alaska and the Lower 48. The Lumberjack Speed Climbing contest (opposite page) is a crowd favorite.

Blueberry Almond Cheesecake Tunnel

TUNNEL:

6 ounces cream cheese, softened
1 egg
1/2 teaspoon almond extract

3 tablespoons flour
1/4 cup sugar

In small bowl, cream all Tunnel ingredients until smooth. Set aside.

1/2 cup sliced almonds
1/2 cup butter, softened
1 cup sugar
3 eggs
1 cup sour cream
2 teaspoons vanilla

1 1/2 teaspoons baking powder
3/4 teaspoon baking soda
1/2 teaspoon salt
3 cups all-purpose flour
1 1/2 cups blueberries

Preheat oven to 350°. Generously grease fluted tube pan. Finely chop or crush sliced almonds. Coat inside of tube pan with almonds by gently tossing on greased sides.

Cream butter and sugar in large mixing bowl. Add eggs, 1 at a time, beating after each addition. Blend in sour cream and vanilla. Combine and add remaining dry ingredients; stir until almost mixed. Add blueberries, stirring just until all ingredients are combined. Batter will be stiff. Turn 1/2 of the batter into prepared pan. Gently make a well about 2 inches wide in circumference of the batter. Gently pour Tunnel mixture into the well. Carefully drop spoonfuls of the remaining batter over the Tunnel and throughout the pan. Smooth as needed to evenly spread batter. Bake about 40 minutes. Remove from oven; allow loaf to cool about 10 minutes before removing from pan.

ICING:

1 1/2 cups powdered sugar, divided
2 ounces cream cheese
1/2 teaspoon vanilla

2 teaspoons milk, divided
1/2 cup blueberries

Combine 3/4 cup powdered sugar, cream cheese, vanilla, and 1 teaspoon milk in blender. Divide mixture in half. Combine 1/2 of mixture with an additional 1 teaspoon milk. Drizzle over cooled loaf.

In blender, crush blueberries and add remaining powdered sugar and icing. Drizzle this over the top of all.

The Best of the Blueberry Bash, 1994-2002

Blueberry Glaze Cheesecake

Use local blueberries or beach-combed strawberries. This is a rich cheesecake in a delicate pastry crust. It's made best with fresh fruit, but you can use frozen; just use less water in sauce mixture.

CRUST:

1/3 **cup margarine or butter**	**1 egg**
1/3 **cup sugar**	1 1/4 **cups flour**

Cream margarine or butter and sugar until light and fluffy. Blend in egg. Add flour and mix well. Dough should be soft, but not stick to fingers. Press dough into 9-inch pie plate. Bake at 450° for 5 minutes or until golden brown in color.

FILLING:

1 (8-ounce) package cream cheese, softened	1/2 **cup milk**
1/2 **cup sugar**	**2 eggs**
1/2 **teaspoon salt**	1/2 **teaspoon vanilla**

Cream softened cream cheese, sugar, and salt; mix well. Blend in milk, eggs, and vanilla. Pour into baked Crust. Bake at 400° for 15 minutes; reduce heat to 325° and continue baking for 20 more minutes. While the cheesecake is baking, begin Sauce mixture.

SAUCE:

1/4 **cup sugar**	**3 cups fresh blueberries or strawberries**
1 1/2 **tablespoons cornstarch**	
1 cup water	

In saucepan, combine sugar and cornstarch; gradually add water. Cook, stirring constantly, until mixture turns from milky white to a clear color and is thickened. Add berries; continue cooking for 5 minutes. Cool slightly. Spoon carefully over the cheesecake once it has finished cooking and cooled; best if served chilled for 3 hours.

Pelican, Alaska: Alaskan Recipe Cookbook

Alaska Blueberry Special Cake

1 yellow cake mix
1 large package lemon pie filling

1 (12-ounce) carton Cool Whip

Mix cake according to package directions. Bake in jellyroll pan. Cool. Mix lemon pie filling according to package directions (or make from scratch). Top cooled cake with lemon pie filling; cover with Cool Whip. Serve with Blueberry Sauce.

BLUEBERRY SAUCE:
$^2/_3$ cup brown sugar
1 tablespoon cornstarch
Dash of salt

$^2/_3$ cup water
2 cups fresh or frozen blueberries

Cook all ingredients except blueberries until thick. Add blueberries. Return to boil. Chill. Serve over cake.

Pelican, Alaska: Alaskan Recipe Cookbook

 The Aleuts were the native inhabitants of the Aleutian Islands. The name Alaska is derived from the Aleut (u-lOOt´) word "Alyeska," meaning "great land."

COOKIES *and* CANDIES

Hubbard Glacier, the largest tidewater glacier on the North American continent, has been thickening and advancing toward the Gulf of Alaska since first mapped in 1895. Most other glaciers have thinned and retreated during the last century.

The Perfect Chocolate, Chocolate Chip Cookie

2¼ cups flour
1 teaspoon baking soda
⅓ cup cocoa
½ teaspoon salt
1 cup margarine or butter, room
  temperature

¾ cup white sugar
¾ cup brown sugar
1 teaspoon vanilla
2 eggs
2 cups chocolate chips
1 cup chopped walnuts or pecans

In a medium bowl, combine flour, baking soda, cocoa, and salt; set aside. Cream margarine or butter, sugars, and vanilla until fluffy. Add eggs and beat in. Add flour mixture in gradual amounts while mixer is on low. Stop mixer and stir well with wooden spoon. Stir in chocolate chips and nuts. Drop by tablespoon on ungreased cookie sheet. Bake 8–10 minutes at 375°. The secret—do not over-bake. The middle will look "wet." Cool in pan 3–4 minutes, then remove to wire rack. Makes about 44 cookies.

Grannie Annie's Cookin' at the Homestead

Jane's Terrific Chocolate Chip Cookies

1½ cups white sugar
1½ cups brown sugar
2 cups butter or margarine,
  softened
4 eggs
2 tablespoons vanilla
3 cups white flour
1½ cups whole-wheat flour

2 teaspoons baking soda
1 teaspoon salt
1 or 2 (12-ounce) packages
  chocolate chips
2 cups chopped nuts
1½ tablespoons cold water
  (optional)

In large bowl, cream together the sugars and butter or margarine. Add eggs; mix well. Add vanilla. Add flours, baking soda, and salt. Mix well. Stir in chocolate chips and nuts. Mix well. Add the cold water last (optional, but makes the cookies softer). Put on ungreased baking sheets in large soup-spoon-size scoops. Bake at 375° for 12 minutes.

Recipes From the Paris of the Pacific—Sitka, Alaska

Cowboy Cookies

2 cups sifted flour
1 teaspoon baking soda
$^1/_2$ teaspoon baking powder
1 cup butter or margarine
1 cup white sugar
1 cup firmly packed brown sugar

2 eggs
2 cups rolled oats
1 teaspoon vanilla
1 (6-ounce) package milk chocolate
    chips

Mix together and set aside flour, baking soda, and baking powder. Blend together butter and sugars. Add eggs and beat until light and fluffy. Add set-aside flour mixture and mix well. Stir in oats, vanilla, and chocolate chips. Drop by teaspoonfuls on greased cookie sheet and bake 15 minutes at 350°.

Literary Tastes

Alaska Mining-Camp Oatmeal Cookies

1 cup butter
1 cup white sugar
1 cup brown sugar
2 eggs, beaten
$1^1/_2$ cups flour

1 teaspoon baking soda
$^1/_2$ teaspoon salt
3 cups old-fashioned oatmeal
1 teaspoon vanilla

Mix together butter and sugars; add beaten eggs. Add remaining ingredients and mix well. Drop by teaspoon onto greased cookie sheet. Bake 8–10 minutes at 375°.

Pioneers of Alaska Auxiliary #8

Established in 1880 as a mining camp and home to the state capital since 1906, Juneau was the first town founded in Alaska. Don't expect to drive there, though, as you can only get there by boat, ferry or plane. As a matter of fact, nearly 30% of Alaska's population is not connected by road or ferry to the continental road network.

Grandma Ost's Soft
Brer Rabbit Ginger Cookies

6–8 cups flour, divided
1 teaspoon salt
1¹/₂ teaspoons cinnamon
2 tablespoons ginger
¹/₄ teaspoon nutmeg
1 cup shortening

1 cup sugar
1 egg
2 cups molasses
2 tablespoons vinegar
4 teaspoons baking soda
1 cup boiling water

Sift 6 cups of flour with salt and spices. Cream shortening and sugar. Add egg. Beat all together until light. Add molasses and vinegar, then sifted dry ingredients. Lastly, add baking soda dissolved in boiling water. If necessary, add more flour to make a soft dough. Drop by teaspoonfuls on greased cookie sheet. Sprinkle with sugar. Bake 8–10 minutes in a moderate (350°) oven. Makes 100 plump, spongy cookies.

Nome Centennial Cookbook 1898-1998

Unbaked Chocolate Cookies

2 cups sugar
¹/₂ cup cocoa
¹/₂ cup margarine
¹/₂ cup milk

1 tablespoon white syrup
3 cups quick oats
¹/₂ cup nuts
1 teaspoon vanilla

Blend sugar, cocoa, margarine, milk and white syrup; cook for 5 minutes. Add oats, nuts, and vanilla; stir till well blended. Drop on waxed paper.

Our Cherished Recipes

Eagle's Nest

3 cups stick pretzels
1 cup dry-roasted peanuts
1 cup raisins

1 cup mini-marshmallows
2 cups chocolate chips
2 teaspoons oil

Combine pretzels, nuts, raisins, and marshmallows in a large bowl; set aside. In a small saucepan, heat chocolate chips and oil over low heat, stirring constantly until chips melt. Pour chocolate over pretzel mixture, stirring until all pieces are evenly coated. Spoon into muffin tins and refrigerate 20 minutes to harden. Makes about 2 dozen.

Moose Racks, Bear Tracks, and Other Alaska Kidsnacks

No Bake Cookies

2 cups sugar
$^1/_2$ cup milk
3 tablespoons cocoa
$^1/_4$ pound butter or margarine

1 teaspoon vanilla
$^1/_2$ cup peanut butter
$^1/_4$ teaspoon salt
3 cups quick-cooking oatmeal

Cook sugar, milk, cocoa, and butter or margarine in saucepan to rolling boil, stirring continually for 1 minute. Remove from heat and add remaining ingredients. Mix well and drop by spoonfuls onto wax paper; let harden.

Alaska's Cooking Volume II

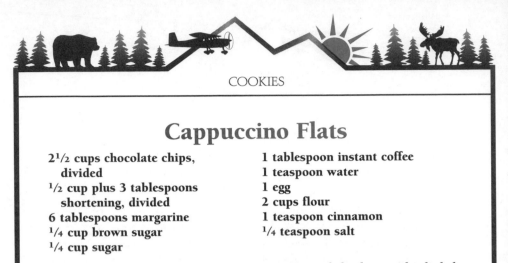

Cappuccino Flats

2¹/₂ cups chocolate chips,
  divided
¹/₂ cup plus 3 tablespoons
  shortening, divided
6 tablespoons margarine
¹/₄ cup brown sugar
¹/₄ cup sugar

1 tablespoon instant coffee
1 teaspoon water
1 egg
2 cups flour
1 teaspoon cinnamon
¹/₄ teaspoon salt

Melt 1 cup chocolate chips in microwave. While that cools slightly, beat ¹/₂ cup shortening and margarine until soft. Add brown sugar and sugar and beat until fluffy. Stir coffee crystals into water until dissolved. Add coffee mixture, melted chocolate, and egg to butter mixture and beat well. Mix in flour, cinnamon, and salt. Cover and chill about 1 hour.

Shape into 2 (7-inch) rolls. Wrap and chill overnight. Cut into ¹/₄-inch slices and bake on ungreased sheet in 350° oven for 10–12 minutes. Cool on racks. Melt 1¹/₂ cups chocolate chips and 3 tablespoons shortening in microwave, stirring occasionally. Dip ¹/₂ of each cookie into chocolate mixture. Place on racks until set. Makes 55 cookies.

Sharing Our Best

Glacier Bear Bars

Easy, no-bake; pack for team trips or freeze, if they last that long.

2 cups white Karo syrup
2 cups packed brown sugar
2 cups peanut butter
4 cups cornflakes

6 cups Rice Krispies
2 cups chopped unsalted peanuts
Chocolate chips (optional)

Combine syrup and sugar and bring to a boil in a saucepan. Remove from heat; stir in peanut butter. Add cornflakes and Rice Krispies. Stir in peanuts until all are mixed. Press mixture into a 9x13-inch pan and allow to cool. "Frost" with melted chocolate chips or any chocolate icing, if desired. Cut into bars and enjoy. Cheer for the team!

Literary Tastes

Bear Tracks

³/₄ cup peanut butter
¹/₄ cup brown sugar
1 teaspoon vanilla
1 (14-ounce) can sweetened
   condensed milk

2 cups all-purpose baking mix
1 (4-ounce) package slivered
   almonds

Preheat oven to 350°. In a large bowl, combine peanut butter, brown sugar, vanilla, and condensed milk. Stir in baking mix. Shape dough into 1¹/₂-inch balls, and insert 5 almond slivers on the side of each cookie (claws). Place on ungreased cookie sheet and bake for 8–10 minutes. Makes about 2 dozen.

Moose Racks, Bear Tracks, and Other Alaska Kidsnacks

There are three types of bears found in Alaska: the black bear, brown/grizzly bear and polar bear. Black bear habitat includes most of the state. They can be brown in color, and may be confused with a grizzly. Brown/Grizzly bears, found in most of the state from the islands of Southeast to the Arctic, aren't always brown—they range in color from black to blonde. Alaska's coastal brown/grizzly bear is the world's largest carnivorous land mammal. Polar bears frequent the pack ice and tundra of extreme northern and western Alaska, and are seldom seen by visitors. Polar bears evolved from the brown bear and actually have translucent fur that reflects light, much like snow.

Earthquake Cookies

¹/₂ cup shortening
1²/₃ cups sugar
2 teaspoons vanilla
2 eggs, beaten
2 cups flour
7 tablespoons cocoa

2 teaspoons baking powder
¹/₂ teaspoon salt
¹/₃ cup milk
Chopped nuts (optional)
Powdered sugar

Cream shortening, sugar, vanilla, and eggs. In a separate bowl, combine flour, cocoa, baking powder, and salt. Then gradually add milk to the dry ingredients. Mix all ingredients together. Add nuts, if desired. Roll teaspoonfuls into powdered sugar and place on generously greased cookie sheets. Bake 15 minutes at 350°.

A Taste of Sitka, Alaska

Sea Otter Biscuits

1 box chocolate cake mix
¹/₂ cup oil

2 eggs
1 cup chocolate chips

Preheat oven to 375°. In a large bowl, combine cake mix, oil, and eggs, stirring until blended. Stir in chocolate chips. Drop by teaspoonfuls onto ungreased cookie sheets. Bake for 8–10 minutes. Cool completely before removing from cookie sheet. Makes 3 dozen.

Moose Racks, Bear Tracks, and Other Alaska Kidsnacks

Ritzee Lemon Cookie

These are always a hit.

28 Ritz crackers, crushed fine
¼ cup brown sugar
¼ cup flour
¼ cup butter, melted

1 package cook-and-serve lemon
  pudding
½ cup coconut

Mix cracker crumbs, brown sugar, flour, and butter with fork, and press ½ the mixture into a 8-inch-square pan. Cook lemon pudding, using ¼ cup less liquid than called for. Spread into crust. Sprinkle coconut and remaining cracker mixture over pudding. Bake at 350° for 20–30 minutes. Let stand to cool. Cut into squares.

Grannie Annie's Cookin' at the Homestead

Viennese Orange Kisses

7 ounces butter, softened
½ cup powdered sugar
2 tablespoons grated orange rind

1 tablespoon cornstarch
1½ cups flour

Cream butter, sugar, and orange rind together until soft. Add cornstarch; mix well. Add flour gradually and beat by hand until smooth. Fill mixture into pastry bag fitted with a large star tube. Pipe into 1-inch rounds on lightly greased cookie sheet. Bake at 375° for 12–15 minutes or until pale golden brown. Cool.

ORANGE CREAM:
2 ounces butter, softened
1 cup powdered sugar

2 tablespoons orange juice

Beat softened butter together with powdered sugar. Add orange juice gradually and mix until smooth. Sandwich cookies together in pairs with Orange Cream as filling. Dust with additional powdered sugar, if desired.

Alaska's Cooking Volume II

Low-bush Cranberry Pinwheels

DOUGH:

1¹/₂ cups flour
¹/₄ teaspoon baking powder
¹/₂ teaspoon salt
¹/₂ cup butter, softened

³/₄ cup sugar
1 large egg
1 teaspoon grated orange peel
1 teaspoon vanilla extract

Mix together the flour, baking powder, and salt; set aside. Cream butter and sugar. Add egg, orange peel and vanilla extract to butter mixture. Add flour mixture gradually and mix well. Place dough on plastic wrap and flatten out slightly into a square. Wrap and refrigerate 4–6 hours. Remove dough and roll on a piece of floured wax paper into a 10-inch square. Place on a flat pan and place back in refrigerator and chill.

FILLING:

¹/₂ cup frozen low-bush
　cranberries
¹/₂ cup walnuts

1 tablespoon grated orange peel
3 tablespoons brown sugar
2¹/₂ teaspoons canned milk

In mini-blender, or meat grinder, process cranberries and walnuts. Remove and place in a small dish; add grated orange peel. Set aside.

Mix brown sugar and canned milk. Spread sugar mixture on Dough, leaving a ¹/₂-inch space on 2 of the edges. Spread the berry mixture evenly over the sugar mixture. Roll tightly, starting with the plain edge, in a jellyroll fashion. Place the rolled log on plastic wrap; cover and place in the freezer overnight or until you are ready to bake.

Remove cookie roll and allow to stand at room temperature for 5 minutes. With serrated knife, cut ¹/₄-inch slices and place on greased cookie sheet. Bake in oven at 375° for 12–14 minutes. Remove from oven and let cookies set a few minutes before removing.

What's Cookin' in the Kenai Peninsula

Cities and towns in Alaska and the Russian Far East are closer to each other than they are to their own national capitals.

Almond Butter Cookies

This is the best recipe I have ever found for cut-out cookies. They are soft, not crispy. Be sure your icing is not too runny, and let the cookies get thoroughly cool before decorating.

1 cup butter, softened
1 (8-ounce) package cream
  cheese, softened
1 1/2 cups sugar
1 egg

1 teaspoon vanilla
1/2 teaspoon almond extract
3 1/2 cups flour
1 teaspoon baking powder
Milk and powdered sugar icing

Cream butter, cream cheese, and sugar until fluffy. Add egg, vanilla, and almond extract. Stir together flour and baking powder; add to creamed mixture and mix thoroughly. Roll out to 1/4-inch and cut in shapes. Bake at 350° for 8–10 minutes. Don't overbake. Ice cooled cookies with a little milk and powdered sugar combined.

Welcome Home

Russian Tea Cakes

1 cup butter, softened
1/2 cup powdered sugar
1 teaspoon vanilla extract
2 1/2 cups all-purpose flour

1/4 teaspoon salt
3/4 cup finely chopped pecans
Powdered sugar for rolling

Cream together butter, sugar, and vanilla. Stir together flour and salt. Blend with butter mixture. Stir in pecans. Chill dough thoroughly (at least 2 hours).

Preheat oven to 400°. Roll chilled dough into 1-inch balls and place on greased cookie sheet. Bake for 10–12 minutes until set, but not brown. Cool slightly, and roll warm cookies in powdered sugar. Allow to cool completely, and roll in powdered sugar again. Yields 48 cookies.

Alaska's Gourmet Breakfasts

Buffalo Cookies

1 cup butter, softened
1 cup shortening
1 cup brown sugar
1 cup white sugar
4 eggs
1 teaspoon vanilla
4 cups flour
2 teaspoons baking powder

2 teaspoons baking soda
1 teaspoon salt
1 cup coarsely chopped nuts
1 cup coconut
1 (16-ounce) bag chocolate chips
2 cups Product 19 Cereal
2 cups oatmeal

Cream butter and shortening; add sugars, eggs, and vanilla. Sift flour, baking powder, baking soda, and salt. Add to creamed mixture. Add last 5 ingredients and mix as best you can. Use ¼ cup of batter per cookie on ungreased cookie sheet. Bake 15 minutes at 350°.

Welcome Home

Big, Big Sugar Cookies

2 cups sugar
1 cup margarine, softened
2 eggs
1 teaspoon lemon extract
4¾ cups flour, divided
2 teaspoons cream of tartar

2 teaspoons baking soda
½ teaspoon salt
½ teaspoon nutmeg
1 cup sour cream
Raisins or maraschino cherries
  (optional)

Beat the sugar and margarine together. Add eggs and lemon extract; cream together. Combine 4 cups flour, cream of tartar, baking soda, salt, and nutmeg and add to sugar/egg mixture alternately with sour cream. Then add about ¾ cup more flour to stiffen dough. Put dough on a floured board and roll ½ inch thick. Use more flour as needed.

Use floured rim of a wide-mouthed jar or bowl to cut cookies about 4 inches in diameter. Place each cookie on a greased cookie sheet about 2 inches apart. Sprinkle with sugar before baking. Add a raisin or chunk of maraschino cherry in center of cookie, if desired. Bake at 350° for 15 minutes. Makes 4 dozen.

33 Days Hath September

Dish Pan Cookies

2 cups oil
2 cups brown sugar
2 cups white sugar
2 teaspoons vanilla
4 eggs
4 cups flour
2 teaspoons baking soda

1 teaspoon salt
4 cups cornflakes
1¹/₄ cups oats
1 cup coconut
1 cup dates
1 cup chopped nuts

Mix oil, sugars, vanilla, and eggs in a large pan. Add remaining ingredients. Drop by spoonfuls on cookie sheet and bake at 325° for 10–14 minutes.

Alaska Women in Timber Cookbook

Blueberry Lemon Bars

CRUST:
1 cup butter, softened
2 cups flour

¹/₂ cup powdered sugar

Preheat oven to 350°. Mix Crust ingredients and press in a greased 9x13x2-inch pan. Bake for 20 minutes.

FILLING:
4 eggs, well beaten
¹/₃ cup lemon juice (approximately
   the juice from 2 fresh lemons)
¹/₄ cup flour

¹/₂ teaspoon baking powder
2 cups fresh or frozen tart
   blueberries

Mix eggs, lemon juice, flour, and baking powder. Pour over baked Crust. Sprinkle blueberries on top and bake 20–30 minutes at 350°.

The Best of the Blueberry Bash, 1994-2002

Alaska is unique among the 50 states in that most of its land mass has not been organized into political subdivisions equivalent to the county form of government. Local government is by a system of organized boroughs, much like counties in other states. Several areas of the state are not included in any borough because of sparse population.

Pumpkin Pie Squares

CRUST:

¹/₂ cup butter, softened
1 cup flour

¹/₂ cup quick cooking oats
¹/₂ cup brown sugar

Mix softened butter with flour, oats, and brown sugar with a fork. Pat into buttered 9x13-inch pan. Bake crust 15 minutes at 350°. Remove from oven and pour Filling mixture on top. Return to oven and continue baking another 20 minutes. Sprinkle nut mixture Topping over partially set Filling and bake another 15–20 minutes or until set. Cut into squares to serve.

FILLING:

1 (16-ounce) can pumpkin
1 (12-ounce) can evaporated
  milk
2 eggs
³/₄ cup sugar

¹/₂ teaspoon salt
1 teaspoon cinnamon
¹/₂ teaspoon ground ginger
¹/₄ teaspoon ground cloves

Whisk all together in medium-size bowl.

TOPPING:

¹/₂ cup chopped nuts
¹/₂ cup brown sugar

2 tablespoons butter, melted

In a small bowl combine nuts, brown sugar and melted butter.

Sharing Our Best

Pumpkin Bars

2 cups sugar
1 cup oil
4 eggs
2 cups flour
2 teaspoons baking powder

$^1/_2$ teaspoon salt
2 teaspoons cinnamon
2 cups pumpkin
1 cup walnuts (optional)

Blend sugar and oil; add eggs. Blend in dry ingredients; fold in pumpkin. Add nuts, if desired. Pour into jellyroll pan. Bake at 350° for 25 minutes. Frost when cool and cut into bars.

FROSTING:
1 (3-ounce) package cream cheese,
   softened
$^3/_4$ stick butter, softened

1 teaspoon vanilla
$1^3/_4$ cups powdered sugar
1 tablespoon cream

Cream together cream cheese and butter. Add vanilla and powdered sugar. Stir in cream. Spread on bars and enjoy. Delicious!

Our Cherished Recipes

Arleigh's Good-for-You Brownies

2 (18-ounce) boxes brownie mix
3 eggs, divided
$^1/_3$ cup applesauce
$^1/_2$ cup oil

2 tablespoons water
1 (3-ounce) package cream cheese,
   softened
$^1/_2$ cup sugar

Mix brownie mix, 2 eggs, applesauce, oil, and water with fork until well blended. Pour into a lightly greased, 9x13-inch cake pan. Blend cream cheese, egg, and sugar, and drop by spoonfuls onto the unbaked brownie mixture. With a knife, pull through the cream cheese with zigzag design. Bake at 350° for 1 hour. Cool and cut in squares.

Grannie Annie's Cookin' at the Homestead

Alaskan Brownies

Not to be confused with Alaskan grizzlies. . . .

1½ cups semisweet chocolate chips, divided
1 cup butter
4 eggs
2 cups sugar
2 tablespoons vanilla extract
1 tablespoon Frangelico Hazelnut Liqueur (optional)
1½ cups unbleached white flour
1 tablespoon ground dark coffee
1 cup chopped walnuts or ground hazelnuts

Preheat oven to 350°. Grease a 9x13-inch baking pan. In double boiler, melt 1 cup chocolate chips and butter. In bowl, cream eggs, sugar, and melted chocolate mixture. Add vanilla and Frangelico, if using. Add flour, coffee, nuts, and remaining ½ cup chocolate chips; stir until blended. Pour into baking pan. Bake for 30–35 minutes until center is done. Cool. Frost, if desired. Yields 16–20 servings.

Note: Hazelnuts may be ground in a coffee grinder.

FROSTING:
2 cups powdered sugar
¼ cup butter, softened
¼ cup unsweetened cocoa powder
1 teaspoon vanilla extract
1 tablespoon hazelnut liqueur (optional)
2–3 tablespoons milk

Blend ingredients together until smooth.

Drop the Hook, Let's Eat

In Fairbanks the aurora borealis, a.k.a. northern lights, can be seen on an average of 240 nights per year. The "lights" are produced by charged electrons and protons striking gas particles in the Earth's upper atmosphere. "The Aurora" is a part of northern life. Some Alaskans have "Aurora Alerts" when a display begins—the first person to spot them begins a phone tree to get the word out.

PIES *and* OTHER DESSERTS

The aurora borealis, or northern lights, provide a rare show over Lynn Canal in Southeast Alaska, where clouds often blot out the sky. Fall, winter and spring are the special seasons for viewing the great lights for residents and off-season visitors.

Peanut Butter Pie

1 (3-ounce) package cream cheese, softened
1 cup powdered sugar
1/2 cup milk

3/4 cup chunky peanut butter
1 (8-ounce) carton Cool Whip
Graham cracker or chocolate crumb crust

Blend cream cheese, sugar, milk, and peanut butter thoroughly. Add Cool Whip and blend. Pour into crust. Freeze.

Alaska Women in Timber Cookbook

Tidewater Peanut Butter Pie

1/2 cup unsalted butter
3/4 cup creamy peanut butter
3 eggs
2 tablespoons all-purpose flour
1/3 cup light corn syrup
1 cup sugar

1 cup firmly packed, light brown sugar
1/3 cup milk
1 teaspoon vanilla extract
Pinch of salt
1 (9-inch) pie shell, partially baked

Melt butter and peanut butter in a small heavy saucepan over low heat, stirring occasionally. Remove from heat. Combine eggs, flour, corn syrup, sugar, brown sugar, milk, vanilla, and salt in large bowl. Mix well. Blend in peanut butter mixture. Pour filling into pie shell. Bake in a 325° oven for about 1 hour and 20 minutes, or until filling is puffed. Filling will still be quite soft and loose. Allow pie to cool to room temperature before slicing.

Kay's Kitchen

Bore tides in many coastal areas of Alaska are extreme, with powerful currents as fast as 20 miles per hour. They come in approximately every six hours. A bore tide is an abrupt rush of water with an incoming tide led by a wave that can be up to six feet high.

Peanut Butter Pie

Very delicious and rich!

CHOCOLATE CRUNCH CRUST:

$^1/_3$ cup margarine or butter
1 (6-ounce) package semisweet
  chocolate chips

$2^1/_2$ cups oven-toasted rice cereal

In heavy saucepan over low heat, melt margarine or butter and chocolate chips. Remove from heat; gently stir in rice cereal until completely coated. Press into bottom and up sides of greased 9-inch pie pan. Chill 30 minutes.

1 (8-ounce) package cream
  cheese, softened
1 (14-ounce) can sweetened
  condensed milk (not evaporated)
3/4 cup peanut butter
1 teaspoon vanilla extract

3 tablespoons lemon juice from
  concentrate
1 cup whipping cream, whipped, or
  1 cup Dream Whip, whipped
1–2 teaspoons chocolate-flavored
  syrup

In large bowl, beat cheese until fluffy; beat in condensed milk and peanut butter until smooth. Stir in vanilla and lemon juice. Fold in whipped cream or Dream Whip. Turn into Chocolate Crunch Crust. Drizzle syrup over top of pie; gently swirl with spoon. Chill 4 hours or until set. Refrigerate leftovers.

Our Cherished Recipes

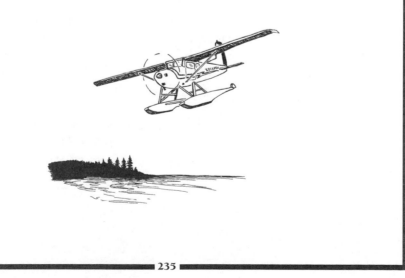

Alaskan Key Stout Pie

"I wrote this recipe for the 1998 Alaska Brewery Contest, and it won!"

CRUST:

³/₄ cup graham cracker crumbs
¹/₂ cup finely chopped pecans
¹/₄ cup firmly packed, light brown
  sugar
¹/₄ cup white sugar
¹/₂ stick (¹/₄ cup) unsalted butter,
  melted and cooled

In a bowl, combine graham cracker crumbs, pecans, and sugars. Stir in butter. Press the mixture into bottom and ¹/₂ inch up side of a buttered, 9-inch springform pan. Bake 10 minutes at 325°. Cool, then chill for 1 hour before filling.

FILLING:

1 tablespoon cornstarch
¹/₂ tablespoon arrowroot
¹/₄ teaspoon salt
5 egg yolks
4 egg whites, divided
¹/₂ cup fresh squeezed lime juice
  (1–2 limes; save a slice and zest
  for garnish)
¹/₂ cup Alaskan Stout Beer
  (or any stout beer)
1³/₈ cup sugar, divided
1¹/₃ tablespoons plain gelatin
  softened in ¹/₃ cup water
1 cup whipping cream

Mix cornstarch, arrowroot, and salt together. In a large bowl, beat egg yolks until fluffy; blend in ¹/₂ of the egg whites, the lime juice, and Alaskan Stout. Add 1¹/₄ cups of the sugar and the rest of cornstarch mixture. Put in double boiler and cook, stirring with wooden spoon, until thick. Remove from heat. Stir in gelatin. Cool in refrigerator, stirring frequently, especially if in metal bowl. Beat remaining egg whites in small bowl with remaining ¹/₈ cup sugar. Beat whipping cream in large bowl. Fold cooled yolk mixture and egg whites into whipped cream. Pour into crust. Chill.

TOPPING:

1¹/₂–2 cups sour cream
2 tablespoons sugar
2 tablespoons Alaskan Stout Beer
  (or any stout beer)

Mix ingredients. Spread over chilled pie. Garnish with lime slice and zest. Chill overnight.

Be Our Guest

Margarita Pie

1¹/₄ cups finely crushed pretzels
¹/₂ cup plus 2 tablespoons butter
  or margarine, melted
¹/₄ cup sugar
1 (14-ounce) can sweetened
  condensed milk

¹/₃ cup lime juice
3–4 tablespoons tequila
2 tablespoons Triple Sec or other
  orange-flavored liqueur
1 cup heavy cream, whipped

Combine crushed pretzels, margarine, and sugar; press firmly on bottom and up side of lightly buttered, 9-inch pie plate. In large mixing bowl, combine condensed milk, lime juice, tequila, and Triple Sec. Mix well. Fold in whipped cream. Pour into prepared crust. Freeze 2 hours or chill 4 hours. Garnish with additional whipped cream and pretzels, if desired.

Alaska's Cooking Volume II

Strawberry-Rhubarb Pie

2 cups sliced strawberries
2 cups chopped rhubarb
1¹/₂ cups sugar
3 tablespoons minute tapioca
¹/₄ teaspoon salt

¹/₂ teaspoon ground nutmeg
1 (9-inch) double-crust pie pastry,
  unbaked
Butter

Mix fruit and cover with sugar, tapioca, and spices. Let stand 25 minutes. Turn into unbaked 9-inch pie shell. Dot with butter; cover with lattice top pastry. Bake at 400° for 10 minutes. Reduce heat to 350° and bake 35 minutes longer, until crust is golden brown.

Let's Taste Alaska

Barrow, the northernmost city in the United States, is only 800 miles from the North Pole. After the sun rises in Barrow on May 10, it doesn't set again for nearly three months. When it sets on November 18, Barrow residents don't see the sun again for more than two months.

Rhubarb Cream Pie

1¹/₃ cups sugar, divided
2 cups diced rhubarb
2 tablespoons cornstarch
2 eggs, separated

1 cup half-and-half
3 tablespoons butter
1 (9-inch) pie shell, baked

In saucepan, combine 1 cup sugar, rhubarb, cornstarch, egg yolks, cream, and butter. Cook over medium heat until thickened. Pour into baked 9-inch pie shell. Top with meringue made with 2 egg whites and remaining ¹/₃ cup sugar whipped till stiff. Bake at 400° until meringue is lightly browned.

Tasty Treats from Tenakee Springs, Alaska

Blueberry-Rhubarb Pie

1¹/₄–1¹/₂ cups sugar
3 tablespoons quick-cooking
  tapioca
¹/₄ teaspoon salt
1 teaspoon lemon juice

3 cups blueberries
3 cups rhubarb, cut into ¹/₂-inch
  pieces
Pastry for double-crust pie

In large bowl, mix sugar, tapioca, salt, lemon juice, blueberries, and rhubarb; toss gently to coat fruit. Let stand 15 minutes. Prepare and roll out pastry; line 9-inch pie pan with half of the pastry. Pour fruit mixture into pastry-lined pan. Place pastry on top of filling; seal edges. Cover pie with foil. Bake 25–30 minutes. Remove foil; bake until golden brown, 20–25 minutes more. Cool pie on rack.

Alaska Connections Cookbook III

The Yukon River, at almost 2,000 miles long, is the third longest river in the United States. There are more than 3,000 rivers in Alaska and over 3,000,000 lakes. The largest lake, Lake Iliamna (ilEam´nu), encompasses over 1,000 square miles.

Double-Good Blueberry Pie

1 cup sugar
3 tablespoons cornstarch
1/8 teaspoon salt
1/2 cup water
4 cups fresh blueberries, divided

1 tablespoon butter or margarine
1 tablespoon lemon juice
1 (9-inch) pie shell, baked
Whipped cream

Combine sugar, cornstarch, and salt in a saucepan. Add water and 2 cups blueberries. Cook until mixture boils and is thick and clear, stirring all the while. Remove from heat; stir in butter and lemon juice. Cool. Mix in remaining 2 cups uncooked blueberries and pour into pie shell. Serve with whipped cream.

Welcome Home

Carolyn's Fresh Blueberry Pie

1 (8-ounce) container Cool Whip
1 (8-ounce) package cream
  cheese, softened
1 1/2 cups powdered sugar

4 cups fresh blueberries, divided
1 baked pie crust, cooled
1–1 1/2 cups Blueberry Glaze
Whipped topping for garnish

Whip together Cool Whip, cream cheese, and sugar. Fold in 1 cup blueberries. Put 1 cup fresh blueberries on the bottom of the crust. Pour mixture into crust on top of the berries and smooth. Pour remaining 2 cups of blueberries over the top of pie. Refrigerate at least an hour, then spoon Glaze over the top and serve with whipped topping.

BLUEBERRY GLAZE:

1 cup sugar
3 tablespoons cornstarch

3/4 cup blueberry juice
1/4 cup water

Mix sugar and cornstarch together; add to juice and water in a saucepan. Cook over medium heat, stirring constantly. Bring to boiling. Boil for a minute; remove from heat. Let cool before spooning onto pie.

The Best of the Blueberry Bash, 1994-2002

Alaska Mixed Berry Pie

1 cup sugar
4 tablespoons flour
¹/₄ teaspoon salt
1¹/₂ cups huckleberries or
    blueberries

1¹/₂ cups salmonberries or
    cloudberries
Pie pastry for 9-inch pie shell,
    unbaked

Mix dry ingredients and pour over berries in shell. Use top crust or leave open-faced to serve with whipped cream. Bake 10 minutes at 450°, lower heat to 350° and bake 30 minutes longer, until golden brown.

Let's Taste Alaska

Apple Pan Dowdy

2 uncooked pie crusts
3 pounds pared, sliced apples
¹/₂ cup sugar
¹/₂ teaspoon nutmeg
¹/₂ teaspoon cinnamon

¹/₂ teaspoon salt
¹/₂ cup molasses
3 tablespoons butter
¹/₄ cup water
Cream

Line casserole with 1 pie crust. Put apples into crust. Mix sugar, spices, and salt. Sprinkle over apples. Add molasses, dot with butter, then add water. Cover with punctured pie crust. Tuck edges together; press to sides of casserole. Bake at 425° for 30 minutes. With spoon, break top crust into pieces and fold them into apple filling. Return to oven and bake 15 minutes at 350°. Serve with cream.

The Original Great Alaska Cookbook

Russians settled Sitka in 1804, dubbing it New Archangel. However, it was almost always known as "Sitka" (sit´ kuh), deriving from the Tlingit word describing the wooded islands that dot the seaside city's harbor. Sitka, "The Paris of the Pacific," was Alaska's capital until 1900, and now claims to be the "biggest city in America." Its 4,710-square-mile boundary includes all of Baranof Island.

Blackberry Polenta Cobbler

¹/₂ **cup butter, softened**	1¹/₂ **teaspoons baking powder**
1 cup sugar	¹/₈ **teaspoon salt**
2 large eggs	**2 cups blackberries**
1 teaspoon vanilla	**1 teaspoon fresh lemon juice**
1 cup stone-ground corn flour	**2 tablespoons cinnamon sugar**

Preheat oven to 350°. Beat together butter and sugar. Gradually beat in eggs. Beat in vanilla. Stir together corn flour, baking powder, and salt. Beat the dry ingredients into the butter/sugar mixture. Spray a 10-inch-deep pie pan or casserole dish with nonstick spray. Spread the polenta mixture evenly in the pan.

Toss berries with lemon juice and spread them over the top of the polenta mixture. Sprinkle cinnamon sugar liberally over the berries. Bake about an hour and serve warm with vanilla ice cream. Serves 8.

Alaska Cooking: Featuring Skagway

GWEN MCKEE

Sitka's New Archangel Dancers perform genuine Russian and Ukrainian dances executed by local women in authentic costumes at Harrigan Centennial Hall.

Rhubarb Crisp

³/₄ cup sugar
1 egg, well beaten
2 tablespoons plus ²/₃ cup flour,
   divided

¹/₄ teaspoon mace
3 cups diced rhubarb
¹/₄ cup butter
¹/₃ cup brown sugar

Mix sugar, egg, 2 tablespoons flour, and mace. Add rhubarb. Put in 9-inch-square pan.

Mix butter, brown sugar, and ²/₃ cup flour together until crumbly. Press down over rhubarb. Bake in 375° oven for 30 minutes or until rhubarb is tender.

Ladies of Harley Cookbook

Winter Apple Crisp

6 cups thin-sliced, peeled apples
1 cup flour
2 cups sugar
¹/₂ cup old-fashioned oatmeal
1 teaspoon cinnamon

¹/₂ teaspoon nutmeg
¹/₂ teaspoon salt
¹/₂ pound (2 sticks) butter
¹/₂ cup chopped walnuts

Preheat oven to 350°. Slice the peeled apples into a large bowl of salted water. (The salt prevents discoloration of the apples.)

In a food processor (or a large bowl using a pastry cutter), combine the flour, sugar, oatmeal, cinnamon, nutmeg, and salt. Use several short bursts of the food processor to combine ingredients, then cut the hard butter into small cubes and drop it into the work bowl. Cut the butter in until it looks like coarse crumbs, then pulse or stir in the walnuts just to combine.

Lift the apples out of the water and mound into a 10-inch baking dish, packing them down as tightly as possible. Mound topping over the apples and press down to cover every bit of apples. Bake 30–45 minutes, waiting until there are apple juices bubbling out of the center of the top. Poke a knife into the center to check the doneness.

Alaska Cooking: Featuring Skagway

Sweet Potato Crisp

POTATO MIXTURE:

1 (8-ounce) package cream
cheese, softened
1 (40-ounce) can sweet potatoes,
drained
$1/4$ cup packed brown sugar

$1/4$ teaspoon ground cinnamon
1 cup coarsely chopped apples
$1/2$ cup coarsely chopped, fresh
cranberries

Preheat oven to 350°. Beat cream cheese, sweet potatoes, brown sugar, and cinnamon in bowl with mixer until well blended. Spoon into greased $1^1/2$-quart casserole dish or 10x6-inch baking dish. Top with apples and cranberries.

CRISP:

$1/2$ cup flour
$1/2$ cup quick-cooking oats
$1/2$ cup packed brown sugar

$1/2$ cup margarine
$1/4$ cup chopped pecans

Stir together flour, oats, and brown sugar in small bowl. Cut in margarine and pecans. Sprinkle Crisp mixture evenly over potatoes. Bake 35–40 minutes, until edges bubble. Serve hot. Yields 8 servings.

Alaska's Gourmet Breakfasts

Rhubarb Crunch

$1/2$ cup butter
1 cup brown sugar
$3/4$ cup oatmeal
1 cup flour
1 teaspoon cinnamon

4 cups chopped rhubarb
1 cup white sugar
2 tablespoons cornstarch
1 cup water
1 teaspoon vanilla

Melt butter in pan; add brown sugar, oatmeal, flour, and cinnamon, and mix together. Press half of mixture into a greased, 9-inch pie pan. Cover with rhubarb. Combine white sugar, cornstarch, water, and vanilla; cook until clear. Pour over rhubarb. Top with remaining crumb mixture. Bake at 350° for 1 hour. Serve warm or cold. Good with cream, ice cream, or whipped topping.

All-Alaska Women in Timber Cookbook

Blueberry Buckle with Cinnamon Bourbon Sauce

FIRST LAYER:

1 cup butter, room temperature	2 teaspoons baking soda
$^1/_3$ cup sugar	1 cup buttermilk
1 egg, beaten	2 pints blueberries
2 cups all-purpose flour	

Preheat oven to 350°. Grease and flour 9x11-inch pan. Cream butter and sugar until light and fluffy; beat in egg. Sift flour with baking soda. Stir dry ingredients, alternating with buttermilk into cream mixture. Spread mixture in prepared dish. Cover with berries.

SECOND LAYER:

1 cup all-purpose flour	$^1/_2$ cup unsalted butter, cut in
$^1/_2$ cup sugar	pieces
$^1/_2$ cup packed brown sugar	$^1/_2$ teaspoon nutmeg
$^1/_2$ cup toasted pecans	$^1/_4$ teaspoon ginger

Combine all ingredients until crumbly. Crumble over berries. Bake 1 hour until brown.

CINNAMON BOURBON SAUCE:

$^1/_2$ cup butter	1 tablespoon very hot water
$^3/_4$ cup sugar	$^1/_2$ cup whipping cream
2 eggs	$^1/_2$ cup bourbon
$^1/_2$ teaspoon cinnamon	

Melt butter over simmering heat in a double boiler. Beat sugar, eggs, and cinnamon in bowl, then add to butter; add water, stirring until mixture coats back of spoon (7 minutes). Remove from heat; cool to room temperature. Beat in whipping cream and bourbon. Serve squares of Blueberry Buckle topped with warm Sauce.

Blueberry Pride: Blueberry Bash Recipes 1989–1993

Once a primary mode of transportation in numerous areas of Alaska, dog mushing is the state sport.

Rhubarb-Almond Tart

BUTTER PASTRY:

1¹/₃ cups all-purpose flour

¹/₄ cup sugar, divided

¹/₂ cup (¹/₄ pound) butter or
   margarine

1 large egg yolk

In a food processor or bowl, combine flour and sugar. Add butter or margarine in chunks. Whirl or rub with your fingers until fine crumbs form. Add egg yolk; whirl or mix with a fork until dough holds together. Firmly pat into a ball. Press Butter Pastry dough evenly over bottom and up sides of a 10-inch tart pan with removable rim. Bake in a 300° oven until pale gold, about 20 minutes. Use hot or cool.

1 pound rhubarb

1 cup sugar, divided

¹/₄ cup water

1 cup blanched almonds

6 tablespoons butter or margarine

2 large eggs

¹/₄ teaspoon almond extract

If using fresh rhubarb, rinse rhubarb, trim and discard dried ends, and cut stalks into 1-inch lengths. Put in a 10- or 12-inch frying pan, and mix with 5 tablespoons sugar and ¹/₄ cup water. Let stand 5 minutes, then stir and set over medium-low heat. When water boils, turn rhubarb pieces over once and cook about 1 more minute. Remove from heat. (If using frozen rhubarb, omit cooking, cut, and put directly into filling.)

Meanwhile, in a food processor or blender, whirl nuts to a fine powder. Add remaining sugar, butter, eggs, and almond extract. Whirl or blend until well combined. Pour almond mixture into pastry. With a fork or slotted spoon, lift rhubarb pieces from cooking liquid and arrange in a pattern on filling. Bake in a 350° oven until filling which rises around rhubarb, is golden brown and center is firm when pan is gently shaken, 35–50 minutes. Let cool at least 15 minutes; remove pan rim to cut. Serve warm or cool.

A Taste of Kodiak

Flour Tortilla Torte

1 (6-ounce) package semisweet
   chocolate bits
3 tablespoons powdered sugar,
   divided

2 cups sour cream, divided
4 (7- to 8-inch) flour tortillas
1–2 ounces milk chocolate

Melt semisweet chocolate in the top of a double boiler. Add 1 table-spoon powdered sugar and 1 cup sour cream. Stir thoroughly. Then cool mixture.

Set 1 flour tortilla on a serving plate and spread evenly with ⅓ of the chocolate mixture. Cover with another flour tortilla, another ⅓ chocolate mixture, a third tortilla, the rest of the chocolate mixture, and then the last tortilla. Blend the remaining sour cream with 2 tablespoons powdered sugar and spread evenly over the top and sides of the Tortilla Torte. Chill, covered with inverted bowl at least 8 hours, or as long as overnight.

Shave milk chocolate into curls using a vegetable peeler. Pile chocolate curls on top of Tortilla Torte. Cut in slim wedges with a sharp knife. Makes 8–12 servings.

Literary Tastes

Bailey's Tipsy Turtle Torte

CRUST:

1$^{1}/_{2}$ cups shortbread cookie
  crumbs
$^{1}/_{4}$ cup packed, light brown sugar

$^{1}/_{4}$ teaspoon ground nutmeg
$^{1}/_{4}$ cup butter, melted

Lightly butter sides of 10-inch springform pan; line sides with strips of waxed paper. Butter bottom and paper-lined sides of pan. In small bowl, mix shortbread crumbs, sugar, and nutmeg; stir in melted butter. Pat evenly on bottom of pan; refrigerate.

FIRST LAYER:

1 quart butter pecan ice cream,
  slightly softened
$^{3}/_{4}$ cup Bailey's Original Irish
  Cream, divided

1 (12-ounce) jar caramel ice cream
  topping
1 cup coarsely chopped pecans,
  toasted, divided

Spoon butter pecan ice cream into medium-size bowl and swirl in $^{1}/_{2}$ cup Bailey's. (Do not over mix!) Pack into chilled crust. Pour caramel topping into small bowl and stir in 2 tablespoons Bailey's. Spoon over butter pecan layer; sprinkle with $^{3}/_{4}$ cup pecans. (Reserve 2 tablespoons Irish Cream and $^{1}/_{4}$ cup pecans for Second Layer). Freeze 1 hour.

SECOND LAYER:

1 quart chocolate ice cream,
  slightly softened

1 (12-ounce) jar fudge ice cream
  topping

Spread slightly softened chocolate ice cream on top of frozen First Layer. Pour fudge topping into small bowl and stir in remaining 2 tablespoons Bailey's. Spoon over chocolate ice cream. Cover with foil and freeze until firm, about 6 hours or overnight.

To serve, remove sides of pan; peel off waxed paper. Place bottom of springform pan on serving plate. Garnish top with remaining $^{1}/_{4}$ cup pecans. Let torte stand 10 minutes before slicing. Makes 16 servings.

Alaska's Cooking Volume II

Wild Berry Bread Pudding with Huckleberry Anglais

PECAN POUND CAKE:

1 cup unsalted butter, softened
1 cup sugar
2 eggs
³/₄ teaspoon vanilla

³/₄ teaspoon orange zest
1 cup all-purpose flour, sifted with
  ¹/₂ teaspoon baking powder
¹/₈ cup chopped pecans

Preheat oven to 350°. In a mixing bowl, add butter. Beat, adding sugar slowly until light and fluffy. Then add one egg at a time (about 30 seconds apart). Beat until eggs are incorporated, then add vanilla and orange zest; incorporate. Start adding sifted flour on low speed, ¹/₃ at a time; add pecans.

Butter edges of 9x9-inch pan, then roll flour over the buttered area and dump out the remaining flour. Line the bottom of the pan with pan liners and lightly butter. Place batter in pan and level. Bake for about 20–25 minutes—done when toothpick comes out of center clean. When done, let cool for 10 minutes; take out of pan and cool. Let sit out overnight; or cut into ¹/₂ x ¹/₂-inch pieces and place in oven at 150° to dry out. (Can freeze—or eat!—whatever cake you don't need for pudding recipe.) You may want to dry out the French bread at the same time.

WILD BERRY BREAD PUDDING:

1 cup sugar
2¹/₂ cups heavy cream
³/₄ cup huckleberry or any fresh
  berry compote
1 tablespoon ground cinnamon
4 ounces brown sugar
6 egg yolks, beaten

4 cups French bread, cut
  1x1 inches (dried)
4 cups Pecan Pound Cake, cut
  ¹/₂ x ¹/₂ inches (dried)
1 cup fresh berries (equal parts
  raspberry, blue, black)

Combine sugar, heavy cream, berries, cinnamon, and brown sugar in a double boiler and let simmer until smooth and creamy (no lumps). Stir with a whip often, about every 5 minutes, and only bring to 160°. Then temper egg yolks with hot mixture. Have bread and cake cut, cooled, and mixed well.

Have oven-safe, 12-ounce bowls buttered and ready to fill. Combine bread/cake mixture with berry batter and mix well. Let the

(continued)

Wild Berry Bread Pudding (continued)

batter soak into dry mixture for a few minutes, then add berries when ready to fill the bowls. Mound the mixture over the top of bowls so they are about 1 inch higher in the center. Bake in a 325° oven 30–35 minutes.

ANGLAIS:

⁵/₈ **cup granulated sugar**
3 egg yolks
1 cup cream

¹/₂ stick butter
¹/₄ cup rum
¹/₂ cup huckleberries, mashed

Mix sugar and egg yolks together in a stainless steel bowl. Meanwhile place cream and butter in a saucepan and heat to 170°. Slowly add the cream-and-butter mixture to egg-and-sugar mixture to temper them—do not scramble the eggs by adding too fast.

Place stainless bowl over a pan of boiling water to create a double boiler; whisk constantly with a wire whip until temperature reaches 170°. Transfer to an ice bath and cool to 45°, then stir in the rum and huckleberries. Refrigerate until needed. Serve, chilled, over warm bread pudding servings. Sprinkle powdered sugar over plate and cake, and top with mint leaves. Gorgeous!

Recipe by Chef Matt Little Dog, Simon & Seaforts, Anchorage

Editor's Extra: When I tasted Chef Little Dog's special bread pudding (see photo below), I knew I wanted to put his recipe in this book. He graciously allowed me to do so. I used frozen mixed berries, blueberries for the huckleberries, and half the amount of rum in the Anglais, and it was still a WOW! Thanks, Matt.

GWEN MCKEE

Pineapple Bread Pudding

1 cup margarine, softened
2 cups sugar
2 eggs
1 cup evaporated milk
1 (20-ounce) can crushed pineapple
  and juice

1 (8-ounce) can pineapple chunks,
  drained, reserve juice for Sauce
8 or 9 slices of bread, cubed

In a mixer bowl, cream the margarine and sugar. Add eggs, milk (more, if bread is dry), crushed pineapple and juice, and pineapple chunks. Blend well and pour into a large bowl with bread cubes. Mix well until moisture is absorbed. Pour into oiled, cast iron skillet; cover with lid. Put in oven (about 300°) for 2–3 hours. After 1½ hours, take lid off to allow moisture to escape; replace top and bake until tested and the knife comes out clean.

SAUCE:

1 (8-ounce) can crushed pineapple
Reserved pineapple juice
1 teaspoon lemon juice

Pinch of salt
1 teaspoon cornstarch
2 tablespoons water

Pour crushed pineapple into a small saucepan and add the reserved pineapple juice. Add lemon juice and a pinch of salt. Mix cornstarch with water. When mixture comes to a boil, turn off heat and add the cornstarch; stir and ladle on individual plates of hot Bread Pudding.

Grannie Annie's Cookin' on the Wood Stove

Apple Bread Pudding with Bourbon Sauce

**8 cups sourdough or French bread
(day old is best)**
4 tablespoons butter
3 cups low-fat milk, scalded
1 cup brown sugar

1 cup apple pie filling
3 eggs, beaten
1 tablespoon vanilla extract
$^1/_2$ cup raisins

Butter bread and tear into small pieces. Place in a large bowl. Scald milk and then pour over bread to cover. Let soak for 30 minutes.

Once bread has been soaking for about 15 minutes, preheat oven to 350°. Toss the brown sugar and apple pie filling. Add beaten eggs and vanilla and whisk together. Pour over bread mixture. Sprinkle raisins over top and lightly stir to blend. Scrape the mixture into a 2-quart baking dish, lightly oiled. Place the baking dish in a larger pan filled with hot water. Place the entire contents into oven. Bake for 60–70 minutes. You may want to loosely cover pudding with foil after 30 minutes of baking to prevent the top from burning. While Bread Pudding is baking, prepare the Bourbon Sauce.

BOURBON SAUCE:
6 tablespoons butter
1 large egg

$^3/_4$ cup powdered sugar
3 tablespoons bourbon whiskey

Melt butter in a small saucepan. In a small bowl, beat egg, then beat in powdered sugar. Stir into melted butter and whisk mixture until it becomes hot. Do not boil. Remove from heat and let cool to room temperature, stirring occasionally. The sauce will thicken as it cools. Stir in the bourbon. Serve pudding hot or warm, spooning the sauce over each serving. Yields 8 servings.

Drop the Hook, Let's Eat

Alaska ranks 47th in population by state with North Dakota, Vermont, and Wyoming following. Taking a closer look, Alaska is home to 1.1 residents per square mile compared to an average of 79.6 residents per square mile for the rest of the nation. By comparison, New York has 401.9 residents per square mile. With men making up 51.7% of its population, Alaska has the highest ratio of men to women of any U.S. state.

Tequila Sunrise Bread Pudding

6 cups bite-size pieces of French
  bread or plain white bread
1 cup milk
3 eggs, beaten
1 (8-ounce) can crushed
  pineapple in juice
¹/₂ cup sugar

¹/₂ cup packed brown sugar
¹/₂ cup butter, melted
1 tablespoon lemon juice
1 tablespoon vanilla
¹/₂ cup golden raisins
¹/₄ cup pine nuts

In a large bowl, soak bread pieces in milk. Stir in eggs, undrained pineapple, granulated and brown sugar, melted butter, lemon juice, vanilla, raisins, and pine nuts. Divide among 8 ramekins or soufflé dishes. Place ramekins in 15x10x1-inch baking pan. Bake in 350° oven for 15–20 minutes or until knife inserted off center comes out clean. Cool slightly. Top with Margarita Sauce.

MARGARITA SAUCE:

1 cup sugar
2 egg yolks
¹/₄ cup butter, melted

3–4 tablespoons tequila
2 tablespoons water
1 tablespoon lime juice

In 1¹/₂-quart saucepan, whisk sugar and egg yolks until well mixed. Stir in melted butter. Stir over medium-low heat just until bubbly. Remove from heat. Stir in tequila, water, and lime juice. Serve warm over Bread Pudding.

Kay's Kitchen

Cranberry Pudding

3 cups low-bush cranberries
$5^{1}/_{2}$ cups water, divided
3 cups sugar
1 cup flour
$^{1}/_{2}$ teaspoon cinnamon

$^{1}/_{2}$ teaspoon nutmeg
Chopped nuts or sunflower seeds
  (optional)
Whipped cream

Crush berries in large saucepan; add 4 cups water, bring to a boil, and add sugar. Make a paste by dissolving flour in water, slowly to avoid lumps. Add spices. Combine with berries. Let boil 10–15 minutes. Chopped nuts or sunflower seeds may be added, if desired. Serve hot or cold with whipped cream.

Let's Taste Alaska

Forty Below Cranberry Dessert

1 (12-ounce) package vanilla
  wafers, divided
2 eggs
1 cup powdered sugar
$^{1}/_{2}$ cup margarine, softened

2 cups ground cranberries
$^{2}/_{3}$ cup sugar
2 bananas, sliced
$^{1}/_{2}$ cup chopped nuts
1 cup whipped cream

Crush wafers. Line baking dish with $^{1}/_{2}$ of wafers. Mix eggs, powdered sugar, and margarine. Spread over crumbs. Mix ground cranberries, sugar, and bananas. Spread over egg mixture. Sprinkle on chopped nuts. Spread whipped cream over nuts. Sprinkle remaining wafers on top. Refrigerate overnight. May serve with additional whipped cream. Serves 12.

Sharing Our Best

Monthly utility bills in Alaska are among the nation's lowest, despite the severe winter weather. This is due to the availability of relatively inexpensive natural gas for heating and the mild summers that eliminate the need for air conditioning.

Layered Blueberry Dessert

COOKIE LAYER:

1 cup flour
1 cup margarine

1 cup chopped walnuts

Cut margarine into flour until crumbly. Add chopped nuts. Pat into a 9x13-inch pan. Bake at 350° for 10–12 minutes. Cool.

CREAM LAYER:

1 (8-ounce) package cream cheese, softened

1 cup powdered sugar
1 (8-ounce) container Cool Whip

Whip cream cheese with powdered sugar. Fold in Cool Whip. Place on cooled cookie layer in dabs; spread carefully to level. Chill well.

BERRY LAYER:

1 cup sugar
4 tablespoons cornstarch
1 cup water (or berry juice with enough water to measure 1 cup)

3 tablespoons dry raspberry Jell-O
1 quart fresh or frozen blueberries
1 (8-ounce) container Cool Whip

Blend sugar with cornstarch in saucepan. Add water. Boil over medium heat until thick and clear, stirring constantly. Add Jell-O and stir until completely dissolved. Add fresh or frozen blueberries; remove from heat. Partially chill berry mixture to prevent melting cheese layer. Spread Berry Layer over Cream Layer. Chill well. Spread Cool Whip over top to serve.

Nome Centennial Cookbook 1898-1998

Koktuli Fruit Galette

While the Koktuli doesn't have any fruit trees, anglers do delight in the river's rainbow trout fishery. The light nature of this dessert suggests the best way to float this river: pack a minimal amount of gear, a lightweight flyrod and plenty of gossamer tippets for these tail-dancing rainbows.

1 (9-inch) round of puff pastry,
   well-chilled
2 tablespoons all-purpose flour
$^1\!/_2$ cup sugar, divided
4 firm, ripe unpeeled nectarines,
   halved, pitted, and thinly sliced

1 egg yolk
1 tablespoon heavy cream
1 tablespoon cold unsalted butter,
   cut into small pieces

Preheat oven to 400°. Place the circle of puff pastry (available in frozen food section of grocery store) on a parchment-lined baking sheet. With the tines of a fork, prick the pastry surface except for a $^1\!/_2$-inch rim. Sprinkle only the punctured area of the circle with flour and $^1\!/_4$ cup sugar.

Starting just inside the unpunched edge, arrange the nectarine slices, with cut edges toward the center, in concentric circles covering the pastry entirely.

Beat egg yolk with heavy cream to make a glaze. Brush egg yolk glaze on just the exposed rim of puff pastry, sprinkle the remaining $^1\!/_4$ cup sugar on top of the fruit and dot with butter. Bake for 18–20 minutes at 400° until the fruit is tender and the pastry has puffed and turned golden brown. Serve immediately. Serves 6.

Recipe from Iliamna Lake Resort
Best Recipes of Alaska's Fishing Lodges

Eskimo Ice Cream

Grate reindeer tallow into small pieces. Add seal oil slowly while beating with hand. After some seal oil has been used, then add a little water while whipping. Continue adding seal oil and water until white and fluffy. Any berries can be added to it.

Eskimo Cookbook

Editor's Note: The recipes in this cookbook are somewhat impractical to prepare but are fascinating to read. See the catalog section for a description of this unique cookbook.

Norwegian Fruit Pizza

CRUST:

³/₄ **cup butter, softened**   1¹/₂ **cups all-purpose flour**
¹/₂ **cup powdered sugar**

Mix together by hand, butter, powdered sugar, and flour until crumb-like. Do not melt butter. Pat into 15-inch pizza pan and bake at 350° for 13–15 minutes until golden brown. Do not over bake.

FILLING:

1 **(8-ounce) package cream cheese,**   2 **cups fresh fruit, sliced (peaches,**
  softened   **kiwi, strawberries, blueberries,**
¹/₂ **cup sugar**   **bananas, etc.)**
¹/₂ **teaspoon vanilla**

With hand mixer, mix cream cheese, sugar, and vanilla until smooth. Spread over cooled Crust. Place fruit on top, so design will remain when cut into 12 wedges.

GLAZE:

1 **cup apple juice**   1 **tablespoon lemon juice**
2 **tablespoons cornstarch**   ¹/₂ **cup sugar**

Mix apple juice, cornstarch, lemon juice, and sugar together in saucepan. Cook over medium heat until clear and thick, stirring constantly. Cool. Spread on top of pizza after slicing. Yields 12 servings.

Alaska's Gourmet Breakfasts

Lake Hood in Anchorage is the largest and busiest seaplane port in the world with an average of 234 takeoffs and landings daily—sometimes more than 800 on a busy summer day. Merrill Field, also in Anchorage, records more than 207,000 flights each year and more than 1,200 on a peak day in July. Alaska boasts six times as many pilots per capita—and 14 times as many airplanes per capita—as the rest of the nation.

Creamy Banana Tiramisu

1¹/₂ cups milk
2 tablespoons instant coffee
  crystals
1 (8-ounce) package cream
  cheese, softened
¹/₄ cup sugar
1 package instant vanilla pudding
  and pie filling (4 cup serving)

2 cups frozen, non-dairy whipped
  topping, thawed
12 ladyfingers
3 medium, ripe bananas
Additional whipped topping for
  garnish
¹/₄ cup semisweet mini-chocolate
  chips for garnish

Stir together milk and coffee crystals until coffee is almost dissolved. With hand mixer, beat together cream cheese and sugar in large bowl until smooth and blended. Add pudding mix; gradually beat in coffee mixture until smooth and blended. Gently stir in whipped topping.

To assemble, place 1 ladyfinger in each 4-ounce custard cup. Top with pudding mixture. Just before serving, place 4–5 banana slices on top of pudding mixture. Top with whipped cream and garnish with a sprinkling of mini-chocolate chips. Yields 12 servings.

Alaska's Gourmet Breakfasts

Blueberry Cream

FILLING:

¹/₄ cup cornstarch

¹/₂ cup white sugar

¹/₂ cup water

4 cups blueberries, divided

Combine cornstarch, sugar, water, and 1 cup of blueberries in a saucepan. Cook and stir over medium heat until thick. Cool. Add 3 cups berries. Set aside.

CRUST:

³/₄ cup soft margarine

¹/₃ cup brown sugar

³/₄ cup chopped walnuts

1¹/₂ cups flour

Thoroughly mix Crust ingredients, then spread on a cookie sheet. Bake at 375° for 10–15 minutes, stirring occasionally until brown and crumbly. Press crumbs into bottom of 9x13-inch pan.

TOPPING:

1¹/₂ cups white sugar

1 (8-ounce) package cream cheese, softened

2 teaspoons vanilla

1 (8-ounce) container Cool Whip

Cream together sugar, cream cheese, and vanilla. Fold in Cool Whip. Spread Filling on Crust; then spread Topping on Filling. Refrigerate. Yields 12–15 servings.

Sharing Our Best

Custard Igloo or Lemon Snow

2 tablespoons unflavored gelatin
  (2 envelopes)
¹/₂ cup cold water
2 cups very hot water
2 cups sugar

¹/₂ cup lemon juice
6 egg whites, beaten stiff (reserve
  yolks for Custard Sauce)
1 tablespoon grated lemon rind

In a large mixing bowl, soften gelatin in cold water; dissolve in hot water. Add sugar and stir until sugar is completely dissolved. Add lemon juice. Chill until partially set, or consistency of unbeaten egg whites (usually about 2 hours).

Beat until frothy (about 2 minutes), then fold in egg whites. Beat until gelatin will hold its shape (another 2 minutes); fold in lemon rind. Pour into mold and chill until firm. For "Custard Igloo" use round bowl for mold. When set, invert pudding to serving plate (use thin knife around edge, if necessary to loosen) which is several inches larger than bowl. Make ice block lines with thick custard sauce or pour sauce over. Serve with extra sauce.

CUSTARD SAUCE:

4 slightly beaten egg yolks
Dash of salt
5 tablespoons sugar

2 cups scalded milk
1 teaspoon vanilla

In top of double boiler, combine egg yolks, salt, and sugar. Gradually stir in scalded milk. Cook over gently boiling water until mixture coats spoon, stirring constantly (usually 2–3 minutes). Remove from heat, and stir in vanilla. Chill thoroughly.

A Cook's Tour of Alaska

Editor's Extra: This makes four igloos, so half a recipe is plenty for an average dessert.

The word igloo comes from the people of eastern and northern Canada and of Arctic Alaska. The dome-shaped house built of snow is rarely found in Alaska any more, except perhaps when mountain climbers and bush travelers build temporary shelters against the elements. An Alaskan igloo was traditionally a dome or Quonset-hut shaped structure built with sod and reinforced with driftwood and whale bones. "Igloo," or "iglu" in the Inupiaq (inOO′pE-ak) language, simply means "house."

Individual Baked Alaska

1 sponge cake or pound cake   **Vanilla or strawberry ice cream**

Cut cake into 4- or 5-inch rounds ¹/₂ inch thick. Place cut cake on wooden plank or foil-lined cookie sheet. Top each round with a scoop of ice cream, centering so a ¹/₂-inch rim of cake remains. Cover lightly with waxed paper and place in freezer until needed (up to 3 days) and Meringue is made.

MERINGUE:
3 egg whites   **¹/₃ cup super-fine sugar**
¹/₄ teaspoon cream of tartar

Whip egg whites and cream of tartar until stiff; gradually adding sugar, continue to beat until very stiff peaks form. Heat oven to 450°. Remove cakes from freezer and quickly frost completely with Meringue.   Bake in hot oven about 5 minutes, or until light brown all over. With spatula, remove to serving dishes. Drizzle with Raspberry Topping. Also good with strawberry, blueberry or rhubarb sauce.

RASPBERRY TOPPING:
1¹/₂ cups raspberries, fresh or   **¹/₄ cup orange liqueur or juice**
thawed   **1 tablespoon cornstarch**
¹/₄ cup sugar

Place in small saucepan. Cook over low heat until thickened. Cool.

A Cook's Tour of Alaska

Editor's Extra: If using a frozen pound cake, slice in thirds lengthwise. Using the bottom of a coffee or nut can as a guide, cut circle shapes in cake with a serrated knife to make six rounds.

Blueberry Cheesecake Ice Cream

2 cups blueberries
1 cup sugar, divided
1 tablespoon lemon juice
1 teaspoon grated lemon peel
5 egg yolks, room temperature

1 (8-ounce) package cream cheese, softened
1 cup milk, scalded
2 cups whipping cream

Crush berries. Toss with ½ cup sugar, lemon juice, and lemon peel. Set aside. Beat egg yolks with remaining ½ cup sugar until pale yellow, about 6 minutes. Beat in cream cheese. Slowly beat in hot milk.

Put mixture in a heavy saucepan and cook over medium-low heat, stirring constantly, until it reaches 180° on a thermometer. Stir in berry mixture. Blend in whipping cream. Cool at room temperature, then refrigerate until chilled. Put in ice cream maker and follow directions for making ice cream. Freeze. Makes 8 servings.

Blueberry Pride: Blueberry Bash Recipes 1989–1993

Floathouse City
Homemade Ice Cream

We came up with this recipe when we lived in our floathouse in Shinaku Inlet. Sometimes we didn't see another family or get to town (Craig or Klawock) for three months. Really tastes great, as many local skiff-visiting people will verify. Enjoy and God bless!

2 quarts milk
2 rounded teaspoons salt
4–6 eggs, beaten

2 cups sugar
2 or 3 cans evaporated milk
2 teaspoons vanilla

Combine milk, salt, eggs, and sugar in large kettle. Cook over high heat until it comes to a boil, stirring constantly. Remove from heat; add evaporated milk and vanilla. Put in ice cream maker and crank! This recipe can have almost any flavor fruit or candy added to it.

Alaska Connections Cookbook III

ALASKAN TIMELINE

Presented below is a brief chronology of historical events derived from written records. Native Alaskan history prior to the arrival of Russians and Europeans was passed on almost exclusively through oral narratives and stories. These oral histories converge with archeology to suggest that Natives have lived and moved through Alaska for at least 10,000 years. The list of events below, however, primarily reflects the history of western settlers who entered Alaska less than 300 years ago.

1725 Tzar Peter the Great of Russia sends Vitus Bering to explore the North Pacific.

1741 Alexei Chirikof, with Bering's expedition, sights land on July 15 in Southeast Alaska. The Europeans had found Alaska.

1784 Grigorii Shelikhov establishes the first permanent non-Native settlement at Three Saints Bay, Kodiak.

1799 Alexander Baranov establishes the Russian post known today as Old Sitka; Tzar Paul I grants exclusive trading rights to the Russian American Company.

1802 Tlingits drive Russians from Old Sitka; few Russians survive.

1859 Edward de Stoeckl, the secretariat of Russia, returns to U.S. from St. Petersburg with authority to negotiate the sale of Alaska.

1867 U.S. purchases Alaska from Russia.

1868 Alaska designated as the Department of Alaska under Brevet Major General Jeff C. Davis, U.S. Army.

1880 Richard Harris and Joseph Juneau, with the aid of local Tlingit leader Kowee, discover gold on Gastineau Channel.

1897-1900 Klondike Gold Rush

1906 Alaska authorized to send voteless delegate to Congress; governor's office moved from Sitka to Juneau.

1916 First bill for Alaska statehood introduced in Congress.

1923 President Warren E. Harding comes to Alaska to drive the last spike in the Alaska Railroad.

1940 Fort Richardson established; construction begins on Elmendorf Air Force Base.

1942 Japan bombs Dutch Harbor and invades the Aleutians.

1958 Statehood measure passes; Pres. Eisenhower signs statehood bill.

1959 We're in! Statehood proclaimed; state constitution in effect.

1964 Good Friday Earthquake destroys $311 million of property in over a dozen towns around Prince Wiliam Sound. With a magnitude of 9.2, this is the largest recorded earthquake in the United States.

1977 Trans-Alaska Pipeline completed from Prudhoe Bay to Valdez.

1989 The *Exxon Valdez*, a 987-foot oil tanker carrying 53 million gallons of North Slope crude, grounds on Bligh Reef spilling 11 million gallons of oil into Prince William Sound.

1994 A federal trial results in a $5 billion verdict in the *Exxon Valdez* case.

2000 Along with the rest of the world, Alaskans welcomed the year 2000 with fanfare and firecrackers. Census 2000 results show a state population of 626,932, an increase of 14% from 1990.

EXCERPTED FROM ALASKA DEPARTMENT OF COMMUNITY AND ECONOMIC DEVELOPMENT

CATALOG *of*
CONTRIBUTING COOKBOOKS

In Anchorage, anglers cast for king salmon in the shadows of office buildings.

CATALOG *of*
CONTRIBUTING COOKBOOKS

All recipes in this book have been selected from the cookbooks shown on the following pages. Individuals who wish to obtain a copy of any particular book may do so by sending a check or money order to the address listed by each cookbook. Please note the postage and handling charges that are required. State residents add tax only when requested. Prices and addresses are subject to change, and the books may sell out and become unavailable. Retailers are invited to call or write to same address for discount information.

ALASKA BACKYARD WINES
by Jan O'Meara
Wizard Works
P. O. Box 1125
Homer, AK 99603

Phone 907-235-8757
Fax 907-235-8757
wizard@xyz.net

A "how-to" book containing step-by-step instructions for making delightful home-made wines using fruits and flowers found in Alaska and elsewhere. Contains 30 kitchen-tested recipes. Beautifully illustrated. Winner 1989 Instructional Book Award, Alaska Press Women, National Federation of Press Women. 60 pages.

$ 7.95   Retail price
$ 2.50   Postage and handling
Make check payable to Wizard Works

Visa/MC Accepted

ISBN 0-9621543-5-0

ALASKA CONNECTIONS COOKBOOK III
Prince of Wales Island Chamber of Commerce
P. O. Box 497
Craig, AK 99921

Phone 907-826-3870
Fax 907-826-5467
powcc@aptalaska.net

Over 600 delicious recipes from Alaskan cooks with many ideas for cooking fish and other seafood. All proceeds go toward scholarships to help Island High School seniors further their education.

$13.00   Retail price
$3.50   Postage and handling
Make check payable to POW Chamber of Commerce

ALASKA COOKING: FEATURING SKAGWAY
Greatland Classic Productions
11570 SW Pacific Highway
Tigard, OR 97223

Phone 503-244-2472
Fax 503-244-6715
greatlandclassic@juno.com

This 32-page book beautifully portrays recipes and photographs of Alaska. Forty-eight choice recipes give the reader an opportunity to prepare and enjoy the same foods that those in Alaska do. Whether you prefer salmon, sourdough breads, or just fine cooking, experience a little taste of Alaska in each bite!

$6.95   Retail price
$3.85   Postage and handling
Make check payable to Greatland Classic Sales

Visa/MC Accepted

ALASKA GOLD RUSH COOK BOOK

by Ron Wendt
Goldstream Productions
P. O. Box 870624   Phone 907-376-4715
Wasilla, AK 99687   goldstreamalaska@gci.net

Old Alaska gold rush recipes, humorous tips and tales, short hunting and fishing stories, rare and unique ideas, unusual cooking methods, old food preparations, native customs and much more . . . all included in this must-have book. This book makes a wonderful gift for any occasion.

  $9.95   Retail price
  $1.50   Postage and handling

Make check payable to Goldstream Publications   ISBN 1886574219

ALASKA MAGAZINE'S CABIN COOKBOOK

Morris Communications   Phone 800-458-4010
735 Broad Street   Fax 706-828-3846
Augusta, GA 30901   jmarchant@morris.com

This small, 64-page cookbook packs in more than 130 favorite North Country recipes that tell you how to cook with wild game, fish, fowl, and native plants.

  $ .99   Retail Price   Visa/MC/Amex Accepted
  $2.00   Postage and handling

Make check payable to ALASKA magazine   ISBN 0-89909-196-5

ALASKA SHRIMP & CRAB RECIPES

by Cecilia Nibeck
Alaska Enterprises   Mail Orders Only
P. O. Box 210241
Anchorage, AK 99521-0241

No other seafood can match the tastiness, versatility, magnificence and ease of preparation of shrimp and crab. This collection of recipes features these fine shellfish in over 280 mouth-watering selections.

  $13.95   Retail price
   $1.50   Postage and handling

Make check payable to AK Enterprises   ISBN 0-9622117-4-5

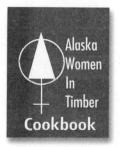

ALASKA WOMEN IN TIMBER COOKBOOK

Alaska Women in Timber
Ketchikan, AK

Recipes were collected and assembled by members of Alaska Women in Timber chapters at two remote logging camps in Southeast Alaska: Naukati and Freshwater Bay. Published in 1991, this book is no longer in print.

ALASKA'S COOKING VOLUME II

GFWC Anchorage Woman's Club   Phone 907-344-5982
P. O. Box 100273   Fax 907-522-6379
Anchorage, AK 99510   gfwcawc@yahoo.com

Alaska's Cooking Volume II was self-published by members of the GFWC Anchorage Woman's Club. The purpose was to raise funds for a club building for the people of Anchorage. It includes 263 pages and 525 recipes.

$15.95   Retail price
 $3.00   Postage and handling

Make check payable to Anchorage Woman's Club

ALASKA'S GOURMET BREAKFASTS

by Leicha Welton
7 Gables Inn   Phone 907-479-0751
P. O. Box 80488   Fax 907-479-2229
Fairbanks, AK 99708   gables7@alaska.net

A collection of breakfast menus based on international themes. Many recipes were adapted from their original use to be suitable for a breakfast setting. The Jewish breakfast entices guests with the Cinnamon Rugalach recipe.

$10.00   Retail price   Visa/MC/Disc/Amex Accepted
 $3.00   Postage and handling

Make check payable to 7 Gables Inn

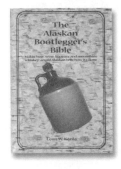

THE ALASKAN BOOTLEGGER'S BIBLE

by Leon Kania   Phone 907-376-2610
Happy Mountain Publications   Fax 907-376-2610
3401 Naomi Drive   leon@happymountain.net
Wasilla, AK 99654   www.happymountain.net

This book presents all types of alcoholic beverages in an easy-to-understand and entertaining manner. It stresses the art, not the science; steers you toward using wholesome natural ingredients, rather than chemicals; and shows you how to make, rather than buy, most of your equipment. Lots of moonshine lore.

$21.95   Retail price
 $4.00   Postage and handling   ISBN 0-9674524-0-6

Make check payable to Happy Mountain Publications

ALASKAN HALIBUT RECIPES

by Cecilia Nibeck
Alaska Enterprises   Mail Orders Only
P. O. Box 210241
Anchorage, AK 99521-0241

At its best, Alaskan halibut is unassuming enough to perform in a tastefully simple meal, yet has the character to stand up to a bold sauce or a pushy sauté. Here are more than 200 recipes for hors d'oeuvres, soups, stews, roasts, fillets and some whimsical dishes for the culinary adventurer.

$13.95   Retail price
 $1.50   Postage and handling

Make check payable to AK Enterprises   ISBN 0-9622117-0-2

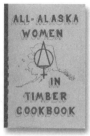

ALL-ALASKA WOMEN IN TIMBER COOKBOOK

Alaska Women in Timber
Ketchikan, AK

The second AWIT cookbook includes recipes from twelve logging camps which, by 1982, were less remote with the advent of telephones and television. However, after extreme cutbacks in the industry, the camps are gone, as is AWIT, once the champion of the people who lived and worked in the forests of Southeast Alaska. The book is no longer in print.

BE OUR GUEST

Juneau CVB
101 Egan Drive
Juneau, AK 99801

Phone 888-581-2201
Fax 907-586-6304
info@traveljuneau.com

This 80-page, 101-recipe cookbook was compiled by JCVB volunteers happy to share their family favorites. *Be Our Guest* celebrates a long tradition of Juneau hospitality and reflects the dedication of our "local ambassadors." Cover photo by Janet Fries Eckholm.

$10.00   Retail price
$2.00   Postage and handling

Visa/MC Accepted

Make check payable to Juneau Convention and Visitors Bureau

THE BEST OF THE BLUEBERRY BASH, 1994–2002

Unalaska Pride
P. O. Box 721
Unalaska, AK 99685

Phone 907-581-1524
Blueberry_Book@hotmail.com

A cookbook full of scrumptious prize-winning blueberry recipes! The Annual Blueberry Bash is sponsored by Unalaska Pride, a nonprofit, neighborhood improvement group which encourages home improvement, painting, clean up, gardening, and landscaping. Proceeds from the book sales will be used for community improvements.

$10.00   Retail price (Order both Blueberry Bash volumes for $15.00)
$5.00   Postage and handling (One or both volumes)

Make check payable to Unalaska Pride

BEST RECIPES OF ALASKA'S FISHING LODGES

by Adela Batin Jackson
Alaskabooks
P. O. Box 82222
Fairbanks, AK 99708

Phone 907-455-8222
Fax 907-455-8222
adela@alaska.net
www.alaskabooks.com

More than just a cookbook—it's a celebration of a wilderness lifestyle many dream about, with 140 beautiful photographs featuring the food, fishing, accommodations, people, scenery, and activities at the lodges. Enjoy 90 recipes for seafood, wild game, salads, breads, and desserts. 320 pages.

$24.95   Retail price
$6.00   Postage and handling

Visa/MC Accepted

Make check payable to Alaskabooks

ISBN 0-916771-10-5

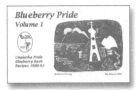

BLUEBERRY PRIDE: BLUEBERRY BASH RECIPES 1989–1993

Unalaska Pride
P. O. Box 721   Phone 907-581-1524
Unalaska, AK 99685   Blueberry_Book@hotmail.com

Blueberry Pride is a cookbook full of prize-winning recipes which celebrate the wild blueberries grown on the Aleutian Island. Local residents, who have entered recipes and won in our annual cooking contests between 1989 and 1993, are included in this delightful book. Proceeds from sales go toward continuing community improvements.

   $5.00   Retail price (Order both Blueberry Bash volumes for $15.00)
   $3.00   Postage and handling (Shipping for both books $5.00)

Make check payable to Unalaska Pride

A COOK'S TOUR OF ALASKA

by Gwen Stetson
JAGS
4605 San Roberto Avenue
Anchorage, AK 99508   Phone 907-337-2535

This unique map-style presentation of a mixture of recipes collected from all around Alaska is a taste-tempting treat to both the eye and the palate. One page with map and recipes from throughout the state of Alaska.

   $9.95   Retail price (Includes postage and handling)

Make check payable to JAGS   ISBN 0-9646235-0-1

DROP THE HOOK, LET'S EAT

by Rachel Barth
P. O. Box 178   Phone 907-772-4778
Petersburg, AK 99833   rachelbarth@hotmail.com

Hardcover, spiralbound, colorful cookbook containing 145 recipes to prepare seafood and vegetarian dishes, as well as desserts. Chapters include "Rising Tide," "High Tide," "Appetides," etc., covering breakfast, lunches, dinners, salads, appetizers, and desserts. Helpful hints included.

   $14.00   Retail price
    $2.00   Postage and handling

Make check payable to Rachel Barth

ESKIMO COOKBOOK

by Students of Shishmaref Day School
On the Wall Productions   Phone 800-788-4044
8312 Olive Boulevard   or 314-692-2900
St. Louis, MO 63132   Fax 314-213-3194

Originally created in 1952 by students of Shishmaref Day School in Shishmaref, Alaska, the *Eskimo Cookbook* remains a living testimony to the lives and lifestyles of the native peoples who live on the northwest seacoast of what is now Alaska. Though difficult to prepare, the recipes are fascinating to read aloud.

   $5.00   Retail price   Visa/MC/Amex Accepted
   $2.50   Postage and handling

Make check payable to On the Wall Productions, Inc.

ESKIMO COOKBOOK BY ALEXANDRA

by Alexandra
215 Fourth Avenue S.
Edmonds, WA 98020   Phone 425-778-3883

Delightful hand-drawn illustrations of native plants and animals—bears, seals, birds, and shellfish to name a few—are found throughout this forty-eight page book of true, authentic Eskimo recipes. The author, Alexandra, was born on Kodiak Island.

$6.95   Retail price
$2.00   Postage and handling

Make check payable to Nicholas Spanovic

FAVORITE RECIPES FROM ALASKA'S BED AND BREAKFASTS

Fairbanks Association of B & Bs
P. O. Box 73334
Fairbanks, AK 99707-3334   fabb@ptialaska.net

Over 200 recipes created and used by some of Alaska's finest Bed and Breakfasts. Categories include Egg Dishes; Pancakes, Waffles, and French Toast; Buns and Breads; Muffins and Coffeecakes; Tea Time and Desserts; Fruits and Cereals. Our goal is to "feed 'em, please 'em, and share the grand state of Alaska."

$9.95   Retail price
$3.50   Postage and handling

Make check payable to FABB

GRANNIE ANNIE'S COOKIN' AT THE HOMESTEAD

by Ann Berg
Fireweed Herb Garden and Gifts   Phone 907-776-5405
202 North Forest Drive   Fax 907-283-6207
Kenai, AK 99611   anninalaska@gci.net

More than 600 interesting recipes using common ingredients. A collection of 45 years from family and friends. Most are Alaskan. All are good eating. Contains 10 food categories in 301 pages. Short stories will make you laugh and cry. Recipes will make you hungry!

$14.95   Retail price   Visa/MC Accepted
$3.80   Postage and handling

Make check payable to Grannie Annie

GRANNIE ANNIE'S COOKIN' FISH FROM COLD ALASKAN WATERS

by Ann Berg
Fireweed Herb Garden and Gifts   Phone 907-776-5405
202 North Forest Drive   Fax 907-283-6207
Kenai, AK 99611   anninalaska@gci.net

Over 300 recipes using common ingredients. Many short stories of Grannie Annie's earlier years in Alaska and growing up on a farm in Colorado, jammed onto 140 pages of fish and seafood recipes. A collection of 36 years of cooking Alaskan fish and seafood from recipes of family and friends.

$14.95   Retail price   Visa/MC Accepted
$2.60   Postage and handling

Make check payable to Grannie Annie

GRANNIE ANNIE'S COOKIN' ON THE WOOD STOVE

by Ann Berg
Fireweed Herb Garden and Gifts
202 North Forest Drive
Kenai, AK 99611

Phone 907-776-5405
Fax 907-283-6207
anninalaska@gci.net

This first book in a series was inspired by a desire to save electricity and propane by cooking on the wood heater we use to heat our tiny house. This 106-page cookbook features over 350 recipes made with common ingredients. Includes recipes from my grandmother, mother, daughter, friends, and myself.

$11.95   Retail price
  $2.60   Postage and handling

Visa/MC Accepted

Make check payable to Grannie Annie

HUNA HERITAGE FOUNDATION COOKBOOK

Huna Heritage Foundation
9301 Glacier Highway
Dept. QRP
Juneau, AK 99801-9306

Phone 907-789-1773
Fax 907-789-1896
info@hunaheritage.org

The *Huna Heritage Foundation Cookbook* features recipes from homes of Huna Tlingit Indians of Southeast Alaska. Recipes reflect use of food items traditionally harvested from land and sea by these Alaska Native people.

$20.00   Retail price
  $4.00   Postage and handling

Make check payable to Huna Heritage Foundation

JUST FOR THE HALIBUT

by Nanci A. Morris
Flatfish Publications
P. O. Box 221
King Salmon, AK 99613

Phone 907-246-8322
Fax 907-246-8322
fishingb@bristolbay.com

An Alaskan recipe book specializing in halibut recipes. Seventy-five pages of succulent recipes for Alaska's largest and tastiest port fish. Being so large, fishermen and women often have a dilemma of what to do with all the halibut they have to take home.

$7.50   Retail price
$2.50   Postage and handling

Make check payable to Flatfish Publications

KAY'S KITCHEN

by Kay Gundersen
8103 N. Tongass Highway
Ketchikan, AK 99901

Kay had a family-run restaurant for 25 years which soon became a reservations-only place. This cookbook contains a variety of 250 recipes that she used in the restaurant or her home.

$15.00   Retail price
  $4.00   Postage and handling

Make check payable to Kay or Eric Gundersen

LADIES OF HARLEY COOKBOOK

by Harley Owners Group Alaska Chapter Anchorage
Ladies of Harley
Attn: Activities Director
4334 Spenard Road   Phone 907-248-5300
Anchorage, AK 99517   Fax 907-248-6300

This cookbook was put together by the Ladies of Harley, Anchorage, in 1997. It contains 100 pages of recipes, photos, and member profiles. This is biker food at its best. Buy a copy or we will ride up and down your street until you do!

$13.00   Retail price
$4.50   Postage and handling

Make check payable to Harley Owners Group Chapter 66

LET'S TASTE ALASKA

by Mary Carey
McKinley View Lodge
P. O. Box 13314
Trapper Creek, AK 99683   Phone 907-733-1555

Recipes and stories from the author's homesteading experiences while building McKinley View Lodge. Includes recipes for many popular dishes from the lodge such as Fiddle-Head Fern Quiche, Peanut Butter Pie, Raspberry-Rhubarb Jelly, etc. Illustrated by famous Alaskan artist Doug Lindstrand.

$6.95   Retail price
$1.50   Postage and handling

Make check payable to Mary's McKinley View Lodge

LICENSE TO COOK ALASKA STYLE

by Larry and Shelly Carroll
Penfield Press
215 Brown Street   Phone 800-728-9998
Iowa City, IA 52245-5842   Fax 319-351-6846

The essence of The Last Frontier state is captured in this delightful little book. Recipes, facts, illustrations, and much more are packed into this 158-page cookbook. A must for those seeking to bring classic Alaska cuisine into their home. A great stocking stuffer and/or a must-have souvenir! Enjoy.

$8.95   Retail price
$1.95   Postage and handling

Make check payable to Penfield Press   ISBN 1-57216-080-2

LITERARY TASTES

Friends of the Haines Borough Public Library
Haines Borough Public Library   Phone 907-766-2545
P. O. Box 1089   Fax 907-766-2551
Haines, AK 99827   hainesp@aptalaska.net

Literary Tastes is a collection of favorite recipes gathered from the patrons of the Haines Borough Public Library. The cover depicts the beautiful scenery of our Chilkat Valley—surrounded by mountains and the sea. 170 pages.

$10.00   Retail price
$4.00   Postage and handling

Make check payable to Friends of the Haines Borough Public Library

METHODIST PIE
AND OTHER RECIPES WORTH RAVEN ABOUT

United Methodist Church
303 Kimsham   Phone 907-747-6773
Sitka, AK 99835   wnyoung@worldnet.att.net

Dedicated to the use and sharing of the Creator's bountiful gifts to Alaskans, and to the preservation of traditional and family favorites which have nourished and brought joy to our lives. A special section of recipes made with food unique to Alaska. 104 pages.

  $15.00   Retail price
    $1.50   Postage and handling

Make check payable to UMC of Sitka

MOOSE & CARIBOU RECIPES OF ALASKA

by Cecilia Nibeck
Alaska Enterprises   Mail Orders Only
P. O. Box 210241
Anchorage, AK 99521-0241

A unique cookbook from the heart of Alaska. These recipes will help provide variety and boost the confidence of any cook, novice or sourdough. It brings the flavor and spirit of the North Country to your dinner table in all the splendor and variety this beautiful land offers its people.

  $13.95   Retail price
    $1.50   Postage and handling

Make check payable to AK Enterprises   ISBN 0-9622117-3-7

**MOOSE
IN THE POT
COOKBOOK**

MOOSE IN THE POT COOKBOOK

Burchell High School
c/o Tim Lundt   Phone 907-373-7775
1775 West Parks Highway   Fax 907-373-1430
Wasilla, AK 99654   lundt@mtaonline.net

Moose in the Pot Cookbook includes 88 moose recipes and 28 other favorite recipes for desserts, wild game, fish and espresso—with special sections on how to field dress a moose, how to get on the road kill list, and how to reconstruct a moose skeleton. 75 pages.

  $13.00   Retail price
    $3.00   Postage and handling

Make check payable to Burchell High School   ISBN 1-57833-086-6

MOOSE RACKS, BEAR TRACKS, AND OTHER ALASKA KIDSNACKS

by Alice Bugni
Sasquatch Books
119 S. Main Street #400   Phone 800-775-0817
Seattle, WA 98104   custserv@sasquatchbooks.com

A kid-tested and approved cookbook for children.

  $8.95   Retail price   Visa/MC/Amex/Disc
  $4.00   Postage and handling

Make check payable to Sasquatch Books   ISBN 1-57061-217-5

NOME CENTENNIAL COOKBOOK 1898-1998

by Kay Hansen
Wizard Works   Phone 907-235-8757
P. O. Box 1125   Fax 907-235-8757
Homer, AK 99603   wizard@xyz.net

My cookbook features recipes from Nome, Alaska family and friends. Historic artwork by my daughter, Heidi Hansen, depicting early Nome, as well as local flora, make up the divider pages. It also has a time line of Nome history.

$15.00   Retail price   Visa/MC Accepted
$3.50   Postage and handling

Make check payable to Wizard Works
or contact Kay Hansen • 907-443-5425 • P.O. Box 246 • Nome, AK 99762

THE ORIGINAL GREAT ALASKA COOKBOOK

by Walter C. Friedrich
Star-Byte, Inc.   Phone 800-243-1515
2880 Bergey Road   Fax 215-997-2571
Hatfield, PA 19440   starbyte@starbyte.com

Compiled over 50 years ago, these superior and hearty recipes came from Alaskan ladies who spent much of their adult lives cooking and baking for their families. The best of their recipes are represented here in this rare and unusual compilation.

$15.00   Retail price   Visa/MC/Disc Accepted
$4.95   Postage and handling

Make check payable to Star-Byte, Inc.

OUR CHERISHED RECIPES

First Presbyterian Church Deacons
First Presbyterian Church   Phone 907-983-2806
P. O. Box 513   Fax 907-983-3107
Skagway, AK 99840   brummett@aptalaska.net

In our homes today, as always, life is centered around our kitchens. It is with this thought that we have compiled these recipes from members of First Presbyterian Church (Skagway, Alaska). Some are treasured family keepsakes and some are new. They all reflect the love of good cooking.

$8.50   Retail price
$3.00   Postage and handling

Make check payable to First Presbyterian Church Deacons

OUR CHERISHED RECIPES VOLUME II

First Presbyterian Church Deacons
First Presbyterian Church   Phone 907-983-2806
P. O. Box 513   Fax 907-983-3107
Skagway, AK 99840   brummett@aptalaska.net

First Presbyterian Church, "The Goldrush Church," was founded in 1899 at the height of the Klondike Goldrush when men with dreams of riches came to Skagway. In this second edition of our cookbook, you will find 146 more delicious family favorites from our congregation.

$8.50   Retail price
$3.00   Postage and handling

Make check payable to First Presbyterian Church Deacons

PANHANDLE PAT'S FIFTY YEARS

by Patricia Emel
P. O. Box 8
Seabeck, WA 98380   Phone 360-830-5187

Forty-six pages filled with old-time pictures of a small Alaskan fishing village where Pat Emel gathered and used the recipes in this book. The short stories are about some colorful neighbors whose recipes always bring back humorous memories.

$8.00   Retail price
$1.50   Postage and handling

Make check payable to Patricia Emel
ISBN 0-9622337-6-5

PELICAN, ALASKA: ALASKAN RECIPE COOKBOOK

Pelican Citizen's Emergency Travel Fund
P. O. Box 753   Phone 907-735-2297
Pelican, AK 99832   elvira@ptialaska.net

Proceeds from the sale of this cookbook help maintain the Pelican Citizen's Emergency Travel Fund. Created on a home computer with all printing, binding and laminating done by donated help, we have managed to build quite a nest egg for the citizens of Pelican, Alaska.

$10.00   Retail price
 $3.85   Postage and handling

Make check payable to Pelican Emergency Fund

PIONEERS OF ALASKA AUXILIARY #8

FAVORITE RECIPES–FAIRBANKS, ALASKA

Kitty Hensley House
1358 Leslie Street
North Pole, AK 99705-5809   Phone 907-488-6690

Rich in the traditions of pioneer cooking as well as today's modern trends in the kitchen, these recipes have been handed down family-to-family, friend-to-friend, etc. over the last century. They feature Alaska's bountiful wild meats and seafood, wild berries, and locally grown vegetables. 314 pages.

$15.00   Retail price
 $3.50   Postage and handling

Make check payable to Kitty Hensley House

RECIPES FROM THE PARIS OF THE PACIFIC

Europe '97
Sitka, AK

In 1997, a group of 32 teenagers and adults from Sitka High School gathered favorite recipes from the community and compiled a cookbook, selling it as a fundraiser to help defray costs of their 5-week, 5-country grand tour of Western Europe taken that summer. No longer in print.

RECIPES TO THE RESCUE

Coast Guard Spouses' & Women's Association
P. O. Box 1164
Sitka, AK 99835   sitkasarbar@yahoo.com

This cookbook is a tribute to the varied backgrounds of the Coast Guard family and the quintessential Southeast Alaska food experience. Includes a variety of chapters including recipes to make with kids, and simply delicious ways to pre-pare the fresh seafood caught in Sitka's beautiful waters.

$14.00   Retail price
  $4.00   Postage and handling
Make check payable to CGSWA

SALMON RECIPES

by Cecilia Nibeck
Alaska Enterprises   Mail Orders Only
P. O. Box 210241
Anchorage, AK 99521-0241

Cecilia Nibeck's first cookbook has been one of the most successful yet published about the art of preparing salmon to perfection. *Salmon Recipes from Alaska* offers nearly 250 recipes for preparing salmon in more ways than you can imagine. Don't venture home from the river or the fishmonger's without it.

$13.95   Retail price
  $1.50   Postage and handling
Make check payable to AK Enterprises   ISBN 0-9622117-1-0

SHARING OUR BEST:
A COLLECTION OF FAVORITE RECIPES

Eagle Historical Society & Museums   Phone 907-547-2325
P. O. Box 23   Fax 907-547-2325
Eagle, AK 99738   ehsmus@aptalaska.net

Three hundred recipes lovingly compiled on 142 pages, originating from historic Eagle City on the Yukon River, the first incorporated city in interior Alaska A delectable blend of Alaska specialties, healthy eating, gourmet and just plain ol' good home cooking from Alaska Bush Country!

$10.00   Retail price   Visa/MC Accepted
  $4.00   Postage and handling
Make check payable to Eagle Historical Society & Museums

SIMPLY THE BEST RECIPES

Matanuska Telephone Association, Inc.
MTA / Attn: Pulic Relations
1740 S. Chugach Street
Palmer, AK 99645

MTA's employee cookbook includes recipes from some of the best cooks around. The cookbook is packed with a blend of recipes from various origins (ex: Fireweed Honey, Clover Honey, Salmon Marinade).

$10.00   Retail price
  $2.00   Postage and handling
Make check payable to Matanuska Telephone Assoc., Inc.

A TASTE OF KODIAK

Soroptimist International of Kodiak
P. O. Box 367
Kodiak, AK 99615

Phone 907-486-8488
seastar@ptialaska.net

A Taste of Kodiak is a collection of treasured recipes that reflects the unique Alaskan lifestyle—featuring the abundance surrounding us on land and in the seas. In 2001, our cookbook won first place in a national cookbook contest. The book is hardback and features over 545 recipes.

$15.00   Retail price
   $4.25   Postage and handling

Make check payable to Soroptimist International of Kodiak

A TASTE OF SITKA, ALASKA

by Sitka Girls Basketball Team
Sitka, AK

This book was a fund raiser for the girls basketball team that proved to be a "gold mine." This 93-page book has the favorite recipes of many people of Sitka. This is one of the first cookbooks to come out of Sitka and our cover was designed by a local artist to give you a "Taste of Sitka." This book is currently out of print.

TASTY TREATS FROM TENAKEE SPRINGS, ALASKA

Senior Site Council
Snyder Mercantile Company
P. O. Box 505
Tenakee Springs, AK 99841

Phone 907-736-2205

Tasty Treats is a compilation of tried-and-true recipes given to us by past and present residents of Tenakee. It is a 216-page cookbook filled with recipes perfect for our region, as we have an abundance of venison, crab, shrimp, and fish. This will become a well-used cookbook.

$9.95   Retail price
$5.00   Postage and handling

Visa/MC Accepted

Make check payable to Snyder Mercantile Company

33 DAYS HATH SEPTEMBER

by Karen Cauble
Vanessapress
P. O. Box 82761
Fairbanks, AK 99708

While working as a cook for a river tugboat crew on Alaska's Yukon River, the author created a journal of events including a recipe featured from each day's menu. The voyage scheduled for 21 days beginning 9/1, did not arrive at home port until 10/3—hence the title.

$9.95   Retail price
$3.00   Postage and handling

Visa/MC Accepted

Make check payable to Vanessapress

ISBN 0-940055-74-0

UPPER KENAI RIVER INN BREAKFAST COOKBOOK

by Peggy J. Givens
Upper Kenai River Inn
P. O. Box 838   Phone 907-595-3333
Cooper Landing, AK 99572   Fax 907-595-3333

Cookbook of breakfast recipes used at the Upper Kenai River Inn to insure a great start to every day. The inn is pictured on the cover. Over 100 fun recipes to try. Includes wonderful information about Alaska.

  $10.00   Retail price
   $1.80   Postage and handling

Make check payable to Upper Kenai River Inn

WE'RE COOKIN' NOW

by Sitka Emblem Club #142
Sitka, AK

The proceeds from the sale of this cookbook went to increase the local club's Scholarship Trust Fund. A small portion was dedicated to kitchen improvements at the Elk's Lodge. Recipes were gathered from members, families, and friends. This book is currently out of print.

WELCOME HOME

Sisters of Martha & Mary Society
St. John Orthodox Cathedral   Phone 907-696-3326
P. O. Box 1108   Fax 907-696-3326
Eagle River, AK 99577   crancliff@alaska.net

This cookbook is a blend of the history of our community and great recipes. Our recipes represent the many states and countries present in our unique Orthodox community. You will be delighted with the tempting choices and variety found in over 500 recipes.

  $15.00   Retail price
   $4.00   Postage and handling

Make check payable to St. John Orthodox Cathedral (SJOC)

WHAT'S COOKIN' IN THE KENAI PENINSULA

Holy Assumption (Russian Orthodox Church)
Holy Assumption Cookbook   Phone 907-283-7748
P. O. Box 1227   or 907-283-4103
Kenai, AK 99611   Fax 907-283-7748
                                                        tyshee@gci.net

Although many contributors have passed away, our heritage and culture have been preserved within the pages of our cookbook. We have combined our original book with our newer recipes. The result is a combination of many ethnic backgrounds, with our Russian ancestry being well represented.

  $15.00   Retail price
   $2.50   Postage and handling

Make check payable to Holy Assumption

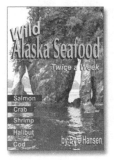

WILD ALASKA SEAFOOD—TWICE A WEEK

by Evie Hansen
National Seafood Education   Phone 800-348-0010
P. O. Box 60006   Fax 206-546-6411
Richmond Beach, WA 98160   eviense@aol.com

Evie's 256-page cookbook will give you boatloads of reasons to eat seafood twice a week. Includes over 200 tasty, quick and healthy, kitchen-tested and supermarket ingredient recipes. This beautifully illustrated book teaches with preparation tips, nutritional charts and nutritional analysis, including diabetic exchanges. Includes stories of Alaskan fishing adventures.

$14.95   Retail price
  $3.50   Postage and handling

Make check payable to National Seafood Educators

INDEX

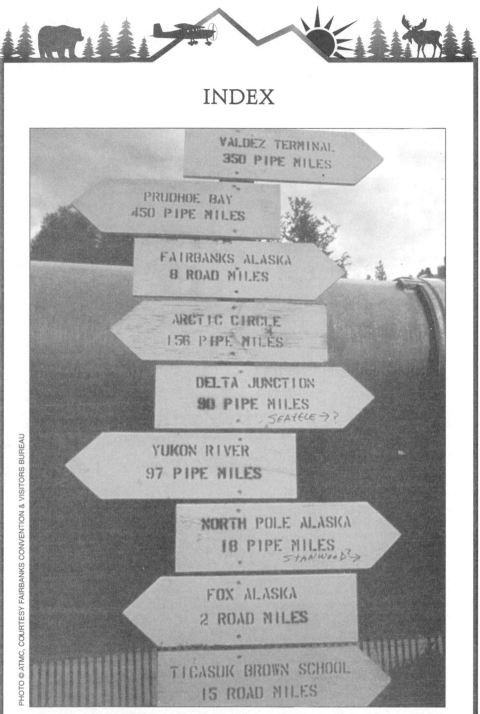

The Trans-Alaska Pipeline measures 48 inches in diameter and stretches 800 miles, crossing three mountain ranges and over 800 rivers and streams. The pipeline delivers 17% of the U.S. domestic oil production.

INDEX

INDEX

INDEX

Best of the Best State Cookbook Series